CROSSING BORDERLANDS

See 204/212 discovery

layage diversity etc

treats almost exclusily the

relationship between feachers and

note bilingual students. the case

is repeatedly made for any voice

to marginalized students. But they accept

multilingualism as a precondition.

while's work a cure exception.

so this narrow focus perhaps

explains why we keep to

theories, have yet to

engage strategies for

multimodality of stylistic

trans-rhetorical.

Pittsburgh Series in Composition, Literacy, and Culture

David Bartholomae and Jean Ferguson Carr, Editors

CROSSING BORDERLANDS

Composition and Postcolonial Studies

Edited by Andrea A. Lunsford and Lahoucine Ouzgane

UNIVERSITY OF PITTSBURGH PRESS

Published by the University of Pittsburgh Press, Pittsburgh, Pa., 15260
Manufactured in the United States of America
Printed on acid-free paper
10 9 8 7 6 5 4 3 2 1

Many thanks to *JAC: A Journal of Composition Theory* for permission to reprint revised versions of several essays that appeared in the 18:1, Winter 1998 issue of that journal.

Library of Congress Cataloging-in-Publication Data

Crossing borderlands : composition and postcolonial studies / edited by
Andrea A. Lunsford and Lahoucine Ouzgane.

    p. cm. — (Pittsburgh series in composition, literacy, and
culture)
Includes bibliographical references (p.) and index.
  ISBN 0-8229-4222-4 (cloth : alk. paper) — ISBN 0-8229-5837-6 (pbk. :
alk. paper)
  1. English language—Rhetoric—Study and teaching—United States. 2.
Minorities—Education (Higher)—United States. 3. Immigrants—Education
(Higher)—United States. 4. Multicultural education—United States. 5.
Postcolonialism—United States. I. Lunsford, Andrea A., 1942- II.
Ouzgane, Lahoucine. III. Series.
  PE1405.U6C756 2004
  808'.0428'0711—dc22

                                    2003020006

Contents

Composition and Postcolonial Studies: An Introduction 1
Andrea A. Lunsford and Lahoucine Ouzgane

Composing Postcolonial Studies 9
Min-Zhan Lu

Toward a Mestiza Rhetoric: Gloria Anzaldúa on
Composition and Postcoloniality 33
Andrea A. Lunsford

Terms of Engagement: Postcolonialism, Transnationalism,
and Composition Studies 67
Deepika Bahri

Encountering the Other: Postcolonial Theory and
Composition Scholarship 84
Gary A. Olson

Pratt and Pratfalls: Revisioning Contact Zones 95
R. Mark Hall and Mary Rosner

Beside Ourselves: Rhetoric and Representation in
Postcolonial Feminist Writing 110
Susan C. Jarratt

Postcolonial Transformations in Canadian Inuit Testimonio 129
Martin Behr

(Im)migrant Crossings 143
Aneil Rallin

Resisting Writing: Reflections on the Postcolonial Factor
in the Writing Class 157
David Dzaka

Arts of the U.S.–Mexico Contact Zone   171
  Jaime Armin Mejía

Hybridity: A Lens for Understanding Mestizo/a Writers   199
  Louise Rodríguez Connal

The Politics of Location: Using Flare-Ups to Spark "Reflexive
Dialogue" in the Ever-Changing Classroom Text   218
  Pamela Gay

The New Literacy/Orality Debates: Ebonics and the
Redefinition of Literacy in Multicultural Settings   238
  C. Jan Swearingen

Notes   255
Bibliography   263
Contributors   279
Index   281

CROSSING BORDERLANDS

Andrea A. Lunsford and Lahoucine Ouzgane

COMPOSITION AND
POSTCOLONIAL STUDIES

An Introduction

Across all disciplines, a growing awareness of the importance of minority and subjugated voices to histories and narratives that have previously excluded them has led to widespread interest in postcolonial theory. While quite diverse, this body of work coheres around an exploration of power relations between Western and Third World countries. More particularly, postcolonial studies has sought to expose the mechanisms of oppression through which "Others"—aboriginal, native, or simply preexisting cultures and groups—are displaced, eradicated, enslaved, or transformed into obedient subjects. Joining poststructuralism and postmodernism in challenging the concept of the unified founding subject, postcolonial studies has gone on to mount a stringent critique of the specifically imperialist subject. By the 1990s, postcolonial studies—drawing on gender theory, psychoanalysis, deconstruction, ethnic studies, and race theory—was exerting an influence on scholarship across the disciplines in unprecedented ways.

At the same time, scholars in rhetoric and composition led efforts to understand the ways in which students (and student writings) are variously constructed, subjugated, and turned into obedient subjects, both within and outside the academy, and to find ways of enabling resistance to such forces. For thirty years, in fact, compositionists have been in the forefront of those advocating for students and for student agency, through open admissions programs (like the one famously attempted at CUNY) and increased access to and agency within higher education for all people (Maher). Rejecting the role traditionally assigned writing programs to "wash out" a goodly proportion of those admitted to college, composition scholars instead developed robust theories of writing that went beyond traditional formalism, created curricula based on Freirean principles, and built programs devoted to student writers and their goals (Flower et al., Shor, Bartholomae, Bizzell).[1] In addition, compositionists such as Schell and Stock have persistently addressed the material conditions affecting teachers in higher education, demonstrating graphically the position of part-time contingent laborers in composition and presenting cogent arguments for change.

Given the obvious connections and similar interests, it is perhaps surprising that scholars in rhetoric and composition and in postcolonial studies have not been, by and large, in dialogue with one another, nor have insights from one field been used systematically to inform the other. Several reasons for such a disconnection readily present themselves, however. During the 1970s and much of the 1980s, composition/rhetoric struggled to achieve disciplinary status and recognition within the academy, a struggle that distracted composition scholars from larger goals of access and equity and often led to a kind of embattled mentality and a concomitant insularity. Ironically, composition's very focus during those years on access for and attention to students and their writing led to more than a little essentializing, as those in the field tended to speak of *the* student writer and his or her writing processes, with the unfortunate effect of erasing difference in many ways (Royster and Williams). In addition, this focus on *the* student writer was deeply ethnocentric, representing writers as generically American (Guerra). (It has taken over twenty years for composition to recognize and thoroughly critique such assumptions and, thus, to rethink the power relations that animate this field of study.)

For its part, postcolonial studies has focused, according to C. Richard King, "almost exclusively on Europe and its former colonies, primarily on British and to a lesser extent French endeavors in Africa and Asia, especially India" (King 3), thus largely ignoring the ways in which America can be said to be postcolonial. Postcolonial studies has also tended to erase or leave out student voices, to ignore the positioning of students, and to speak for students. As Min-Zhan Lu points out in her chapter, "Composing Post-colonial Studies," the recurring references to "student writers" in the collection point to a common oversight in postcolonial theory: recognition of the need of academic intellectuals to resist the temptation of speaking for "the student writer." Perhaps most notably, postcolonial critics moved fairly quickly from examining material practices related to oppression to theorizing about those practices, thus dealing with such constructs almost exclusively in the abstract.

If postcolonial studies is sometimes charged with focusing too exclusively on high theory, composition is accused by others of consistently privileging practice over theory (Olson), a dichotomy that has also functioned to separate the two fields. But while such extremes surely exist, many scholars of writing have worked hard to create a dialogic reciprocity between theory and practice, and they have explored relationships between composition and literary theory (S. Miller, John Schilb), postmodernism (Harkin and Schilb; Faigley), cultural studies (Berlin; McComiskey; Fitts and France), multiculturalism (Severino, Guerra, and Butler; Walters and Moss), feminism (Jarratt and Worsham; Flynn; Phelps and Emig), and race (Gilyard, Royster, Logan, Villanueva). Scholars of composition have been particularly interested in pursuing concepts of resistance, especially in the classroom (Greenbaum; Giroux). This work is important for its emphasis on ways to call attention to and hence resist oppressive practices, but it too often fails to move beyond considering acculturation, accommodation, and resistance in terms of the disempowered. As Haivan Hoang has argued, scholars need also to examine the practices of those who are embued with institutional or social power, to explore the ways in which accommodation and resistance can and do co-exist among members of both groups, and, most importantly, to study what she calls, drawing on Burkean identification and Bakhtinian centripetalism, the "self-conscious ethnic discursive acts that unite people for particular purposes and to enact particular values" (8).

Thus recent years have produced the beginnings of some productive cross talk between composition and postcolonial studies. A 1998 special issue of *JAC: A Journal of Composition Theory*, for example, comprised a series of essays (some of which appear in revised form here) aimed at exploring issues of importance to both composition and postcolonial studies. In the following year, Lynn Worsham and Gary Olson edited a series of *JAC* interviews, including one with postcolonial theorist Homi Bhabha. More recently, Andrea Greenbaum's *Insurrections: Approaches to Resistance in Composition Studies* emphasizes connections between critical literacy theories and composition, arguing that composition should be fully informed and shaped by these theories.[2]

Crossing Borderlands seeks to further extend this conversation, complementing and grounding the insights gleaned from such previous efforts. More specifically, the essays collected here seek to build on composition's traditional concerns—for access, agency, and material conditions of student writers and their teachers—by situating these concerns in the context of postcolonial theory and in richly situated pedagogical practice. These essays consolidate some of the most important postcolonial work of composition and attempt to engage postcolonial scholars in issues related to students and student writing—and to the liberatory potential of teaching and practicing writing. We stress this liberating "potential" purposely, since writing, a system and a technology, is always engaged in some form of regulation: grammar itself is highly regulatory, and beyond that governing structure lie the imposing discourses of society, all of which exert pressure on writers and their messages. In spite of such pressures—or perhaps partially because of them—the authors in this volume look for ways to question and resist regulation and to build opportunities for students to realize agency.

The articles collected here insist on valuing the voices of students, of engaging those voices directly, and examining how students can come to voice. In addition, this collection moves beyond a Eurocentric view of postcolonialism, considering the position of Mexican Americans, African Americans, and Native Americans, and hence tracing colonialist economies of power in America. Equally important is the focus on the centrality of speaking and writing English. Given the hegemonic tendencies of English, understanding its ideology and power is of key concern. As Edward Said notes, "there is simply no use operating politically and responsibly in a world dominated by one superpower without a profound familiarity and knowledge of that superpower—America, its histories, its institutions, its currents and countercurrents, its politics and culture; and, above all, a perfect working knowledge of its language" ("Thinking"). This volume contributes to such a working knowledge and explores liberatory ways of using such knowledge while also calling attention to the colonizing modes of English itself. In short, the interview and essays gathered here all seek to explore various borderlands and to contribute to a growing body of work on borderland pedagogy. *Borderland* is a particularly apt metaphor in which to ground these essays, because the concept allows for—indeed encourages— what may seem to be shifting and contradictory movements and claims, the kind that enable and value the "flexible rhetorics" identified and described by Hoang.[3]

The themes we have identified—resisting the urge to speak for students, valuing student voices and student writing, a focus on access and agency, attention to material conditions, and attention to the role of English and to the ways in which America can be said to be postcolonial do not together animate each individual essay herein. Indeed, these essays sound additional themes as well. In the opening piece, Min-Zhan Lu responds to the collection as a whole, interrogating the ways in which composition functions as an "ungrateful receiver" of the gifts of postcolonial studies. In a trenchant analysis of the "systematic 'swallowing' of the reality of composition in the world of the academy," Lu argues that contesting the imbalance of power relations across many borders calls for the need to "make giving mutual between postcolonial and composition studies." Following Lu's analysis is an interview with Gloria Anzaldúa, one Lu reads meticulously and critically, often deconstructing Anzaldúa's root metaphors while building her reading on Trinh Minh-ha's metaphor of gifts and ungrateful receivers. Together, Lu's theoretically rich reading and Anzaldúa's extensive comments based on her own rhetorical praxis set the scene for the essays to come.

In "Terms of Engagement: Postcolonialism, Transnationalism, and Composition Studies," Deepika Bahri treats "the confusions that have come to characterize both postcolonialism and the writing classroom in the current climate produced by transnationalism and economic globalization" by clarifying terms and concepts and showing in detail how a terministic reciprocity between composition and postcolonial studies may be effected. The following essays, by Gary Olson and by R. Mark Hall and Mary Rosner, both add to an understanding of theoretical terms and, especially, of the function of the "Other" in various discursive formations. Olson argues that the commonalities between composition and postcolonial studies move both fields toward a carefully articulated ethics of practice. Hall and Rosner narrow the terministic focus, following the path of Mary Louise Pratt's concept of "contact zone" as the term shifts and changes in several of Pratt's own texts as well as in reviews and adaptations of her work. Hall and Rosner's meticulous unpacking of the word "context" and their emphasis on what is missing from accounts of the contact zone (namely, the voices and perspectives of students) set the stage for a more effective and reflective use of this concept in both composition and postcolonial studies.

Susan C. Jarratt's "Beside Ourselves: Rhetoric and Representation in Postcolonial Feminist Writing" participates in this narrowing of focus, addressing "the problem of speaking for others by looking at how 'others' speak." Toward this end, Jarratt describes representational strategies of postcolonial feminist rhetoric and shows how those strategies can lead to the gradual transformation of singular subjectivity to "self-divided" subjects who are literally and figuratively "beside themselves," and eventually to a position that enables students and teachers "to move collectively across the axes of metaphor/metonymy rather than silence/speech." To make her case for such a new vision of collectivity, Jarratt applies postcolonial feminist strategies to the work of Gayatri Spivak, Trinh T. Minh-ha, and Rigoberta Menchú Tum. Martin Behr's "Postcolonial Transformations in Canadian Inuit Testimonio" follows from Jarratt's discussion of Menchú Tum's use of that genre, here drawing on new genre theory to help understand how the discursive features of testimonio function to create strategies of transformation typical "of a collective form of autobiography." In his essay, Behr applies such an understanding of testimonio to the first book-length one by a Canadian Eskimo, *I, Nuliqak*, in which the speaker gives voice to the dispossession of his people through a western autobiographical form—without acquiescing to the colonizing powers of that form.

The next two essays focus on personal experiences of postcolonial subjects in the composition classroom. In "(Im)migrant Crossings," Aneil Rallin employs what are now sometimes called "alternative discourse strategies,"[4] including disjunctive pairings, notes, lists, and shifts of several kinds to evoke synchronicity and to make room for teachers and students to "inhabit multiple positionings." David Dzaka, born and raised in Ghana, examines his own identity as a multilingual postcolonial subject, tracing his encounters with writing and looking at the many ways in which students in Ghana resist writing. As he came to understand the hollowness of injunctions to think critically and divergently, Dzaka learned to recognize the oppressive connection between "good writing" and "good students," both of which "toe the line" of their instructors. As he learned to tug at and then break this line, Dzaka also learned how to work with postcolonial learners whose "struggle with writing grows out of their own history, a history of miseducation, of misguided pedagogy, of domination and submission."

In "Arts of the U.S.–Mexico Contact Zone" and "Hybridity: A Lens for Understanding Mestizo/a Writers," Jaime Armin Mejía and Louise Rodríguez Connal turn their attention to Mexican American and Latino/a students. Mejía focuses on the U.S.–Mexico borderlands, describing a form of internal colonialism at work among a people fluent in both Spanish and English who have been systematically left unimagined by composition studies. Detailing the exclusionary educational practices that have marginalized these students, Mejía argues that teachers of writing must come to know the rhetorical and linguistic complexity characteristic of border texts such as corridos, dichos, and tallas, and not only to recognize but to value these features in student texts. Connal chronicles her own use of transcultural rhetorics that help navigate what she calls the "hybridized viewpoints that Spanish and English [. . .] can create." Taking issue with Patricia Bizzell's call to teach hybrid discourses, Connal argues that, rather than developing such hybrid languages, "we should select from the dialects and ways of knowing available to us [. . .] when dealing with political issues in our lives."

The final essays in this volume deal explicitly with issues of race and related issues of multiculturalism. Pamela Gay's "The Politics of Location: Using Flare-Ups to Spark Reflexive Dialogue in the Ever-Changing Classroom Text" describes a graduate course (Teaching Writing from a Postcolonial Perspective) that uses the concept of voice as a site of departure for an extensive listserv discussion, reads a "flare up" of texts produced on the listserv over multiculturalism and its place(s), and concludes that establishing a truly dialogic pedagogy requires not only recognizing and celebrating difference but actively engaging it as well. C. Jan Swearingen continues an examination of backlashes against the concept of multiculturalism, focusing specifically on the racist nature of parts of that movement. In tracing the controversy over the Oakland School Board's Ebonics proposal and the less well-known debate over Eric Havelock's linking of the pre-Socratic philosophers' zero-copulative speech to Black English—as a way of arguing for the primacy of literacy over orality—Swearingen asks whether "multiculturalism" as a movement within American education has been brought to a "screeching halt." Turning from overtly racist attacks on multiculturalism to critiques mounted by members of the academy such as Henry Louis Gates, Swearingen ends on a note of hope, concluding that "the mindless celebration of difference for its own sake is not more tenable than the nostalgic return to some monochrome homogeneity. We all must search for a middle way and commit ourselves to its construction."

Crossing Borderlands aims to participate in the construction of such a middle way, one that can move us toward an ongoing constructive exchange between composition and postcolonial studies. In addition, these essays contribute to the creation of a viable borderland pedagogy capable of making use of this exchange in creating a space for dialogic engagement and a theory of writing able to account for the multiply rich rhetorical practices of both students and teachers.

Min-Zhan Lu

COMPOSING POSTCOLONIAL STUDIES

The compulsion to "help" the needy whose needs one participates in creating and legislating ultimately leads to "bombing people into the acceptance of gifts." [. . .] The "needy" cannot always afford to refuse, so they persist in accepting ungratefully. [. . . T]he vitality of the ungrateful receiver lies not in destroying the giver, but in understanding that giving is mutual, and thereby, in baffling expectations and unsettling the identification process of giver, given, and gift.

Trinh T. Minh-ha, "Cotton and Iron"

This is an invested reading of the essays gathered here. Both composition studies and postcolonial studies have been vital to my thinking about the production and reception of meanings against the grain of global and internal systems of oppression. I am, however, interested particularly in exploring composition's vitality as "the ungrateful receiver" of the gifts of postcolonial studies. It has been my conviction that if those of us reading, writing, and teaching inside the panopticon of English Studies are to contest the asymmetrical power relations between the so-called metropolitan center and the third world, across divisions of sex, gender, class, or race, and also between literature and composition, research and teaching, or between "published" and "student" writers, then we need to make giving mutual between postcolonial and composition studies.

As postcolonial theory reminds us, to proclaim oneself a radical worker inside U.S. English Studies is to confront its official function in global and internal domination—that is, to wrestle with our complicity with the compulsion of English to "help" the so-called third world, minority, student, or basic writers by creating and legislating their "needs." This task is further complicated for those of us who have been institutionally placed and/or who self-identify with composition studies. Given the historical dichotomizing of literature over composition and research over teaching, to proclaim oneself a radical worker inside English Studies requires one to confront the field's compulsion to bomb composition teachers into accepting the gifts of literary theories. As many in composition have argued, while the economic importance of work in composition may be grudgingly acknowledged, its intellectual and scholarly importance consistently escapes notice (R. Miller, "Composing" 165). I find it particularly troubling that, in spite of the explicit concern of postcolonial studies to speak alongside the "other," its traffic with composition studies has dutifully replicated the identification process of giver, given, gift as that process has been traditionally maintained between literary and composition studies. Composition has been assigned the role of a grateful recipient: an ideal "laboratory for articulating the pedagogical implications" of the theoretical and scholarly advances in diverse theories housed in the literature wing of English (R. Miller 168). The intellectual work of composition, as that work is evidenced in both the teaching of composition and in composition scholarship, continues to escape notice (Harris, *A Teaching*; Horner, *Terms*; Schilb, *Between*). Efforts to make giving mutual between postcolonial and composition studies remain scarce and perfunctory. In those works where the conviction that the former has something to learn and gain from the latter is expressed, that conviction is seldom accompanied by a detailed articulation of what, how, and why composition might help postcolonial studies revise its current theories and practices (Lu, "Professing"; Bahri, "Terms").

Hiring, tenure, and promotion decisions in English departments across the United States also routinely operate to remind composition scholars and teachers that we cannot afford to refuse the gifts of literary theory in its various post-versions. For instance, literature faculty often consider it *unreasonable* that composition faculty should expect candidates specializing in postcolonial studies to demonstrate any knowledge of current composition theory or that they should be probed on their pedagogical stance and practices (even when the job description "dares" to require occasional teaching of first-year composition). The same literature faculty nevertheless deem it *unthinkable* that candidates specializing in composition could qualify for jobs that would "allow" them to occasionally offer literature courses unless the candidate proves to be well versed in current literary—including postcolonial—theory.

A literature candidate who describes Paulo Freire as the guru of problem solving (rather than problem posing) may suffer no consequences (because most literature faculty can't tell the difference?). I'd wager, however, that a composition candidate crediting Spivak with "Can the Subaltern Speak?" would pay dearly for her "error." Postcolonial specialists in English departments often join other literature faculty in making public confessions of their ignorance of composition theory, using that professed ignorance as an excuse for exempting themselves from having occasionally to teach a composition course (teaching to which some of them may have professed commitment at the time of their being hired). All must have intuited (without ever having bothered to open a single copy of a composition journal) that such "ignorance" would neither endanger their candidacy for tenure and promotion nor, once they have managed to establish themselves in postcolonial studies, disqualify them from giving keynote speeches to composition conferences and interviews to composition journals. In fact, enough precedents exist to reassure such faculty that if their stock tumbles at the MLA, they can always use their professed ignorance (accompanied by the right pinch of contrition and a quick reference to Freire) to bring about an uptick of their stock at the CCCC and NCTE.

I rely on sarcasm to call attention to my anger at not only the prevailing organization of English Studies but also my own failure to effectively unsettle such givens in my daily practices in both scholarly and departmental matters. If institutional constraints continue to mark composition as the "needy" who "cannot always afford to refuse" the gift of postcolonial theory, and if, as attested to by all the articles in this collection, it is in the political interest of radical workers in composition studies to learn from postcolonial critiques of global and internal colonization in the past and the present, how and why should composition studies nevertheless explore its vitality as an ungrateful receiver of that gift? Reading this collection with such a question in mind, I note four potential points of departure for exploring that vitality.

Point One: Taking Notice of the Work of Composition

In Lunsford's "Towards a Mestiza Rhetoric: Gloria Anzaldúa on Composition and Postcoloniality," Anzaldúa baffles academic expectations by claiming, "I didn't even know I belonged in this postcolonial thing until Patricia Cloud said in a book flap that I am a feminist, postcolonial critic." She then goes on to portray herself as having neither the time nor the patience to "study" postcolonial theory:

> When Homi Bhabha was here, I did some reading and I went to his lecture, which I couldn't understand. When Spivak was here it was the same thing. I took a class with Donna Haraway in feminist theory, and when I had to read "Can the Subaltern Speak?" it took me weeks to decipher one sentence. Well, not weeks, but you know what I'm saying. . . . And then for your interview I got a copy of this postcolonial studies reader. But you know, I didn't have time to really study a lot, so I made little notes about the things that I wanted to think about and maybe respond to in writing.

Such an ungrateful attitude is in keeping with Anzaldúa's conviction that both writing and postcoloniality are "emancipatory projects, about how to get from here to there." The "there" Anzaldúa envisions is a *Nepantla*, a liminal borderland between worlds, realities, systems of knowledge, and languages. The "here" she tries to confront is an historical time and geopolitical space where "English" is going to "have this kind of United Statesian-culture-swallowing-up-the-rest-of-the-world kind of mouth." "Here" is also an educational and bodily space where "English" has devoured her "head": "When I'm dealing with theory, it's all in English, because I didn't take any classes in which theory was taught in Spanish. So the body and the feeling parts of me come out in Spanish, and the intellectual, reasoning parts of me come out in English." For Anzaldúa to begrudge the time and energy to "study" postcolonial theory is therefore to undo not only the linkage between "English" and "theory" in education and her head but also the power of "English" to swallow up the rest of the world.

Ironically, Anzaldúa's explicit refusal to be grateful for the "gift" of post-colonial theory also bears implicit witness to the pervasive power of this form of gift giving and, most importantly, to the absence of any institutional pressure to take notice of the work of composition. As indicated by the passage cited at the beginning of this section, Anzaldúa was at least aware that Homi Bhabha "was here," and Spivak "was here." When each was present, Anzaldúa felt compelled to "[do] some reading" and "[go] to" the lecture. She had actually "[taken] a class with Donna Haraway" where she "had to" read Spivak's "Can the Subaltern Speak?" And she admits to having "got[ten] a copy of this postcolonial studies reader" in preparation for her interview with Lunsford. Several questions come to mind: Who in composition studies might have been "here" during the same period? Did Anzaldúa feel compelled to do any reading and attend any of the lectures? Did she get hold of a composition theory reader in preparation for her interview with Lunsford? I pose these questions not to comment on Anzaldúa's lack of involvement in composition studies but to comment on the prevailing organization of the U.S. academy.

What are the material givens of the "world of the academy" (which Anzaldúa reminds Lunsford that "we occupy?" First, "people generally assume" that Anzaldúa must have read Foucault, Derrida, Irigaray, or Cixous:

> Q: You said that you hadn't read them before you wrote *Borderlands,* but that the ideas—they're "out there."
>
> A: Yes, the ideas are out there because we are all people who are in more or less the same territory. We occupy the world of the academy and of the late twentieth century. We've read some of the same books, we've seen some of the same movies, we have similar ideas about relationships, whether we're French or born in the United States or raised here.

Second, books in composition are not among the "same books" we—"all people who are in more or less the same territory"—have read. Although Anzaldúa seems equally surprised to see herself "picked up" by "composition people," and even though she sees many of the questions raised by Lunsford and Ouzgane in preparation for the interview as "[being] there" in one of her book projects, she does not mention having encountered anyone who "generally assume[s]" that she "must have read" any of the work in composition studies. Neither does she refer to any work [in composition] by author or title as she does to work in postcolonial studies. Likewise, when Lunsford points to some links she perceives between Anzaldúa's work and the work of composition, Lunsford cannot rely on quick references to specific authors or book titles, as she is able to when asking Anzaldúa to place her work in relation to other fields of English Studies, such as to Homi Bhabha as "a very good example" of a "very high abstract language" and to the various "styles" of Toni Morrison, Borges, or Cortazar. Instead, Lunsford has to rely on generalizations—"some in composition studies" or "people in composition"—when depicting the advances made on how to change our roles as the "gatekeepers" of the academy .

The general lack of institutional expectation for "all people" to have read or heard of composition theory is probably most visible in Anzaldúa's praise of James Sledd:

> He was the first person ever to encourage me to talk about cultural stuff [. . .] and I used some Mexican words and some terms in Spanish. I had written some stories way back when I was working on my B.A., and some when I was working on my M.A. They all code-switched, but when I wrote for James Sledd we were doing something different. We were trying to write formally: what we would call now theorizing; what was called then criticism. His encouragement was very important to me, and he was also very important to me as a role model. He was very much a maverick against the university; he was very much at odds, an outsider. From him I learned that an outsider is not just somebody of a different skin; it could be somebody who's White, who's usually an insider but who crosses back and forth between outsider and insider. So he was my model to think about insider/outsider, and then I had my whole life to think about *Nosotras,* us and them.

Let's imagine a different world of the academy, one where all people are expected to have taken serious notice of the complex work of composition. What kind of discussion would then ensue after this portrait of James Sledd?

Since composition is a dynamic and complex field, the actual tenor of the conversation is impossible to predict. Rather, it would have to depend largely on the particular readings of the field held by the interviewer and the interviewee. Hypothetically, let's just presume that both were to agree with Richard Miller's definition of composition as "an institutional site reserved for investigating acts of reading and writing as evidenced in and by student texts" ("Composing" 169). Then it is conceivable that the interview would go on to discuss Sledd's teaching in terms of composition's history of focusing attention on how meaning gets made: on treating the institutional location—where students work—rather than literary texts as the principal subject of study, and on examining the problems involved in mediating between the desires of individual students and the work institutionally required of them. It would likewise be a given, as is common in composition scholarship, to talk about Sledd's teaching in terms of the particular reading and writing assignments, written comments, or class discussions he used to "encourage" students to produce writing that not only "code switched" but also "theoriz[ed]" cultural stuff. It would also be a given to acknowledge Sledd's contribution to scholarly debate on "students' right to their own language." The interview would then move on to discuss the relationship between Sledd's scholarship and his teaching practices.

I sketch these imaginary trajectories for continuing Anzaldúa's account of Sledd's influence on her work, not to call attention to what is remiss in the interview but to call attention to what (as a student in my writing class has taught me to say "cannot able to" take place in a "territory" where the complex work of composition has continually escaped notice (Lu, "Professing" 450–51). Composition cannot afford to receive the gifts of Anzaldúa's interview without also examining carefully the material givens informing this interview. Given the systematic "swallowing" of the reality of composition in the world of the academy, when conversing with those within the "university wall" but housed supposedly outside and above composition, we need to also unsettle the standardized identification process of givers, givens, and gifts.

One direction might be to ask those with the status to "grant" us interviews that they talk about our work not only in terms of the writing teachers they have had but also in terms of the (lack of) institutional pressure to take notice of the complex work of composition. While sound in theory, such a move could indeed be risky. It might make "leading" figures like Anzaldúa more hesitant to grant interviews. Given the institutional conditions of English Studies, composition studies can hardly afford to refuse any of the gifts these interviews often bring. First, the move to interview our power-full "literary" others is itself subversive. It is an opportunity to make the "givers" take notice of the existence of intellectual sites such as *JAC: A Journal of Composition Theory*. It can work to inform the givers of what is currently going on in composition studies, in teaching as well as in scholarship (Lunsford's questions and responses to Anzaldúa in the current volume are instructive). Second, as illustrated by all the essays in this collection, composition has much to learn from postcolonial theory if we are to further our research on processes of reading, writing, and teaching that push against the rules of English Studies and its global and internal ruling over differences in literacy practices. Third, the publication of interviews accrues cultural capital. It would be both politically naive and irresponsible to ignore the fact that composition workers like myself gain cultural capital by producing texts that present themselves as conversant with literary, postcolonial, or poststructural studies.

Given such material conditions, I wonder if we might instead start by at least making explicit in the introduction to (if not also the main body of) the interviews the institutional givens enabling and constraining the traffic among the various disciplines housing the interviewer, the interviewee, and their imagined audience. Such discussions might in turn help readers treat these interviews as means for examining not only what we can learn from the person interviewed but also how we might go about changing the institutional givens informing the interviews. They might incite readers to adopt more ungrateful reading postures, including actively examining the degree of attention given by the "givers" of interviews to the work of composition. On the one hand, given the current organization of English Studies, such a reading posture might indeed appear to be nothing but posturing. The outcome is regrettably predictable. Nothing much would come out of such a reading posture other than making manifest, once again, what we already know, that is, the lack of institutional pressure on "leading" figures (in literary—poststructural, postmodern, or postcolonial—studies) to take the work of composition seriously. On the other hand, such an ungrateful reading posture could at least mark this lack as a focal point for composition's contestation of the existing givens within English Studies. If nothing more, it would shift our own attitudes toward composition's terms of engagement with the "givers" of interviews. Such a shift in focus might affect not only how composition teachers and scholars talk to our power-full others, but also, eventually, how they talk to us so that the efforts to make giving mutual would be shared by the interviewee, interviewer, and the readers of such interviews.

Point Two: Problematizing the Developmental Plot

In discussing her views on when writers are ready to challenge the norms of a field, Anzaldúa uses two analogies, both of which carry the developmental plot of "you have to know and master the norms before you can be innovative."

> You *have to* know how to wire the house *before you can* start being an innovative electrician. (my emphasis)

> It's kind of like a fish in the Pacific Ocean, with the analogy that the Pacific Ocean is the dominant field and the fish is this postcolonial, this feminist, or this queer, or whoever is trying to make changes. I think that *before you can* make any changes in composition studies, philosophy or whatever it is, you *have to* have a certain awareness of the territory, be familiar with it and you *have to* be able to maneuver in it *before you can* say, "Here's an alternative model for this particular field, for its norms, for its rules and regulations, for its laws." (my emphasis)

The fish and electrician analogies make sense when viewed in relation to several points Anzaldúa makes. First, she rejects the false dichotomy between "nos" and "otras," posing instead the concept of "nosotras." She reminds us that "we [the colonized] are complicitous for being in such close proximity and in such intimacy with the other; [. . .] the other is in me." Second, she points out that she is "inside" the walled city of the university as a result of not only historical necessity but also personal choice: "As for me, I like English and I majored in English at a time when I wasn't allowed Spanish." Third, she views her writing as "only partly new": "most of it is cast in the Western tradition, because that's all that I was immersed in." Fourth, she attributes the popularity of her writing in part to her ability to gain access to the "appropriate" credentials to secure subsistence—grants and jobs —and an audience among other writers, artists, and academicians and their students. Given Anzaldúa's concern to acknowledge the dominant *in* her postcoloniality and her writing, the fish and the electrician analogies are understandable because they contain an imagery of immersion.

Working from a different set of concerns, composition studies has long questioned the function of the developmental frame, especially the plot line of "you have to [. . .] before you can" in education politics and writing pedagogies. For instance, some in composition have conducted historical studies of the ways in which the academy has used this master plot to legislate the needs of students whose home discourse is perceived as foreign to the English promoted by the academy. Others have studied the potential discrepancy between the academy's account of what student writers can/should be allowed to do and the student writers' counter accounts of what they can do/are interested in and capable of doing. How might we use this tradition of inquiry when studying Anzaldúa's position on when writers are ready to be innovative?

One direction would be to problematize the developmental plot in her fish and electrician analogies by listening carefully to her own accounts of her schooling, where she seems to concur with composition's dispute with the academy's faith in the developmental myth. When talking about her current effort to "mix Spanglish" in theory as well as in poetry, Anzaldúa states that "I think of style as trying to *recover* a childhood place where you code switch" (my emphasis). She has to recover that place because code switching once "was" the way Anzaldúa "grew up with her family." But since Spanish "was not allowed" in school, "[w]hen I'm in my head, stuff comes out in English. When I'm dealing with theory, it's all in English." Given her personal educational history, Anzaldúa literally has to wait until English has devoured her "head" to "recover"—"can" (is allowed to) go to—"the place where [she] code switch[es]." This suggests that the developmental plot in the fish and electrician analogies indeed reflects an historical reality experienced by students like Anzaldúa. Schooling has historically been the site where the dominant uses the developmental myth to exercise its compulsion to "bomb" the "needy" bilingual student into believing she cannot work for change—pose alternatives or be innovative—until she has survived her rite of passage through the house of English.

However, a second set of stories indicates that in spite of such an historical reality, the developmental myth does not accurately reflect the student's own sense of what she can do—desires to do and is capable of doing. These stories recount Anzaldúa's struggle for alternative style when doing her

B.A., M.A., and Ph.D. Every time Anzaldúa "code-switched," all the professors (except for James Sledd) in the "Comp Lit" and "English Lit" courses she took "marked [her] down" for not writing the "status-quo way." Anzaldúa's expressed frustration at the lack of encouragement she got from these literature classes suggests that she faults her teachers for "subtly wanting her to" refrain from innovative efforts. That is, they bombed her into accepting the norms of the field. Indeed, she uses these stories to indict college classrooms that coerce students like herself into believing that she "cannot"—has no ability to and is therefore not allowed to—be innovative until she has proven her fluency in the "status quo way" and thus earned the appropriate credentials.

In fact, I would argue that memories of her own frustration as a writing student are in part why Anzaldúa hopes her own writing might serve an alternative pedagogical function for other student readers. For instance, she imagines one reader to say upon reading her work: "'I didn't know that Chicano Spanish was the bastard language. And if Chicano Spanish is a bastard language, what registers of English are also bastards and not allowed into the academy?' [. . .] And then maybe the reader will say, 'I don't know, I'm a redneck and this is my language, and maybe I should write about this language for this particular class'" (22). This passage suggests that Anzaldúa hopes that her writing might lead student readers to recognize that they are capable of and should be allowed, encouraged, to try out the alternative model she poses in her postcoloniality and writing. She hopes her writing would persuade professors teaching "this particular class" to not mark this student down for trying to be innovative, as her own professors had. She would not want any professor to use the developmental plot embedded in her fish and electrician analogies as a rationale for keeping her student readers from trying out the alternative models she poses in her writing. To use Anzaldúa's literacy narrative of her own student days to problematize the developmental myth in her analogies is in keeping with composition's commitment to examine the potential discrepancy between teachers' views of what students can do and students' views of what they can do. This in turn can help both composition and postcolonial studies increase their vigilance over how they talk about their positions on when a writer is ready to be innovative.

A second direction for applying composition's contention with the developmental plot would be to consider Anzaldúa's position on when students placed in basic sections of college writing courses can try alternative or innovative models of writing. Whether Anzaldúa would consider all student readers of her work in any college classes ready to try out the alternative model she poses as a writer remains ambiguous. Does she imagine that "the particular class" her "redneck" reader is taking is the kind of literature classes she herself had been placed in during undergraduate and graduate school? Or would she consider those students placed in basic writing classes ready for similar innovative moves *before* they have been tested out of the remedial section of the academy? This is a difficult task since the interview makes no direct reference to this body of students. The absence of this body of students is common in postcolonial scholarship most probably because few working in that field have had any direct contact with or experience of having been placed in—as either a student or teacher—a basic writing course. This contact is necessary for scholars like Anzaldúa, however, who are interested in "connect[ing]" their writing with "the real-life, bodily experiences of people who were suffering because of some kind of oppression."

Composition studies can help postcolonial writers like Anzaldúa problematize the developmental plot by providing insights and strategies for taking a closer look at the work of student writers housed at the bottom tiers of the institutional ladder. For instance, composition studies has tapped into the "hidden script" in "poor" student performances—their seeming indifference to learning or their "error-ridden" prose—by asking and taking seriously students' answers to a series of questions: How and why is it that some of them have failed to "have" the grades and "brains" necessary for entering credit-granting English courses? What do individual basic writers have to say about how and why they have (or have not) found the developmental plot convincing and/or viable for their own education? To what extent have the reading postures of teachers who contest or endorse the developmental frame affected the agency of these student writers as they try to write with and against the laws of English? Others in composition have also used these student literacy accounts to revise academic interpretations and representations of the writings of basic students (T. Fox; Hull and Rose; Hull et al.; Soliday). By studying student writing while it is still in process and still in its (less finished) form of notes, journals, drafts, or revisions, still others in composition studies have gathered a wealth of evidence that basic student writers are not only interested in but also capable of trying to push against the norms of English even as they learn to work within them.

For instance, Aneil Rallin uses his own experience as a writer and teacher of writing to call into question the complaint of his colleagues that students for whom English is a second language (ESL students) do not "belong in their classes" because these students are "unable to speak and write standard American English fluently." "I wonder who among us hasn't fumbled with language?" Rallin asked in response. He links such collegial interchange in the hallways to his ESL students' fear that he, the teacher, will read "their indecision with the English language, their pauses, as signs of their ignorance." And he argues for the need to study the students' seeming "uncertainty" or "indecision" in terms of not only their fear and anger toward the teacher's assumptions about what they cannot do but also in terms of what they indeed can and want to do—their efforts to write in response to the specific, complex "reality" of their lives and the "valuable insights" they have to share.

These traditions of inquiry in composition studies can help writers like Anzaldúa explore ways of complicating their use of the word "can" in the developmental plot so that the word would invoke the conflict between, on the one hand, what the students "can"—are *allowed* to—do by dominant modes of English instruction and, on the other, what they "can" do—are interested in and have the capability of doing—*before* the academy accredits them as indeed fluent in what it believes they "need to have" before being innovative. Doing so could help Anzaldúa prevent her fish and electrician analogies from being appropriated by the dominant to perpetuate the developmental myth and thus to protect the power of English to swallow other languages, realities, and experiences. The essays herein illustrate that postcolonial theory can help composition teachers and students to further these traditions of inquiry by attending more rigorously to the specific and complex geopolitical context of individual literacy practices. At the same time, taking note of the work of composition might help writers like Anzaldúa explore ways of more explicitly and more rigorously connecting their postcolonial perspectives and styles with the experience and efforts of student writers placed outside the walls of (credit earning) college literature classrooms traditionally attended and taught by these published writers, students representing one of the most subordinated groups within the walls of the university.

Point Three: Acknowledging the Materiality of Writing

Lunsford brings to her interview with Anzaldúa a series of questions central to composition research on the composing process: "Are there any things about writing that are particularly hard for you? Or easy?" "Do you try to write at a regular time? Every day?" "Do you compose at the word processor?" "Do the words seem to come out as well from the ends of your fingers typing as they did when you were scripting?" In response, Anzaldúa links the "problem of voice"—her refusal to do "disembodied writing" and her struggle "to start with the feeling"—with the problem of engaging and disengaging oneself with writing. This in turn calls attention to the specific material conditions sustaining and constraining her work as she tries to "recommit" herself daily to her embodied writing, which she likens to "making a date" with herself: "I really have to get into the feeling [. . .] which I access sometimes by being very, very quiet and doing some deep breathing, or by some little tiny meditation, or by burning some incense. [. . .] Sometimes I walk along the beach. So I access this state, I get all psyched up, and then I do the writing. I work four, five, six hours; and then I have to come off that [. . .] heightened, aware state. [. . .] To disengage you have to take another walk, wash the dishes, go to the garden, talk on the telephone, just because it is too much. Your body cannot take it." Later in the interview, we learn that when the feminist architects (hired to put an addition on her house) asked what kind of space Anzaldúa wanted to live in, her answer was "tall, a lot of opening, a lot of window space."

Lunsford's questions also draw out the technological aspects of the materiality of writing: "Yes, I do [compose at the word processor], at my desk, and sometimes I take my little laptop to the coffee house or to the beach, or just outside." Then Anzaldúa recalls a time when she had "to resort to handwriting" because her computer broke down during a four-week stay at an artists' retreat. This "switched [her] over" from her plan to "do stories" to doing revisions of stories in hard copy, writing poems, and "writing exercises."

These accounts depict a writer with access to the kind of time, quiet personal space, natural environment, and technologies that are not always available to all writers. I have in mind here not only professional writers but also student writers who likely keep full-time or part-time jobs in nonacademic settings and share crowded living spaces with others. As the interview reminds us, the younger Anzaldúa herself had to work under a very different set of conditions: "When we were growing up, we had to work after school. We had chores, we had field work, we had house work. And then it was time for bed, and I didn't get to do my reading. So I would read under the covers with a flashlight in bed with my sister. And my brothers were in the same room, but my sister and I shared the same bed. And she was ready to tell my mom. To keep her entertained, and to keep her from going to my mom, I would tell her a story. I would make up a story—just something that had happened during the day. [. . .] So I was writing stories very early." As illustrated by the different working conditions enjoyed by the younger Anzaldúa and the current day Anzaldúa as well as by research in composition studies, access to time, quiet personal space, and technology are not always equally and globally distributed along lines of class, race, ethnicity, and gender (Canagarajah; T. Fox, 10–17).

For instance, Aneil Rallin contextualizes his choice of style—the note form—and topic—(im)migrant crossings—in the materiality of his work. He uses "images and dispatches" to connect his mestiza rhetoric with not only his being from the Third World and queer but also his writing the piece in San Diego (the border between Mexico and the United States of America) and his thoughts on the conditions of life of the "homeless" and "queer" in the United States. And he connects his writing with his work as a *visiting* assistant professor hired to "teach" (only) and teach "service courses" as well as with the working conditions of the "migrant laborers of the academy": the invisible janitors and cleaners and the part-time faculty and teaching assistants—the only ones teaching first-year composition at San Diego State University. Rallin's writing and the exchange between Lunsford and Anzaldúa remind us of the need to examine the socioeconomic conditions sustaining and constraining the work of individual writers when exploring the viability of mestiza rhetoric. For to fail to do so would be to reify and universalize mestiza rhetoric in ways classical rhetoric has been historically legislated in the U.S. academy. We need to teach and learn mestiza rhetoric in accompaniment with rather than in detachment from considerations of the materiality of writing (see Horner, *Terms* 219–22).

The interview also hints at the importance of introducing the body into discussions of the materiality of writing. Anzaldúa states: "Some days I don't feel like going to meet that appointment [to do this writing]. It's too hard on my body, especially since I have diabetes; it takes out too much."

The issue of physical health is material on at least two levels: it affects the physical, emotional, and psychic energy demanded by the labor of writing, thus contesting the dichotomy between ideas and feelings; and it is affected by access to health care, which continues to be unevenly distributed within and outside the United States along race, class, and gender lines. These references to the complex material conditions sustaining and constraining Anzaldúa's struggle for a mestiza rhetoric suggest that if the purpose of asking students to study Anzaldúa's writing is to help them practice the mestiza rhetoric in their own writings, then we need to consider more than merely the degree to which the student readers can *"see* themselves in the text" and whether "reading these other voices *gives them permission* to go out and acquire their own voices, to write in this way" (emphasis mine). Rather, we also need to link individual students' efforts to practice that rhetoric with the often different but equally complex materiality of Anzaldúa's work and of individual students' work. In this way, the question of how and why we might want to teach students to practice mestiza rhetoric would be linked to questions like the following: Given the specific material conditions of her or his life, how would the individual student writer go about enacting the mestiza rhetoric promoted in the writing classroom? How might the student writer go about revising both that rhetoric and those material conditions when learning to enact it?

The questions Lunsford brings to her interview indicate that as a result of sustained work in areas such as the "composing process" and the "materiality of writing," composition studies has come up with a wealth of strategies for pursuing these questions. Her questions also call attention to the noticeable absence of such questions in other interviews with postcolonial writers (see, e.g., interviews with Gayatri Spivak by Roony, Bahri, and Vasudeva). While the question of how to construct and textually represent subject positions against the grain of transnational and internal colonization occupies these interviews, no attention is paid in any of them to either the actual process of composing or the complex material conditions sustaining the writing of a text such as "Can the Subaltern Speak?" This absence significantly delimits how both the participants and readers of such interviews investigate the often privileged material conditions of various U.S. academic postcolonial critics and writers. In contrast, Lunsford's interview reminds us to explore the "accessibility" of postcolonial theory to diverse readers and writers in terms of not only its "very high abstract language" but also the distinctive, often privileged, material conditions constraining and sustaining its production.

Point Four: Representing the "Student Writer"

As several articles in this collection illustrate, composition studies has much to offer postcolonial studies on how to confront our institutional authority to speak for student writers by taking into account what students have to say about themselves in relation to us and our teaching. Like other works in composition, these articles indicate a concern to acknowledge the specificity of individual student writers in terms of not only the students' lived experience of race, ethnicity, class, gender, sex, or geographical divisions, but also the link between these divisions and academic divisions between literature and composition, published and student writers, and across different levels of student writers. For instance, Lunsford reminds Anzaldúa that the "student" she has in mind is someone "in a first-year writing class, who may come from southern Texas and be a speaker of Spanish as a first language." "Many of my students are from small farming communities in Ohio. Most of them are Anglo" and "don't see themselves as having any race, any ethnicity, and often they don't even think they have any range of sexuality." Others writing in this collection refer to "female students" in women's studies classes (Jarratt), "Southwestern bilingual minority students" in a "first-year college" writing or literature class (Mejía), and two male masters' students dialoguing through email while taking a course titled "Teaching Writing from a Postcolonial Perspective" in upstate New York (Gay 1). This attention to the specific institutional location of the individual student is something I've not come across in any of the rare moments in the writings of postcolonial critics, such as Spivak, when they make actual references to students or depict their actions and thoughts.

In "Terms of Engagement," Bahri cautions composition studies to use postcolonial materials—the literature and the theoretical concepts—with a high degree of vigilance. She joins others in postcolonial studies to argue that the association of the concept of "hybridity" with "metropolitan postcolonial celebrities" such as Bhabha and Rushdie can risk glamorizing "transnational border-crossing" and overlook "intransigent borders within," including "the deeply racial and class segregated nature of our cities" and the experiences of "scores of underclass immigrants in Anglo-American and illegal border-crossers" (see also Mejía). Composition's persistent attention to the specific institutional location of individual student writers suggests that composition studies can enhance that vigilance by highlighting yet another set of borders often neglected by postcolonial theory: namely, the borders within English studies across diverse fields and types of students.

Lunsford's interview enacts that vigilance along two such institutional borders. In naming Anzaldúa a postcolonial critic, the interview not only puts the internal "colonization of the Chicano, the Blacks, the Natives" and the realities of a "woman," "queer," "child" at the center of postcolonial studies but also contests the division between theoretical and creative writing within English Studies. By asking Anzaldúa to talk about her current work in relation to her earlier experience as a student writer and to the first-year writing students at Lunsford's institution, the interview also reminds us to examine the ways in which U.S. postcolonial academics represent, talk to, about, for, or alongside student writers.

In "Beside Ourselves: Rhetoric and Representation in Postcolonial Feminist Writing," Susan C. Jarratt argues through a detailed analysis of the writings of Trinh T. Minh-ha and Gayatri Spivak that in the writings of both critics "[a] principled resistance to the temptation to speak for India, for Vietnam, for women is joined with the principled impulse to put the voice of the 'other' in play in first-world academic discourse." That is, these writers exemplify a model for speaking "'beside, alongside, among, in common with, with the help and favor of, in the midst of others." As Jarratt and others in this collection have cogently argued, postcolonial theory can inform composition on how to put the voices of those "othered" by international and internal divisions of race, ethnicity, class, gender, and sexuality in play in first-world academic discourse. At the same time, the recurring references to "student writers" in the collection point to a common oversight in postcolonial theory: recognition of the need of academic intellectuals to resist the temptation of speaking for the student writer.

Composition can inform postcolonial studies on how to confront our role as the "professional 'representers'" of student writers (Jarratt). Composition studies has a substantial tradition of trying to ensure that our impulse to put the voice of the student writer (especially the basic writer) in play with first-world academic discourse is joined by our resistance to the temptation to speak for student writers (see, e.g., Mejía.) To begin with, composition studies has addressed the politics of representing student writers by examining the ways in which dominant conventions in academic discourse name the differences between writers and nonwriters and across diverse populations of writers; legislate the desires, efforts, and needs of these differently ranked writers; and solicit, analyze, and evaluate the writings produced by these differently ranked writers (at different stages of the composing process) (see Helmers; Horner, "Mapping;" R. Miller, "Fault Lines;" S. Miller, *Textual*). More recently, composition scholars have furthered this inquiry by asking how we as teachers and scholars of writing perceive and represent ourselves, and what potential gaps might exist between how we represent ourselves and how students might represent us (Royster and Taylor 30).

This tradition of inquiry is briefly evidenced in several essays in this collection. For instance, when discussing the ways in which feminist postcolonial theories might contribute to the reading practices of writing teachers, Jarratt points out: "I am not suggesting that students *will* consciously employ the complex tactics I have outlined in the writing of the two academic postcolonial feminists but rather that we might use Spivak's and Trinh's rhetorical gestures as guides for reading traces or symptoms of texts from students writing their own relations to institutional power. *Imagining* students capable of inscribing multiple selves could be an important reading posture for teachers concerned with subject construction in a postcolonial era" (emphasis mine). The word *imagine* is key to Jarratt's view of how "teachers of writing, language, and literature in U.S. universities" might confront our ethical responsibility as "professional 'representers.'" Jarratt argues that "a postcolonial intellectual cannot speak for these unrepresented groups but only *to* them in an *imagined* conversation across class lines and historical distances" (emphasis mine). Feminist postcolonial intellectuals resist the professional temptation to speak for the powerless by highlighting the "imagined" nature of the conversation. In urging us to adopt reading postures which "imagine" our students "as capable of inscribing multiple selves," Jarratt is also reminding us to confront our ethical responsibility. We cannot speak *for* the student writers—legislate what they can, want, or need to do—but only *to* them in an *imagined* conversation *across* social, historical, and institutional divisions.

The effort to imagine the viewpoints of student writers is also evidenced in Jarratt's disclaimer: "I am not suggesting that students *will* consciously employ the complex tactics I have outlined in the writings of the two academic postcolonial feminists" (emphasis mine). The disclaimer indicates Jarratt's concern to problematize the role of postcolonial feminist teachers: our institutional power to rank rhetors along the literate (intellectual, published, student, basic writers) and illiterate ("not a writer") divide, as does our power to use our reading gestures to solicit or silence the voices of others. In "not suggesting" that students "will" consciously employ the tactics she herself so admired in the "two academic postcolonial feminists," Jarratt likewise calls attention to the potential disjunction between the tactics individual students *will* employ, given the specific institutional as well as social and historical context of each act of reading and writing, and what teachers like herself are urging "us" to "imagine" the students as capable of and needing to do. I highlight Jarratt's effort to acknowledge such disjunctions because it is in keeping with composition's persistent concern to imagine conversations with student writers across academic divisions and because such efforts are often missing in other works which argue for the need and feasibility of teaching students to employ the "postcolonial" rhetoric enacted by writers such as Bhabha, Said, Spivak, and Anzaldúa.

To become ungrateful receivers of postcolonial theory, we need to accompany composition's emerging impulse to put the voice of elite academic postcolonial feminists in play in first-world discourse with composition's long-standing knowledge of and expertise in resisting the temptation to speak for student writers—to measure their needs by the yardstick of elite academic postcolonial feminists. Composition research and teaching practices have long examined the teacher's choice of "reading posture" (toward texts by student as well as published writers) as a primary institutional means for soliciting or excluding specific literacy practices. Composition can thus help postcolonial studies to become more reflexive about the ways in which teachers' reading postures, whether informed by postcolonial or classic rhetoric, set constraints on how students go about writing and rewriting their relations to institutional power. More specifically, it can offer postcolonial studies insights on how to use writing assignments, written and oral responses to student papers, and qualitative research to imagine conversations with students concerning the reading postures of teachers and to use such conversations to revise how we respond to and represent student writings in our teaching and scholarship.

There are vestiges of such strategies at work in several moments in this collection, where the authors explicitly acknowledge the need to "imag-

ine" what the student writers might be saying in their writings about "ou
effort to bring the voices of "postcolonial" writers and critics into writir.
classrooms. For instance, in "Arts of the United States–Mexico Contacı
Zone," Jaime Armin Mejía cautions academic elites to recognize the potential gap between the voice of the published writer "we" select to speak for
or to "ethnic minority" student writers and the concerns and realities of
the actual student writer. Citing Sandra Jamieson, Mejía argues that if previous readings demand that the reader adopt a white, middle-class reading-
subject position, which is also still male, alternative reading (featuring the
cultural backgrounds or histories of "ethnic minority" students) "might be
forcing the same kind of demand in identity construction, albeit a different
one, on ethnic minority students who may not construct their identities
ethnically." Mejía further resists the temptation to speak for "ethnic minority
students" by examining the institutional sources he has used to back this
representation of ethnic minority students: an ethnographic study by Shirley
Brice Heath and Milbrey McLaughlin on young people (including Latinos)
of youth organizations in inner cities. "Invaluable and revealing as Heath
and McLaughlin's studies are about ir.ner-city youth," Mejía notes, "one nevertheless would like to have seen extended views from the ethnic minority
youth's own perspectives confirming their multilayered self-conceptions
in contact zones." Furthermore, "the perspectives of adults of color" living
in comparable contact zones are absent. Mejía thus articulates a healthy
skepticism common in composition theory toward how we represent the
needs, realities, and desires of various bodies of student writers in our ethnographic research and teaching, in the texts we select, as well as in the reading postures we endorse.

In "Hybridity: A Lens for Understanding Mestizo/a Writers," Louise
Rodríguez Connal uses her own experience as a writer, researcher, and
teacher to call for a "closer reading" of students' language choices, linguistic
patterns, and codes (18, 20). More specifically, she considers the possibility
of reading "the strategies of submissive subversion and indirection" that
some Latina students use in terms of their efforts to "engage with their
hybrid cultures by addressing two or more audiences." She cautions us
against "facile comparisons" between the reasons offered by researchers
such as Belenky and company on why women in their research are reluctant to speak out and the reasons for some "Latinas' hesitation to write or
speak out." She argues instead for the teachers' need, when approaching
the "indirect" mestiza rhetoric of Puerto Rican student writers, to take

into account not only issues of gender but also specific factors such as "the features of the particular Spanish and English spoken by Puerto Ricans," the changes to the Puerto Rican economy after its conquest by the United States, and the history of Puerto Rican migrations to the United States.

In "Resisting Writing: Reflections on the Postcolonial Factor in the Writing Class," David Dzaka likewise cautions against interpreting all international students' "resistance" to academic writing as stemming from the same reasons. While the resistance of students from countries with "a long-standing tradition of writing in their own cultures" might be related to their need to negotiate the conflict between two cultural traditions, Dzaka argues that for students like him, resistance to writing needs to be studied within the specificity of the colonizing process in which English and the teaching of writing were historically introduced to Ghana, where he was educated.

While such moves to solicit student representations of "us" (the teacher of the writing course and the published writers whose work the students have been assigned to read) and to acknowledge the specific locations of the student writer (institutional as well as geopolitical) are standard in composition research, they are to my knowledge glaringly absent in the writings of all the postcolonial critics and writers cited by the essays in this collection. As Hall and Rosner point out in "Pratt and Pratfalls: Revisioning Contact Zones," in Mary Louise Pratt's much cited "Arts of the Contact Zone," the perspectives of the students taking Pratt's western civilization class, who Pratt depicts as experiencing joys and pains, remain visibly absent. At the same time, it also seems that much less space and energy are given to such moves in composition theory that try to engage with postcolonial theory than in most regular issues of most composition journals.

For instance, it is becoming standard practice in composition theory to address the politics of representation by not only bringing in the voice of individual students but also examining the particular assignment used to solicit particular student texts, examining individual students' actual experiences when producing these texts, and examining the degree to which the responses of the teacher and peers concerning these texts have affected those students' performance when revising that text or various versions of other texts. Continuing this tradition of inquiry can benefit composition's effort to learn from postcolonial studies. Bahri notes that in the Anglo-American academy, "the lessons of postcolonialism are abstracted from their contexts and brought into discussion of marginality and victimage in domestic debates on diversity." Reflexivity to the extent that teachers' reading and writing postures (in the writing of assignments and comments on student writings, as well as in conducting class discussions on student and published texts) affect the rhetorical practices of students can help composition part ways with such cooptation of postcolonial theory and texts in some "multicultural" literature classes in the Anglo-American academy. Rather than using postcolonialism as a way to canonize new themes such as abuse, trauma, or migration when selecting teaching materials (and, I'd add, when soliciting student writing), we might engage in serious discussions on how to use assigned writing, comments, and discussions to help students address the politics of representation when reading and writing such themes. Writing and reading trauma or migration can then go beyond reading and writing *about* the trauma or migration of an "other" and *about* relations of domination in which only "others" but not ourselves are implicated. Our impulse to let in those themes traditionally perceived as not belonging in the texts students write would thus be joined by a rigorous reflexivity on how we go about soliciting student writing addressing such themes. We would pose the questions to ourselves and our students of who is writing about the victimization of whom, when, where, to whom, and why.

Continued research on the responses of individual students to our efforts to engage postcolonial theory and texts can also help us create mutual giving between composition and postcolonial studies. Together, we might extend our impulse to bring the diverse voices of U.S. college students—mainstream as well as transnational and internal immigrants—into play with first-world academic discourse on postcolonialism by joining that impulse with a rigorous resistance to our professional temptation to speak for our students.

Composition's Vitality as the Ungrateful Receiver

By identifying four possible points of departure, I hope to jump-start rather than to exhaust how composition teachers and scholars might go about confronting the institutional givens of composition's exchanges with postcolonial studies. Both postcolonial studies and composition studies are dynamic and heterogeneous institutional sites. My reading of composition's potential as the ungrateful receiver of postcolonial studies speaks more to my specific location within composition studies and thus to those issues with which I've been most invested in wrestling. Hopefully, the partiality of my reading will stimulate others to rework the contours of this provisional mapping from different locations and different readings of the fields and of their relations.

As a field of studies, composition is in a unique position to explore the vitality of the ungrateful receiver and to do so in relation not only to postcolonial studies but also to all emerging theories and fields in asymmetrical institutional power relations with composition. Composition is in this vital position on at least three levels. First, as an academic field, it has been from its inception explicitly cross-disciplinary in aim. It has thus developed a solid tradition of reflecting on the strengths and limitations of its past and present exchanges with other disciplines—as, for instance, in its turn to the scientific objectivism of quantitative research. It has amassed a wealth of strategies for gift receiving and giving across disciplinary boundaries and against the grains of institutional hierarchies. Second, as a site of instruction, composition works with an unusually diverse body of students across all colleges, disciplines, and programs, as well as across all academic ranks. It is often in more direct contact with the specific and different concerns and interests of diverse student groups and thus in tune with how and why the dominant theories and practices of diverse fields might work (and not work) for specific students (see, e.g., Wolff and Miller's reworking of Pratt's theory as analyzed by Hall and Rosner). Third, as a work force composition consists of members with training, interest, and work in programs as diverse as literary studies, creative writing, education, literacy studies, linguistics, and rhetoric. Vigilance toward academic hierarchies and their impact on how we speak and listen to one another is a lived necessity in the daily experience of becoming and being a part of this work force. In short, the question of how to mobilize composition's vitality as the ungrateful receiver of the knowledge and practices of the powerful disciplines and fields is by no means new to the geography of composition. At most, to take this question to composition's exchange with postcolonial studies is to add a signpost to composition's institutional map. But it is a necessary sign if composition studies is to sustain its hybridity as an academic field, instructional site, and work force.

Andrea A. Lunsford

TOWARD A MESTIZA RHETORIC

Gloria Anzaldúa on Composition and Postcoloniality

I will have my voice: Indian, Spanish, white. I will have my serpent's tongue—
my woman's voice, my sexual voice, my poet's voice. I will overcome the tradition of silence.

Gloria Anzaldúa, Borderlands/La Frontera

Gloria Anzaldúa has not had an easy time of having what she calls her "own
voice." Born in 1942 and raised in the border country of south Texas (in
Jesus Maria of the Valley), Anzaldúa learned early that she was different, an
"alien from another planet" who didn't quite fit with the norms and expectations of her family and community, didn't "act like a nice little Chicanita
is supposed to act" ("La Prieta," 199, 201). Describing some of her early experiences in "La Prieta," Anzaldúa rejects ongoing efforts to label her differences in various ways—as lesbian, as feminist, as marxist, as mystic, as
"other:" "Ambivalent? Not so. Only your labels split me," she says (205).

In this early essay, Anzaldúa announces the multiplicity of her "self"
and her "voice." She is a "wind-swayed bridge, a crossroads inhabited by
whirlwinds"; she is "Shiva, a many-armed and legged body with one foot
on brown soil, one on white, one in straight society, one in the gay world,
the man's world, the woman's, one limb in the literary world, another in the

working class, the socialist, and the occult worlds. A sort of spider woman hanging by one thin strand of web" (204). And indeed, much of Anzaldúa's work has been devoted to making a space where such multiplicity could be enacted. *This Bridge Called My Back*, edited with Cherie Moraga, grew out of an experience at a 1979 women's retreat during which Anzaldúa was made (once again) to feel she was being labeled—tokenized as a "Third World woman" and as an outsider, an exoticized other to the white feminists there. Characteristically, Anzaldúa turned that experience into a means of affirming her commitment to women of color by providing a forum in which their multiple voices—and her own—could be heard. In 1987 came her groundbreaking *Borderlands/La Frontera*, the book in which she has most thoroughly rendered and theorized the borderland space that is home to her multiple identities and voices. And then in 1990—after years of waiting for someone "to compile a book that would continue where *This Bridge Called My Back* left off"—Anzaldúa edited the luxuriant and sprawling collection *Making Face, Making Soul/Haciendo Caras*. (She has also given voice to two bilingual children's picture/story books, including: *Prietita Has a Friend/Prietita tiene un amigo* and *Friends from the Other Side/Amigos del otro lado*).

Taken together, Anzaldúa's work (including a number of essays not cited here) stands testimony to her personal triumph over the "tradition of silence" and to her ability to imagine, enact, and inhabit spaces that go beyond dichotomies of all kinds: beyond male/female; beyond reason/emotion; beyond gay/straight; beyond other/white; beyond mythic/real; beyond mind/body; beyond spirit/matter; beyond orality/literacy; beyond I/you. In every case, Anzaldúa rejects either/or in favor of both/and then some, of an identity that is always in process. As she says in "To(o) Queer the Writer," identity can never be reduced to a "bunch of little cubbyholes. [. . .] Identity flows between, over, aspects of a person. Identity is a river, a process" (252–53). This process, which Anzaldúa represents both as occurring on the borderland, the in-between, and in the act of making faces/souls can enable transformations that, while often brutally painful, can allow for nonbinary identity, for new states of mestiza consciousness, and for multiple writing strategies (what AnaLouise Keating calls "mestizaje écriture" and what I am calling a "mestiza rhetoric").

In these moments, it is possible to take in the labels of society and to transform them, to find all others in one's self; one's self in all others. Learning to live such transformations calls for a "new mestiza" who has "a tolerance for contradictions, a tolerance for ambiguity," who "learns to be an Indian in Mexican culture, to be Mexican from an Anglo point of view. She learns to juggle cultures. [. . .] Not only does she sustain contradictions, she turns the ambivalence into something else" (*Borderlands* 79). In turn, living in and rendering such contradictions and transformations calls for a new kind of writing style. In Anzaldúa's case, this means a rich mixture of genres —she shifts from poetry to reportorial prose to autobiographical stream of consciousness to incantatory mythic chants to sketches and graphs, and back again—weaving images and words from her multiple selves and from many others into a kind of tapestry or patchwork quilt of language. It also means an insistence that visual images and words belong together in texts of all kinds as well as a rich mix of languages—some English, some Spanish, some Tex/Mex, some Nahuatl—and registers. In "How to Tame a Wild Tongue," she denounces "linguistic terrorism," saying "I am my language. Until I can take pride in my language, I cannot take pride in myself. Until I can accept as legitimate Chicano Texas Spanish, Tex-Mex, and all the other languages I speak, I cannot accept the legitimacy of myself. Until I am free to write bilingually and to switch codes without having to translate, [. . .] my tongue will be illegitimate" (*Borderlands* 59). In the interview that follows, Anzaldúa comments on all of these issues. She also has much to say about her prior experiences with and current relationship to writing and to a form of collaboration, aspects of her work that will be of special interest to rhetoric and composition students.

As we might expect, Anzaldúa's relationship to language and to writing is extremely complex. If books, as she says in the preface to *Borderlands/La Frontera* "saved [her] sanity" and taught her "first how to survive and then how to soar," she often figures the act of writing as daring and dangerous (*Bridge* 171) or as painful, as a terrifying ride in the "nightsky" (*Borderlands* 140–41), as like "carving bone" (73), as giving birth, an endless cycle of "making it worse, making it better, but always making meaning out of the experience" (73), as a "blood sacrifice" (75). Writing is for Anzaldúa thus inextricably related to the process of making (or writing) faces/souls as well as a primary means of enabling the kinds of ongoing transformations necessary for inhabiting the borderlands. *"There is no separation between life and writing,"* she says in "Speaking in Tongues: A Letter to Third World Women Writers," so *"Why aren't you riding, writing, writing?"* (emphasis hers). And most important, she cautions, "It's not on paper that you create but in your innards, in your gut and out of living tissue—*organic writing*, I call it" (*Bridge* 172).

Given her commitment to multiplicity and inclusivity, Anzaldúa is naturally drawn to forms of collaboration—with artists in her children's books, with co-editors and with collectives in other works, even—as she says in the following interview—with the architect and designers who have helped to expand her home. Anzaldúa represents herself as in constant conversation, a dialogue between her many selves, her multiple audiences / readers, and the texts that emerge in the process (with their own intertexts and interfaces) that hum along on her computer screen. "That's what writers do, we carry on a constant dialogue between language and hands and images, one or another of our identities trying desperately to get in a word, an image, a sound," she says in a passage in *Making Face* that is highly reminiscent of Bakhtinian dialogism (xxiv). In fact, Anzaldúa's discussions of the crucial role audiences / others play in her own writing provide a fine example of what Bakhtin means by "answerability," which Anzaldúa refers to as "responsibility," literally the ability to respond, to answer, to join in a conversation that is always ongoing. As she says in this interview, "I do the composing, but it's taken from little mosaics of other people's lives, other people's perceptions." These mosaics are her own collaborative response-abilities (for a further explanation of this aspect of Anzaldúa's work, see Susan Bickford's "In the Presence of Others") and reveal the degree to which she is aware of the politics of address, of her need to answer or respond in ways that will create a readership at the same time that it teaches how to "read" her respondings (*Making Face* xviii).

During this interview, Anzaldúa remarks that she has been shocked to "find composition people picking me up" (she was interviewed at a CCCC meeting in 1992 by Donna Perry). Given that composition has long been equated with the hegemony of "standard" English and with gatekeeping, Anzaldúa's surprise is—well, not surprising. As this interview reveals, however, she has experienced in her own schooling both the limiting and the liberatory impulses in composition, the latter in the company of longtime writing teacher, theorist, and critic Jim Sledd. Close attention to this doubled experience with composition and a close reading of this interview suggests to me that, among her many selves, Anzaldúa includes a writing theorist as well as an accomplished rhetor and a prolific writer. She is also a teacher. When I asked her whether she thought mestiza consciousness could be taught, she said yes, though with great difficulty and pain. In *Making Face*, she speaks directly of her own teaching goals: "I wanted a book which would teach ourselves and whites to read in nonwhite narrative traditions" (xviii); moreover, she wants to teach others to acquire voices without becoming *periquitas* (parrots) and to use theory to "change people and the way they perceive the world" (xxv). "We need *teorías*," she says, "that will enable us to interpret what happens in the world, that will explain how and why we relate to certain people in specific ways, that will reflect what goes on between inner, outer, and peripheral 'I's within a person and between the personal 'I's and the collective 'we' of our ethnic communities. *Necesitamos teorías* that [. . .] cross borders, that blur boundaries—new kinds of theories with new theorizing methods" (xxv). Here and elsewhere Gloria Anzaldúa calls for a new rhetoric, a mestiza rhetoric, that she is clearly in the process of helping to make.

Q. What are some of your very early memories of writing? I'm using writing very broadly here to include drawing, marking, any kind of language use that seems like writing.

A. Sí, the whole activity of writing and the conditions that surround it as distinct from writing on a piece of paper started early on orally with me: it started as a defense against my sister. When we were growing up, we had to work after school. We had chores, we had fieldwork, we had housework. And then it was time for bed, and I didn't get to do my reading. So I would read under the covers with a flashlight in bed with my sister. And my brothers were in the same room, but my sister and I shared the same bed. And she was ready to tell my mom. To keep her entertained, I would tell her a story. I would make up a story—just something that had happened during the day, and I would make it all kind of like an adventure or a quest of the happenings of these little girls, my sister and myself, and, you know, I kind of embroidered it. And so she would settle down and go back to sleep and wouldn't tell my mom the next day. And then the following night she would want the same thing. Every night I learned to tell a little story. So I was writing stories very early.

Q. Your own version of *A Thousand and One Nights?*

A. And then this is what happened: she wanted two. So I got into doing serials. I would tell a part of the story and then break it off and say, "You know, if you don't tell, you'll get the rest of it tomorrow." It was like I turned the tables on her. So for me, writing has always been about narrative, about story; and it still is. Theory is a kind of narrative. Science—you know, physics —that's a narrative, that's a hit on reality. Anthropology has its narrative. And some are master narratives, and some are outsider narratives. There's that whole struggle in my writing between the dominant culture's traditional, conventional narratives about reality and about literature and about science and about life and about politics; and my other counternarratives as a *mestiza* growing up in this country, as an internal exile, as an inner exile, as a postcolonial person, because the Mexican race in the United States is a colonized people. My ancestors were living life on the border. The band was part of the state of Tamaulipas, Mexico, and then the U.S. bought it, bought half of Mexico, and so the Anzaldúas were split in half. The Anzaldúas with an accent, which is my family, were north of the border. The Anzalduas without an accent stayed on the other side of the border, and as the decades went by we lost connection with each other. And so the Anzaldúas and the Anzalduas, originally from the same land, the state of Tamaulipas in the nation of Mexico, all of a sudden became strangers in our own land, foreigners in our own land. We were a colonized people who were not allowed to speak our language, whose ways of life were not valued in this country. Public education tried to erase all of that. So here I am now, a kind of international citizen whose life and privileges are not equal to the rights and privileges of ordinary, Anglo, White, Euro-American people. My narratives always take into account these other ethnicities, these other races, these other cultures, these other histories. There's always that kind of struggle.

Q. I know that art and drawing are central to much of your work, and I think of drawing as a kind of writing too. As a child, did you draw a lot?

A. Yes. I wanted to be an artist. I wasn't sure whether I wanted to be a visual artist or a writer, or something else, but I started out as an artist, and in fact the teaching that I did in high school as a student teacher was in literature and in art. But I never could get a job teaching art in the public schools. I got one teaching composition, teaching English, teaching literature, but not art. But I have a degree in art. I had two areas of focus in my M.A., "majors" I guess was the word, and one was art education and the other was literature.

Q. If you define writing broadly enough to include drawing, then you certainly began writing very, very early in your life.

A. Yes. I started drawing very early on, and besides telling my sister these stories, I started keeping a journal because my sister, my whole family is . . . I don't know how to explain it. We would talk a lot and fight a lot and quarrel a lot.

Q. You were a very verbal family?

A. Very verbal. In some ways like your average family in the U.S., abusive verbally, or not aware of the vulnerabilities a child might have. So I was always gotten after for being too curious, for reading. I was being selfish for studying and reading, rather than doing housework. I was selfish because I wasn't helping the family by reading and writing. So anyway I had all of these emotions. I wanted to fight back and yell, and sometimes I did. But I would watch my sister have temper tantrums, and she would have temper tantrums so severe that she would pee in her pants.

Q. She is younger than you, right?

A. A year and three months. And she would eat dirt. She would get so upset, you know, and I didn't want to be with her. I started shutting down emotions, but I had to find a release for all these feelings. I was feeling alienated from my family and I was fighting against society—you know, your typical preadolescent and adolescent angst. So I started keeping a journal. I attribute my writing to my grandmothers who used to tell stories. I copied them until I started telling my own, but I think it was my sister who forced me to find an outlet to communicate these feelings of hurt and confusion. So I started keeping journals.

Q. Did you keep them throughout school?

A. Yes. I have all of them lined up on top of my closet, but I think the earlier ones are still back home, so I'm going to try to hunt those up. I always keep journals and I do both my little sketches and some texts. The pamphlet I gave you [which includes several drawings] came from a workshop in Pantla that I did at the Villa Montalbo, a writer's residency right here in Saratoga. These people saw an essay that I had done, "Nepantla," about the in-between state that is so important in connecting a lot of issues—the border, the borderland, *nepantla*. It was an essay I had done for a catalog, on border art as being the place that a lot of Chicanas do our work from—you know, the site of cultural production. These people wrote up a grant and got some money, and so five of us (I got to pick some of the other artists) worked for five weeks on a project together and had an exhibit at the San Jose Latino Arts Center. My presentation was both textual and visual. I had the visual image and I had the text and they exhibited them together on the wall.

So, yes, if you define writing as any kind of scribble, any kind of trying to mark on the world, then you have the oral, the dance, the choreography, the performance art, the architects—I had a feminist architect help me design this addition to my study. It's all marking. And some of us want to take those marks that are already getting inscribed in the world and redo them, either by erasing them or by pulling them apart, which involves deconstructive criticism. Pulling them apart is looking at how they are composed and what the relationship is between the frame and the rest of the world. In this country it's White. The dominant culture has the frame of reference. This is its territory, so any mark we make on it has to be made in relationship to the fact that they occupy the space. You can take any field of disciplinary study, like anthropology: that frame is also Euro-American, it's Western. Composition theory, that's very Euro-American. Thus any of us trying to create change have to struggle with this vast territory that's very, very powerful when you try to impinge on it to try to make changes. It's kind of like a fish in the Pacific Ocean, with the analogy that the Pacific Ocean is the dominant field and the fish is this postcolonial, this feminist, or this queer, or whoever is trying to make changes. I think that before you can make any changes in composition studies, philosophy, or whatever it is, you have to have a certain awareness of the territory; you have to be familiar with it and you have to be able to maneuver in it before you can say, "Here's an alternative model for this particular field, for its norms, for its rules and regulations, for its laws." And especially in composition these rules are very strict: creating a thesis sentence, having some kind of argument, having kind of a logical step-by-step progression, using certain methods, like contrast, like deductive versus inductive thinking. I mean all the way back to Aristotle and Cicero with his seven parts of a composition.

So for anyone like me to make any changes or additions to the model takes a tremendous amount of energy, because you're going against the Pacific Ocean and you're this little fish and you have to weigh the odds of succeeding with the goal that you have in mind. Say my goal is a liberatory goal: it's to create possibilities for people, to look at things in a different way so that they can act in their daily lives in a different way. It's like a freeing up, an emancipation. It's a feminist goal. But then I have to weigh things. Okay, if I write in this style and I code-switch too much and I go into Spanglish too much and I do an associative kind of logical progression in a composition, am I going to lose those people that I want to affect, to change? Am I going to lose the respect of my peers—who are other writers and other artists and other academicians—when I change too much, when I change not only the style, but also the rhetoric, the way that this is done? Then I have to look at the students, the young students in high school and in elementary school who are going to be my future readers, if my writing survives that long. And I look at the young college students, especially those reading *Borderlands*: how much of it is a turnoff for them because it's too hard to access? I have to juggle and balance, make it a little hard for them so that they can stop and think, "You know, this is a text, this is not the same as life, this is a representation of life." Because too often when people read something, they take that to be the reality instead of the representation. I don't want to turn those students off. So how much do you push and how much do you accommodate and be in complicity with the dominant norm of whatever field it happens to be?

Q. So if you are a fish in this vast ocean, which is the Anglo-European framework, you can't just reject the water outright but rather try to change it?

A. Yes. Let me show you a little drawing, so you can see what I am saying:

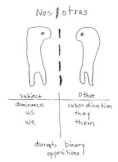

I want to speak of the *nosotras* concept. It used to be that there was a them and an us. We were over here, we were the "other" with other lives, and the *"nos"* was the subject, the White man. And there was a very clear distinction. But as the decades have gone by, we, the colonized, the Chicano, the Blacks, the Natives in this country, have been reared in this frame of reference, in this field. So all of our education, all of our ideas come from this frame of reference. We are complicitous for being in such close proximity and in such intimacy with the other. Now I think that us and them are interchangeable. Now there is no such thing as an other. The other is in you, the other is in me. This White culture has been internalized in my head. I have a White man in here, I have a White woman in here. And they have me in their heads, even if it is just a guilty little nudge sometimes. So, when I try to articulate ideas, I try to do it from that place of occupying both territories: the territory of my past and my ethnic community, my home community, the Chicano Spanish, the Spanglish; and the territory of the formal education, the philosophical educational ideas, and the political ideas that I have internalized just by being alive. Both of these traditions are inherent in me. I cannot disown the White tradition, the Euro–American tradition, any more than I can the Mexican, the Latino, or the native, because they are all in me. And I think that people from different fields are still making these dichotomies—I think.

Q. Would you describe yourself as being in one or more fields?

A. Composition, feminism, postcolonialism . . . I didn't even know I belonged into this postcolonial thing until Patricia Cloud said in a bookflap that I am a feminist, postcolonial critic. And then there is me the artist, me the teacher, and all the multicultural stuff. It's hard to keep up with the reading, so I don't even try anymore. For preparation for this interview, one of your questions was "Who has influenced you as a postcolonial critic?" and I couldn't think of anyone. All of the reading that I've done has been in terms of particular articles for a class. When Homi Bhabha was here, I did some reading and I went to his lecture, which I couldn't understand. When Spivak was here it was the same thing. I took a class with Donna Haraway in feminist theory, and when I had to read "Can the Subaltern Speak?" it took me weeks to decipher one sentence. Well, not weeks, but you know what I'm saying. And then I read a couple of JanMohamed's essays too. Of course, way back I read a little bit of Frantz Fanon's *The Wretched of the Earth*, and Paulo Freire's *The Pedagogy of the Oppressed*, but just little snippets. And then for your interview I got a copy of this postcolonial studies reader. But you know, I didn't have time to really study a lot, so I made little notes about the things that I wanted to think about and maybe respond to in writing.

Q. One of the reasons Lahoucine Ouzgane[1] and I wanted particularly to talk to you about postcolonial studies is that we are interested in why there hasn't been more confluence between postcolonial studies and composition studies. One reason is no doubt the historical association of the English language with colonialism. We think that another of the reasons may well be that postcolonial studies has very quickly theorized itself into very high abstract language that is inaccessible. I think Homi Bhabha is a very good example of the kind of scholar who is speaking on a level of abstraction that just seems completely foreign to a student in a first-year writing class, who may come from southern Texas and be a speaker of Spanish as a first language. Yet it seems a shame that these fields don't talk more to one another. In our perspective, you're a person who does talk to both fields, and in ways that are accessible. My first-year students read parts of *Borderlands,* for example, and they are more threatened than they are puzzled. They are threatened because they think they can't imagine you. Many of my students are from small farming communities in Ohio. Most of them are Anglo, and they say things like, "She sounds so mad. Is she mad? And who is she mad at?" So that's one of the reasons we wanted to talk with you, and to see if in doing so we could find some means of getting both composition and postcolonial studies to think about their own discourses, and the ways in which some of those discourses are very exclusionary—they shut people out.

A. I think that you came at the right time, because the first half of one of the book projects that's currently on my back burner is about composition and postcolonial issues of identity. Most of the questions that you've asked are there, plus others. I have about four different chapters of notes and rough drafts for this book in my computer that have to do with the writing process, that have to do with rhetoric, that have to do with composition. Not just that, but taking it over into how one composes one's life, how one creates an addition to one's house, how one makes sense of all the kinds of coincidental and random things that happen in one's life, how one gives it meaning. So it's my composition theme, *compustura*. In fact, that's the title of one of the chapters: "Compustura." Compustura used to mean for me being a seamstress; I would sew for other people. Compustura means seaming together fragments to make a garment which you wear, which represents you, your identity and reality in the world. So that's why when you and Lahoucine called me, I thought, yes, there's finally somebody out there who's making the connection.

Q. You have already talked about the risks you take and about the stylistic borders you cross. Are there any things about writing that are particularly hard for you? Or easy?

A. Yes, there are. I think one problem is for me to get into a piece of writing, whether it is theory, or a story, or a poem, or a children's book, or a journal entry. I am always rethinking and responding to something that I value, or rethinking somebody else's values. If the value is competition, then I start thinking about how when you compete, there is a certain amount of violence, a certain amount of struggle. Okay, behind that violence and that struggle I experience some kind of emotion: fear, hesitancy, sadness, depression because of the state of the world, whatever. In order to backtrack to the theoretical concepts, I have to start with the feeling. So I dig into the feeling and usually the feeling will have a visual side while I'm pulling it apart. One of the visuals that I use is Coyochauqui, the Aztec moon goddess who was the first sacrificial victim. Her brother threw her down the temple stairs and when she landed at the bottom she was dismembered. The act of writing for me is this kind of dismembering of everything that I am feeling, taking it apart to examine it and then reconstituting it or recomposing it in a new way. So that means I really have to get into the feeling—the anger, the anguish, the sadness, the frustration. I have to get into this heightened state, which I access sometimes by being very, very quiet and doing some deep breathing, or by some little tiny meditation, or by burning some incense, or whatever gets me in there. Sometimes I walk along the beach. So I access this state, I get all psyched up, and then I do the writing. I work four, five, six hours; and then I have to come off that. It is like a withdrawal, I have to leave that anger, leave that sadness, leave that compassion, whatever it is that I am feeling; I have to come off that heightened, aware state. If I want to do some honest writing, I have to get into that state. If you want to do a mediocre job, you do a kind of disembodied writing which has nothing to do with your feelings or with yourself or with what you care about. You care, maybe, only intellectually about putting out this essay so that your peers can respect you. So that is one problem of writing for me: engaging in an emotional way, and then disengaging. To disengage you have to take another walk, wash the dishes, go to the garden, talk on the telephone, just because it is too much. Your body cannot take it. So that is one problem.

Some of the other things that come up for me—and I wrote them down, because I knew you were going to ask me this—one other problem is that you want to avoid that stage. You practice avoidance, you procrastinate. It takes you a while to go to the computer. You circle around the stuff over and over. You do not want to get to the dissertation, to the master's thesis, to that paper that is due for this quarter, because you are going to be struggling with these things. That is the problem of avoidance, of not doing the work. Every day I have to recommit myself with the writing. It is like making a date with myself, having an appointment to do this writing. And some days I don't feel like going to meet that appointment. It's too hard on my body, especially since I have diabetes; it takes out too much.

Q. Do you try to write at a regular time? Every day?

A. Not in terms of clock time, but in terms of my routine, because my internal clock changes. I get up later and go to bed earlier and sometimes I write at night and sometimes I write during the day; but yes, I have a certain routine. I get up and I inject myself with insulin and I have my food. Generally after that I have some activity like this interview. Or maybe two hours of filing and returning people's calls and letters—the stuff that I don't like to do. And then a walk, and then I dive into four, five, or six hours of this appointment with myself. Sometimes I can only do two or three hours, and other times I can do it around the clock. After writing, I take a break for lunch or the second meal, whenever that is, and then I do some reading: serious theoretical stuff for maybe an hour or two, and then some escapist reading. I love mysteries, horror.

Q. Do you compose at the word processor?

A. Yes, I do, at my desk, and sometimes I take my little laptop to the coffee house or to the beach, or just outside.

Q. Do the words seem to come out as well from the ends of your fingers typing as they did when you were scripting?

A. Yes, except that when I was at an artist's retreat for four weeks just last month, my computer broke down and I had to resort to handwriting. What started happening was that I started writing poems. I had gone there to revise 24 Stories, which is this book I'm working on. I had taken nineteen of the stories in hard copy, so I was able to revise on paper, but the rest of the time I was doing poems and I was doing composition theory. I ended up doing a lot of stuff on composition theory. I also did work on a large book that I have in progress—the creative writing manual that I told you about. I did writing exercises for that book: some meditation, some hints and elements of writing, some fictive techniques. I didn't plan on doing any of that. I just wanted to do the stories, but not having a computer switched me over.

So anyway, those are two problems: the problem of engaging and disengaging, and the problem of avoidance. Then there is the problem of voice. How am I going to write the forward for the encyclopedia I agreed to do? What voice, tone, am I going to take? How much can I get away with the Spanish? How much can I get away with the Spanglish? This is a pretty formal reference book. Another example is the bilingual series of children's books. How much can I get through the censors in the state of Texas in any particular children's book? The state of Texas has more stringent censorship rules than the other states, and most publishers can only do one book for all of the states. So the publishers tend to be conservative, because they want to get these books into the schools. How much can I get away with pushing at the norms, at the conventions? That's another problem, and sometimes it's my biggest problem: if I can't find a voice, a style, a point of view, then nothing can get written. All you have are those notes, but you don't have a voice to speak the style. The style is the relationship between me, Gloria, the author; you, the person reading it, my audience, the world, and the text. So there are three of us. Or are there more than three of us?

Q. A lot more, probably. At least four, maybe, when you bring the text in?

A. Well, in the author there is the outside author, there is the author who is the writer, and there is the narrative-voice author; and then in the reader there are all these different readers. And then the text changes according to the reader, because I think that the reader creates the text.

So I'm grappling with this voice and how much I can push in order to make people think a little bit differently, or to give them an emotional or intellectual experience when they can go and say, "Oh, so that's the Pacific Ocean?" Not quite that blatantly. Another example is Toni Morrison's *The Bluest Eye*. You never quite look at another Black child without what you took from that text. It has changed your way of looking at Black children. The problem of voice is the third problem.

I think another more external problem is one of censorship. With the very conservative path that this country has taken in terms of the arts, these times are hard. I know artists who can't exhibit nude photographs of their children because that's like an obscenity. When you apply for the NEA or any of these grants, you're limited. That's external censorship from the right, of morality and family values. Then there is the external censorship from my family. "Gloria, don't write about that; that's a secret." You're not supposed to devalue the Chicano culture. I was being disloyal to my mother and my culture because I was writing about poverty and abuse and gender oppression. So there's a kind of weightiness on you *not* to write, not to do your art in as honest a way as possible. You're supposed to make nice, like you were talking about being Southern girls.

I write a lot about sexuality in my stories. And—I don't know if you read "Immaculate, Inviolate" in *Borderlands*—but when I sent my brother the book, and he read it, he had a fit. He was going to show it to my uncle, and my uncle was going to sue me, because that was his mother I was talking about, my grandmother. I talked about how my grandfather lifted her skirt to do his thing, and how he had three other *mujeres con familia*. He would spend three days and three nights with my grandmother, and two days and two nights with the next mistress, and two days with the next one. The children from all the families played together, and my grandmother was ashamed of that and felt so humiliated. I'm not supposed to write about that. I'm constantly asked by my family to choose my loyalty. When I choose who I'm going to be loyal to, myself or them, I'm supposed to choose them. I don't, and I never have, and that's why I'm accused of betraying my culture, and that's why I'm a bad girl: selfish, disobedient, ungrateful.

Q. And also why you are a writer.

A. To take the problem of censorship one step further, there is also internal censorship. I've internalized my mom's voice, the neoconservative right voice, the morality voice. I'm always fighting those voices.

Q. I was just going to ask you about that again. The visual that you showed me earlier had "us" and "them," and you said very beautifully that both of these—the "them" and the "us"—are now in you. You're very aware of that mixture of voices inside yourself. I think that many teachers of composition would like to be able to find ways to help students recognize their own multiple voices, especially the Anglo students who don't see themselves as having any race, any ethnicity, and often they don't even think they have any range of sexuality. They're just "man" or "woman," that's it. How do we help those students really hear those other voices? How do we help them get Gloria's voice in them? They have the *nos* so much in their head that they don't have any other voices. One of the reasons work like yours is so important to the future of composition studies is that it gives concrete evidence of many voices in a text, many voices speaking out of who you are, many voices that you allow to speak. Many, on the other hand, are not only monolingual in the strict sense of English being the only language, but deeply, internally monolingual as well. And composition studies really hasn't done much of anything in the past to help them out of that.

A. I think that the only recourse is a kind of vicarious move of immersing themselves in the texts of people who are different, because the fastest way for them to recognize that they have diversity, that they have these values, that they have these experiences and beliefs, is to jerk them out into another country where they don't speak the language, they don't know the food. It's like taking a fish out of water. The fish doesn't know that it lives in the element of water until it jerks onto the beach and can't breathe. You can't do that to every student. But sometimes a traumatic experience can do that, it can open up a window. What education and the schools can give is this vicarious experience via the text, via reading *The Bluest Eye*, or *Borderlands*.

In terms of composition, I think teachers need to look at alternate models. What I want to do with the chapters of the textbook that I've been talking to you about is to offer other ways of considering how to write a story, a poem, or a paper. And again, that alternate way is colored by the Western frame of everything. What I'm trying to present to you is another way of ordering, another way of composing, another rhetoric; but it is only partly new. Most of it is cast in the Western tradition, because that's all that I was immersed in. The symbol is to see the university as this walled city, and somebody brings the Trojan Horse, the Trojan *Burra,* into the city gates. At night the belly of the burra opens, and out comes the "other" trying to make changes from inside. And I have a visual for that. . . . There's your Trojan Burra. It's kind of hard, because the university wall or city is very seductive, you know? There's something very seductive about fitting in, and being part of this one culture, and forgetting differences, and going with the way of the norm. Western theory is very seductive, and pretty soon instead of subverting and challenging and making marks on the wall, you get taken in.

Q. Certainly some in composition studies have thought that that's what the university was for, that's what the composition teacher was for: to help the students become assimilated into the university, rather than to help them challenge the reality of the university.

A. Yes. This is also what traditional therapy tries to do. It tries to assimilate you to life, to reality, to living.

Q. So here, in the night, out of the burra, come the challengers?

A. Yes, these different ways of writing: the inappropriate ways, the bad girls not making nice. It's really hard because you are one of only a few.

Q. One of the things I like best about teaching composition is that sometimes I can make a place, as a teacher, for students to do dangerous and experimental kinds of writing. But then they have to go and pass the tests and pass the history essays and do the inside-the-lines kind of writing.

A. This is what I was talking about earlier: that in order to make it in this society you have to be able to know the discipline, if it's teaching, if it's composition, if it's carpentry. Whatever field it is, you have to know your way around. You have to know how to wire the house before you can start being an innovative electrician.

The question is, how can you change the norm if the tide is so tremendous against change? But you can do something. You are in the field of composition, right? And somehow you respect my ideas and my writing. Otherwise, you wouldn't be here. So for me to be effective in making whatever little changes I can, I have to get this respect, this acceptance, this endorsement from my peers. All of these academics who teach my writings are endorsing me, and they make it possible for me to reach a wider audience. Whatever little changes I can make in people's thoughts, it is because they first allowed me through the gate. If you absolutely hated my stuff and everybody else hated my stuff, no matter how innovative it was, nobody would ever see it because it wouldn't get through the peer gate. I couldn't do any of this without you.

Q. Well, you could do it, and you have done it; but reaching the very, very largest audience in the United States certainly does take that.

A. Which is my next step. One of my goals is to have a larger audience, which is what I'm trying to accomplish with this book of fiction. Fiction is a genre that more than just people from the academy can accept. I mean, community people do read my books—the children's book especially goes into the community, and *Borderlands*—but it's still beyond the scale of most people. My family doesn't do any serious reading. They will look at my stuff

—my sister will read a little bit of it, and my brother—but they don't do serious reading. They don't sit down on a daily basis like you and I do and read stuff on composition and theory.

Q. But they might read a book of stories.

A. Yes, and what I'm trying to convey to you about composition and postcoloniality I am trying to do through story. You can theorize through fiction and poetry; it's just harder. It's an unconscious kind of process. The reader will read this and wonder about it. Instead of coming in through the head with the intellectual concept, you come in through the back door with the feeling, the emotion, the experience. But if you start reflecting on that experience, you can come back to the theory.

Q. I wonder if that's partly why the boundaries between fiction and nonfiction seem to be so permeable right now. It's hard sometimes to say what is a short story and what is an essay.

A. The way that one composes a piece of creative nonfiction and the way one composes fiction are very similar. In composing nonfiction, you're very selective and you take little fragments here and there and you piece them together in a new way. So right off the bat you're not being true to the nonfiction. It's fiction already, just in manipulating it.

Q. And then the representation itself—you said earlier that the representation is not the same as the experience; it's the representation.

A. The borders are permeable, and I like the fact that at this turn of the century these borders are transparent and crossable. And when we get past the millennium, the *fin de siècle*, some of these things will settle down into another kind of reality. At every turn of the century everything is up for grabs: the categories are disrupted, the borders are crossable. Then you get to another plateau where things become more fixed in cement, but not really. Then you wait for the next period of insurgency, when everything is up for grabs again. I think it goes like that in cycles. So this is why I'm so hopeful and so glad that I'm alive right now, because I can partake of this confusion. But still, back to your students, what's going to help them?

Q. Well, the book you're working on may help them, but I often find students so anxious to be able to work within the framework and to be part of the system, and so fearful of what will happen if they're not part of the system (and often with very good reason!), that they resist taking risks and they resist trying to get in touch with things that might hurt.

A. Yes, we come back to the same thing: fear of being different. You don't want to stick out, you don't want to be different—especially at their age. You and I have already passed midlife. We can have a sense of identity and of self that is not so much based on other people's reactions anymore. But theirs is very much a relational type of identity, so that if this group of people disapproves of them and finds their difference to be problematic, they won't be able to function. They won't be able to get their degree, they won't get the grant, they won't get the job. So how do you teach them to take risks? How do you teach them to stand up and say, "I'm different and this is who I am, and your way is maybe a good way, but it's not the only way." How do you get them to do that? And I think that writing and post-colonial studies are trying to do that in terms of getting people to think about how they are in the world.

Writing is very liberating and emancipatory; it frees you up. In the process of writing, you're reflecting on all of the things that make you different, that make you the same, that make you a freak. You're constantly grappling with identity issues. Postcoloniality looks at this power system discipline—whether it's a government, whether it's anthropology, or composition—and it asks, "Who has the voice? Who says these are the rules? Who makes the law?" And if you're not part of making the laws and the rules and the theories, what part do you play? How is that other system placed in your mind? You get into the neocolonization of people's minds. You get into the erasure of certain histories, the erasure of ideas, the erasure of voices, the erasure of languages, the erasure of books. A lot of the Mayan and Aztec codices were burned, and a whole system of knowledge wiped out. Postcoloniality comes and asks these questions. What reality does this disciplinary field, or this government, or this system try to crush? What reality is it trying to erase? What reality is it trying to suppress? Writing is about freeing yourself up, about giving yourself the means to be active, to take agency, to make changes. So I see both writing and postcoloniality as emancipatory projects, about how to get from here to there.

Q. May I ask a question about English? One of the first things that brought me to your work was your mixture of languages. As a teacher of writing who believes that writing and literacy can be liberatory, it was very frightening and disorienting and hurtful when I began to realize the degree to which writing and language could be just the opposite: the ways in which they could enslave, keep down, exclude, hurt, silence. To have to face my own doubleness within the discipline of writing was hard for me, because

I wanted to embrace the goals of liberation, and I didn't want to face the fact that teaching any kind of a system involves constraints and hurts, or the degree to which English is hegemonic and silencing, the way in which English tends to drown out. I also think about the way in which English, throughout its whole history as a language, has been like a sponge, sucking up words from Norse, or German, or French, or I think now of Spanish, from which English is absorbing enormous amounts. I don't know how I feel about that. I don't know whether I think that it's good that the language is alive and growing, or whether I think that English is exerting its power once more and trying to surround Spanish, let's say, and take it in. Those are very confusing issues to me. I'm also very much aware that students quite often fear other languages in the same way that they fear other people that they perceive as different. So how are you feeling about the state of English today? How do you feel about the English-only legislation which passed in the Congress last summer?

A. Well I think that English is the dominant symbology system. Language is a representational system, a symbology system. But what happens with the language, this particular symbolic system, is that it displaces the reality, the experience, so that you take the language to be the reality. So say you had Hindi, or Spanish, or Hopi, or whatever the language happens to be. That language attempts to create reality: not just shape it but create it; not just mold it but create it and displace it. I think all languages do that. Then you take a country like the United States, where via the industrial age and the electronic age and the age of the Internet, the dispersal of English is faster and more widespread than any other language thus far. It's going to become the planetary language if we're not careful. Other countries are going to become—I don't want to say "Americanized," because I don't want to use the word "America" to represent the United States—but it's going to have this kind of United Statesian-culture-swallowing-up-the-rest-of-the-world kind of mouth. As for me, I like English and I majored in English at a time that I wasn't allowed Spanish. I never took any Spanish courses other than a Spanish class in high school. I took some French and some Italian—which didn't do any good because I can't remember any of it now. The way that I grew up with my family was code switching. When I am my most emotive self, my home self, stuff will come out in Spanish. When I'm in my head, stuff comes out in English. When I'm dealing with theory, it's all in English, because I didn't take any classes in which theory was taught in

Spanish. So the body and the feeling parts of me come out in Spanish, and the intellectual, reasoning parts of me come out in English.

Q. Do you dream in Spanish?

A. I dream in both Spanish and English. What's happening more and more with English is that I get the ideas in Spanish and I get them in visuals. Like one of the ideas that I'm working with is *conocimiento,* the Spanish word for knowledge, for ways of knowing. Those ideas come to me in Spanish and in visuals. So when I think "conocimiento," I see a little serpent for counter-knowledge. This is how it comes to me that this knowledge, this "counter-knowledge," is not acceptable, that it's the knowledge of the serpent of the garden of Eden. It's not acceptable to eat the fruit of knowledge; it makes you too aware, too self-reflective. So how do you take this *conocimiento* and have the student speculate on it, when all the student knows and is immersed in is the kind of knowledge that crosses this one out? For a student to do this, there has to be some kind of opening, some kind of fissure, crack, gate, *rajadura*—a crack between the world is what I call it—the hole, the interfaces.

Q. Before we began taping, you remembered that people generally assume that you have read a lot of theory, since your books enact so many of the concepts poststructural theory has espoused. You must have read Foucault, you must have read Derrida, you must have read Irigaray or Cixous. You said that you hadn't read them before you wrote *Borderlands,* but that the ideas—they're "out there."

A. Yes, the ideas are out there because we are all people who are in more or less the same territory. We occupy the world of the academy and of the late twentieth century. We've read some of the same books, we've seen some of the same movies, we have similar ideas about relationships, whether we're French or born in the United States or raised here. In reflecting on what we know and on our experiences, we come up with these paradigms, concepts of what it is that life is about, about how interactions and power struggles work. Those theorists give it different terms than I do; a lot of my terms are in Spanish, like *conocimiento.* A lot of the concepts that I have about composition and postcoloniality are attempts to connect pre-Columbian histories and values and systems with the postcolonial twentieth century. A lot of times I will start with a cultural figure from the precolonial: *Coatlicue* or *la Llorona.* Then I look at the experience in 1997 that Chicanos and Chicanas are going through, and I try to see a connection to what was going on then. I want to show a continuity, to show a progression. I try to give a term, to find a language for my ideas and my concepts that comes from the indigenous part of me rather than from the European part of me, so I come up with *Coatlicue*, and *la facultad*, and *la frontera*, and *Nepantla*—concepts that mean: "Here's a little nugget of a system of knowledge that is different from the Euro-American. This is my hit on it, but it's also a *mestizo/mestiza* cognitive kind of perception, so therefore this ideology or this little nugget of knowledge is both indigenous and Western. It's a hybridity, a mixture, because I live in this liminal state in between worlds, in between realities, in between systems of knowledge, in between symbology systems." This liminal, borderland, terrain or passageway, this interface, is what I call *Nepantla*. All of the concepts that I have about composition, all of the concepts that I have about postcoloniality, come under this umbrella heading of *Nepantla*, which means *el lugar en medio*, the space in between, the middle ground. I first saw that word in Rosario Castellano's writings. When they dug up the streets of Mexico City to build the subway system, they found the *Templo Mayor*. In it they found the statue of *Coatlicue*, and they found all these artifacts, and they found murals on the walls, and one of the murals was *Nepantla*. There are also all these words that begin with *Nepantla* and end in other endings in *Nahuatl*. One of them is "between two oceans:" that's the *Nepantla*. Whenever two things meet there's the *Nepantla*, so they have tons and tons of words with the root word *Nepantla*. *Borderlands* falls into that category, but *Borderlands* is just one project of this overall umbrella project that is my life's work, my life's writing. *Borderlands* is just one hit on it. And this new book that I'm working on now, on composition and on the process of writing, and on identity, and on knowledge, and on the construction of all of these things, is like a sequel to *Borderlands*. All of my books are parts of this project.

Q. And the book of short stories that you're working on, too?

A. Yes, and the process for my composing all these projects is very much Coyochauqui, the moon goddess that got dismembered. In composing, you take things apart and everything is fragmented, and then you struggle to put things together.

Q. Is there any sense of weaving in what comes after the tearing apart, from the language? I also think of weaving as a metaphor for what happens at some points in writing.

A. Yes, there is—a kind of weaving, a rearranging. Anyway, I'm enumerating the different stages of my writing process. And what's funny is that I started out just talking about writing, and then I branched off into other art forms: into musical composition, dances that get choreographed, film, video—all of these arts have elements in common. Even architecture and building construction have something in common with composition, even though in the construction of a building you have to have all the details first—where the electrical outlets have to be, where the windows are, what the dimensions are. Then you're allowed to be creative; you can manipulate things, you can move the light switch a little bit. But with writing, you can approach it from an outline, from something that's already framed for you; or you can start composing with a loosely held-together frame; or you can jump into it and start anywhere. You can start in the end and go to the beginning, or you can start in the middle and go both directions, toward the beginning and the end. The frames for all of these art forms vary a little bit, but a lot of the process of the composition is very similar.

Okay, so once I found that out, I started looking at how I create aspects of my identity. Identity is very much a fictive construction: you compose it of what's out there, what the culture gives you, and what you resist in the culture. This identity also has this kind of projection of your self into a future identity. You can say here's the image of Gloria, or here's the image of Andrea that I want to project in the next seven years, the kind of person that I'd like to be in the future; and then you start building that Andrea. You can start building that Andrea by saying, "I'm going to make more time for myself, I'm going to value solitude, I'm going to get rid of the clutter, I'm going to find out what my own goals are and what my agenda is, and go with that instead of what my mother, or my family, or the academy, or my husband wants, and these are the projects that I'm going to concentrate on." You reshape yourself. But first you get that self-image in your head, and then you project that out into the world. When you look at it ten years later, you won't recognize yourself. When you go back home to your mom and to your brothers and sisters, you'll be an entirely different person, and they won't see how you came from there to here. So you keep creating your identity this way.

Then I took all of this knowledge a step further, to reality. I realized that if I can compose this text, and if I can compose my identity, then I can also compose reality out there. It all has to do with the angle of looking at things. Say all your life you've perceived Andrea as being this one kind of person, you've perceived an essay to be this one kind of composition, you've perceived the planet earth and the United States to be this kind of country and this kind of reality. Then you find out that you don't have to write the essay this way, that you don't have to be the Andrea that you've been all your life, and that if you see that shed, and that sky and that sea and all that happens in it from this other angle, then you will see something else. You can recreate reality. But you're going to need some help, because it's all done in relationship with other people. When we are born we are taught by our culture that that is up, and this is down, and that's a piece of wood, and that's a no-no. To change the tree, the up and down, and the no-no, you have to get the rest of your peers to see things in this same way—that that's *not* a tree, and that's *not* a no-no. You know what I'm saying. It's all of us that created this physics, this quantum mechanics; now we all have to recreate something different. A scientist will be the first to give us an idea of this other universe, of this other atom; the writer will be the first to give us an idea of this other emotional experience, this other perception, this other angle. It has to be one of the members of the tribe to start making that aperture, that little hole, that crack. It has to be one of the members of the community to say, "Yeah, this is a different way of looking at reality." Then everybody else will say, "Yeah, why didn't I think of that? That's true." All of a sudden you'll have a congress, a consensual basis for this reality that you're observing. And once you have this consensual view of reality, along comes Anzaldúa, who says, "No, that's just the reality that your particular people—who are Indo-European, or Western, or Inuit, or whatever—that's just your gift. Here's a different way of looking at reality."

Q. When you were talking about your architect, it made me think about what you later said about the importance of other people and always having other people around you. When I think of the feminist architect that you worked with for the addition to your house, that person brought a lot to the project but you were important to the project, too, and then the electricians and the plumbers. Was it a deeply collaborative project?

A. Yes. They consulted with me, but they knew that I didn't have the know-how. They said, "What kind of space do you want to live in?" and I said "Tall, a lot of opening, a lot of window space." And then they said, "Well, how tall?" Then there is the city code. You have to have a certain amount of free territory in your lot; you can only build so many square feet. I was limited to that, so I said, "I'll go up." Then there are the neighbors. I had to get permission, because some of these windows overlook them. There's a public hearing if you build a two-story, because you're impinging on somebody else's space. So anyway, all of those people and the architect had their visions of what they wanted the space to be like, and I had mine, and I wanted them to co-create it with me. I didn't want it to just be me. There's always negotiating. The corner windows are two or three hundred dollars more expensive than the regular windows, and I said, "I can't afford that." But the architect was invested in having these corner windows—which had been my idea in the first place—so I said, "Well, this is your project, too, so we'll go with that." I wanted only one door, because I felt that French doors were not as secure, but then I talked to the carpenter, who said, "No, this glass is very durable." It's all very collaborative.

Q. I was just looking at your children's book: obviously you collaborated with the artist on that project, too.

A. Well, it wasn't quite a straight collaboration, because I did the text first and then I gave it to the artist. But now I am doing a project for a middle-school girl readership, and there I will be working with the artist. But I also think that there is no such thing as a single author. I write my texts, but I borrow the ideas and images from other people. Sometimes I forget that I've borrowed them. I might read some phrase from a poem or fiction, and I like the way it describes the cold. Years and years go by, and I do something similar with my description, but I've forgotten that I've gotten it somewhere else. Then I show my text in draft form to a lot of people for feedback: that's another level of cocreating with somebody. Then my readers do the same thing. They put all of their experience into the text and they change *Borderlands* into many different texts. It's different for every reader. It's not mine anymore.

Q. Does that feel okay to you? You don't feel possessive about your writing as your "property?"

A. No, I don't; I've always felt that way about writing. I do the composing, but it's taken from little mosaics of other people's lives, other people's perceptions. I take all of these pieces and rearrange them. When I'm writing I always have the company of the reader. Sometimes I'm writing with my friends in mind, and sometimes for people like you who teach writing. In writing, I'm just talking with you without your being here. This is where style comes in. Style is my relationship with you, how I decide what register of language to use, how much Spanglish, how much vernacular. It's all done in the company of others, while in solitude—which is a contradiction.

Q. Are there some stylists that have been really important to you?

A. Well, I know that thematically, Julio Cortazar has influenced me. He was an Argentinean writer living in France who wrote *Hopscotch*, and *End of the Game and Other Stories*, and he wrote a lot about these in-between places of reality impinging on each other. In terms of my feminist ideas, my gender liberation ideas, *Jane Eyre* influenced me. I read it thirteen times when I was growing up. I really like how this little girl is so assertive. I like her being able to support herself differently from gender roles that were assigned to women. In terms of style, I recently read a mystery by Ruth Rendell, *No Night Is Too Long*. She writes popular stuff under the name Barbara Vine. She can really get into the rhythm of the lines, the words, the voice. I read Cormac McCarthy's *All the Pretty Horses*. I didn't finish the book, but I thought it had a style very similar to mine.

Q. You mentioned Toni Morrison. Have you read a lot of her work?

A. Yes, in the past I did. I think *Song of Solomon* was the last book of hers that I read. I stopped reading her a few years ago; I don't know why. I have her books, and I'm going to pick them up again.

Q. Have you read Borges?

A. Yes. I have his entire collected works.

Q. I was thinking about the story "The Aleph" and that certain spot where, if you lie down and you put your eye there, you can see everything.

A. Yes, when I talk about borders with my students, I use a visual of the aleph.

Q. Didn't Borges write in both Spanish and English as you do?

A. I think he wrote mainly in Spanish, but was heavily influenced by English writers. He read Poe and Hawthorne and people like that.

Q. I picked up a book the other day called the *History of Reading*, written by Alberto Manguel, who lived in Argentina for a time and who read to Borges for several years. And he would go there at night and Borges would say, "shall we have Kipling tonight, or shall we have Poe?" and he would read.

A. Style is a very difficult concept. Often I go to visuals to clarify my concepts, as I've said. For example, I think what's going on now at the turn of the century is exemplified by the *remolino*, the whirlwind, the vortex. North of the equator, the movement is clockwise, so all of our knowledge on this side moves clockwise. South of the equator, the movement is counterclockwise. The rivers flow the other way here. As a mestiza, I'm living on the equator. Some of my culture, the indigenous and the Mexican culture, pulls me counterclockwise. This comes with its own perception of being. And over here, in North America, all of the knowledge that I learned in school, all of the ways that I've learned to look at life, is pulling me the other way. I'm pulled in two different ways. I think that postcoloniality is situated right here. If you consider the counterclockwise to be the colonized cultures and the clockwise to be the colonizer cultures, then there is this tension and you're trying to accommodate both of these cultures and still be comfortable. But it's a struggle to find this peace, this settlement. You have to change the clockwise movement to be counterclockwise once in a while, and sometimes you have to change this counterclockwise movement to move like the North. It's a state that's very unsettling. It's also the state you are in when you are trying to compose. Moving clockwise is everything that has been written: the literature, the norm, the genre laws. As a writer, you are trying to add to those genre laws, to that knowledge, to that literature, to that art. You have to go along with it in some ways, but to create some changes you have to go counterclockwise. This is the struggle for a writer like me: how much can you get away with without losing the whole thing? All of these metaphors come around and around: to style, to composition itself, to identity, to the creation of knowledge, and to the creation of experience.

Q. When I look at your writing, I think yours is a mixture of styles. Have you seen other people that mix things up the way you do?

A. Well other Chicanas were mixing Spanglish in poetry, but not in theory, not in academic writing. And I think of style as trying to recover a childhood place where you code-switch. If I am fictionalizing a certain experience, I go back to the reality of the experience in my memory, and it takes place in both languages. So I get into that style. But I think that what I was trying to do by code-switching was to inject some of my history and some of my identity into this text that White people were going to read or Black people were going to read or Native American people were going to read. I was trying to make them stop and think. Code-switching jerks readers out of their world and makes each think, "Oh, this is my world, this is another world, this is her world where she does this, where it's possible to say words in Spanish." It's like taking the counterclockwise and injecting it into the clockwise. I think that's why I started that. And now a lot of Chicanas are doing it.

Q. Think of the same thing about injecting, but injecting the discourse of lesbianism or alternative sexuality of any kind into traditional heterosexuality. It does the same thing. It insists that we go this way and it helps readers to inhabit other ways of being, other ways of knowing. Isn't that very important too?

A. And you know we live in the *remolino*, the vortex, the whirlwind; and in this time everything is very much confused: values, ideology, identity. The student is caught in her own little vortex. What I would like to do is what Carlos Castaneda was told to do by Don Juan the shaman: to stop the world. The world is this reality and the world is also the description we have of it in our heads. How do you stop that and say, "No, this other world exists, this other possibility, this other reality." You have to stop this world a little bit to get the other one in. So I would like to stop the *remolino* for just a second, the second that it takes the reader to say, "I didn't know that Chicano Spanish was the bastard language. And if Chicano Spanish is a bastard language, what registers of English are also bastards and not allowed into the academy?" Then they start looking at British English, Australian English, Canadian English, United States English. Then at all of the dialects and all of the registers: academic, formal, slang. And then maybe the reader will say, "I don't know, I'm a redneck and this is my language, and maybe I should write about this language for this particular class. Just for that little second it stops them. Does this make sense to you? Or maybe I'm being too presumptuous and I don't really do that. Anyway, I think that writing has that faculty, but it has to be honest writing and it has to be writing the struggle.

Q. When bell hooks says that language is a place of struggle, I think that's what she means: you're struggling to get language out of the clockwise just for the second and into the counterclockwise, and it's a terrible struggle. It goes on your whole life—if I understand her correctly. Did you have any teachers that . . .

A. . . . . pointed me in this direction?

Q. Or that nurtured you in your writing and in your reading and thinking?

A. I had a favorite teacher when I was in elementary, who influenced the way I look at history and the teacher-student dynamic and at power, domination, and subordination. He would have students teach the class. I was a shy little Chicanita, but I was known as "the brain" because I had the best grades. So he would have me do stuff. I liked to help the other kids. I was his pet: I would grade the papers, and I ended up making up the tests. He would leave me in the classroom. He'd go outside for twenty minutes, and I would be like the little teacher. I learned a lot about power and about teaching.

Then when I was in high school, they put me in the accelerated section. There were plus one, two, three, four sections and regular one, two, three, four sections. Chicanos were put in the one, two, three, four sections, and the Whites were all in the plus, except me and Danny—we were put in the plus. There were also some Whites who were in the one, two, three, four. I was put in the "accelerated" level with Danny, but I had no interaction with the White kids because they looked down on me. I was with the White kids for English, Math, Science—for everything except Health, PE, and Homeroom, which I had with Chicanos. One of the teachers that I had was really into building vocabulary. I remember opening dictionaries and encyclopedias and reading whole chunks. I loved to look at the meanings of words. The whole time I was very studious and very withdrawn from other people, very shy. That particular teacher said that I had a facility with words, but that I needed to be trained. But then she would ignore me and pay attention to the White kids. So it was like a put-down rather than praise. Then I had a teacher in college who felt one of the pieces I wrote should be published.

Then I went to grad school after I got my B.A., and I had a teacher named James Sledd at the University of Texas. He was the first person ever to encourage me to talk about cultural stuff. I wrote an essay for him called "Growing up Chicana," which was the basis for the *Prieta* in *This Bridge Called My Back*. It was also the basis for a manuscript that I did on my memories, which I then took parts of and made into *Borderlands*. And now I have taken part of it and made it into this book of stories, and other segments of it are going into *La Llorona: Theorizing Identity, Knowledge, Composition*. All of that has its roots in the very first essay that I wrote for James Sledd. He encouraged me to talk about cultural things, and I used some Mexican words and some terms in Spanish. I had written some stories way back when I was working on my B.A., and some when I was working on my M.A.. They all code-switched, but when I wrote for James Sledd we were doing something different. We were trying to write formally: what we would call now theo-

rizing; what was called then criticism. His encouragement was very important to me, and he was also very important to me as a role model. He was
very much a maverick against the university; he was very much at odds, an
outsider. From him I learned that an outsider is not just somebody of a different skin; it could be somebody who's White, who's usually an insider
but who crosses back and forth between outsider and insider. So he was my
model to think about insider/outsider, and then I had my whole life to think
about *Nosotras*, us and them.

Q. Did you mention an undergraduate teacher who said that something you had written could be published?

A. Yes. This was at Texas Women's College in Denton. But I couldn't
afford to go to Denton. So then I had to get out for two years and work. I
saved money for two years, and then I went to Pan American. I published
the essay from my first year in a little Pan American quarterly. Few of the
teachers encouraged me. When I was working on my M.A., I would constantly be marked down on my papers for being too subjective, for not following the rhetoric of Aristotle and Cicero. You know, the model that people
value, with the logical development of ideas. I would constantly get marked
down. Across the board, all of the professors—in Comp. Lit., in English Lit.,
in all of the classes that I took for my M.A., and later on while working for
a Ph.D. in Austin—all of the professors marked me down. Even the ones I
took here at UC-Santa Cruz, teachers who were using my book as a textbook
—when I turned in my papers, they would subtly want me to write the
status-quo way, even though they would use my book as a model for how
to do things differently.

So it was a great shock to me several years ago, when the CCCC conference invited me to speak. The very same discipline, the very same teachers
who had marked me down and had said that I was writing incorrectly, all of
a sudden invited me to speak. Then I started getting requests for reprints in
composition readers. That was such a shock to me. Finding that composition people were reading me was a bigger shock than finding that anthropologists were reading me or that women's studies people were reading
me. Just a few days ago I was sent a book, a textbook for students. One of
the sections is on place, and they took a little segment of chapter seven, *"La
Conciencia de la Mestiza,"* where I talk about the valley and returning to the
valley. The students are supposed to take that little piece of writing, and
write a letter saying what I wrote, assuming my place, and signing the let-

ter "Gloria Anzaldúa." I'll show you the book if you don't believe it. I don't know how the students are supposed to do this.

Q. English in colleges and in universities has traditionally been a gate-keeper, functioning to keep the gate closed. Only in the last twenty-five years or so have people in English, and mostly people in composition, said, "We don't want to do that anymore. If we are going to be gatekeepers, we want to be opening the gate." That is a very, very big change.

A. It was a big shock for me to find composition people picking me up, and only a slightly smaller shock to find Spanish and Portuguese modern language people putting my stuff in their readers. Because we Chicanas were not part of Latino writing. They just included Mexican, South American, and Central American writers, not Chicanas. They put Sandra Cisneros in there, they put me in there. I am now a Latina writer. Can you believe that?

Q. We have talked about some of these issues of unity, rationality, or-ganization, and coherence; and of how we can make a space for intuition, emotion, and the body in writing and in the construction of knowledge— what Kenneth Burke calls the paralogical, to go along with the logical, and the logical has had a strangle hold on the teaching of writing. You have to start with A and you must end with Z. You can't start with Q.

A. I use "paralogical" in the forward to the encyclopedia in talking about spirituality and reality. When I use these terms, sometimes I think I made them up. I know "paranormal," so I think "paralogical."

Q. Before our time is over, would you talk at least a little bit about ac-tivism and working for change? Because in your writing, it's very clear that you see writing and activism as related. I think that it's less clear how we engage others in doing that kind of activism.

A. Well, I think that a lot of the activism for writers and for artists stems from trying to heal the wounds. You've been oppressed as a woman, or oppressed as a queer, or oppressed racially as a colonized person, and you want to deal with that oppression, with those wounds. Why did this happen to you? Why is it so hard? Who are these people that are oppress-ing you, and why do they have a license to oppress you? For me it started as a child. Children don't have any recourse. They can be abused by their par-ents. They don't have any rights. Society doesn't protect them. In my case, I was such a freak, such a strange little thing, that I felt all of the ill winds that were blowing. I really felt them. I had a very low threshold of pain. The differences that I felt between me and other people were so excruciating. I felt like such a freak. I was trying to make meaning of my existence and my pain, and that in turn led me to writing. In writing I'm trying to write about these moments where I took things into my own hands and I said, "This is not the way things are supposed to be. Girl children are not supposed to be treated this way. Women are not supposed to be battered; they're not supposed to be second-class citizens. Chicanas shouldn't be treated in this way in society." I started grappling with those issues, and writing became a way of activism, a way of trying to make changes. But it wasn't enough just to sit and write and work on my computer. I had to connect the real-life, bodily experiences of people who were suffering because of some kind of oppression, or some kind of wound in their real lives, with what I was writing. It wasn't a disembodied kind of writing. And because I am a writer, voice—acquiring a voice, covering a voice, picking up a voice, creating a voice—was important. And then you run into this whole experience of unearthing, of discovering, of rediscovering, of recreating voices that have been silenced, voices that have been repressed, voices that have been made a secret. And not just for me, but for other Chicanas. Look at all these women who have certain realities that are similar to mine, but they don't really see them. But when they read a text by Toni Morrison or when they read *Borderlands,* they say, "Oh, that went on in my life, but I didn't have the words to articulate it. You articulated it for me, but it's really my experience." They see themselves in the text. Reading these other voices gives them permission to go out and acquire their own voices, to write in this way, to become an activist by using Spanglish, or by code-switching. And then they go out and they read the book to their little girls, or their neighbor's kids, or to their girlfriend, or to their boyfriend.

Q. It's like links in a chain or a circle that keeps expanding?

A. Yes. As with my children's book *La Llorona,* it's really very much a cultural story. All that these Chicanitos read is White stuff, and then along comes *La Llorona* and they say, "Yeah, my grandmother used to tell me stories like that." And it feels really good for them to be in a book. There's this little kid—six, seven, eight, nine, ten—who never sees himself represented, so unearthing and nurturing that voice is part of the activism work. That's why I try to do so many anthologies. That's why I promote women, especially women of color and lesbians of all colors, and why I'm on editorial boards for magazines: because I want to get their voices out there. I believe that says something about activism. Because in the process of creating the composition, the work of art, the painting, the film, you're creating the culture. You're rewriting the culture, which is very much an activist kind of thing. So that writers have something in common with all of these people doing grass-roots organizing and acting in the community: it's all about rewriting culture. You don't want a culture that batters women and children. By the year 2005, fifty percent of the group that is going to be labeled "poverty stricken"—fifty percent of it—are going to be women and children. That's a whole new thing, women out of jobs, homeless children. It's a reality that we need to speak of. Twenty years ago, incest was not part of consensual reality. It was the writers who wrote about it, feminists who talked about it, who made films about it, and who did art about incest and child abuse, who changed reality. Before that, it was just a given. You beat your wife, that's part of it. Having abusive sex with your wife is not rape. Consensual reality has been redefined by these people rewriting a culture. Now it's part of culture that when you batter someone, you're supposed to be responsible. It's not something you can get away with unless you're a psychopath.

Q. What you just said makes me think of one of the things that's important about your work for postcolonial studies. Your work goes beyond the deconstructive—which has been a large part of the very important work that postcolonial studies has done—to show what colonialism has done and been. But the kind of work that you're talking about creates a new reality. It goes beyond the deconstructing and the showing of old oppressions and hurts.

A. When you get into reading and writing the "other," into assuming some kind of authority for the "other"—whether you are the "other" or you are the subject—there's a community involved. And I think what you are saying is that postcolonial theorists sometimes forget what's going on here in the community, in the world that we inhabit.

Q. And so do teachers of writing, I hasten to add.

A. Yes. There's a responsibility that comes with invoking cultural and critical authority, and I think you could call that responsibility being open to activism and being responsible for your actions. No?

Q. I want to ask one other thing. Suppose you and I had a little child here, and we wanted to watch her grow up and be a writer. What would be your wildest dream for that little child in becoming a writer? What would you most hope for?

A. Well, I think what I would most hope for is probably not something that is possible. I would hope for her to have a peaceful community in all the different worlds, in all the different cultures, in all the different realities. I would hope for her to be a true mestiza, and I don't think it's possible right now because the powers that decide the laws of man are very much monolithical. It's not an equal kind of thing.

Q. Do you have any hopes that the situation might change in the future?

A. Yes, I do. I think we're drifting toward that. The distinction between the people with power and the people without power will get eased, so that the people without any agency now take on a little agency, and the people that were all-powerful now become a little powerless. There will be this kind of hybridity of equal parts, instead of a graft and a major tree. And I would like her to be able to explore the world and not to fear that she's going to be attacked, not to suffer being wounded. To live is to be in pain. To live is to struggle. Life hurts, but we can mitigate that hurt a little bit by having a society where the little girl child can pursue her interests and her dreams without being too much constrained by gender roles or racial law or the different epistemologies that say, "This is the way reality is." I don't know if that's ever going to happen. But I hope so. Sometimes I think so.

Deepika Bahri

TERMS OF ENGAGEMENT

Postcolonialism, Transnationalism, and Composition Studies

As a professor of postcolonial literature and theory and a regular in the first-year composition classroom, I was pleased and intrigued to find a session on composition and postcolonial studies at a recent regional conference. Wishing to see how the speakers would apply postcolonial concepts to pressing issues in rhetoric and composition—or conversely, whether postcolonialism had something to learn and gain from the battles and triumphs of the latter, I arrived with a notepad at the ready. The session was indeed illuminating, both in its attempts to bring together a synthesis of ideas from postcolonial, composition, and cultural studies and in its unwitting betrayal of the confusions that have come to characterize postcolonialism and the writing classroom in the current climate produced by transnationalism and economic globalization. Drawing, not surprisingly, on quotations and ideas from the expected triumvirate of Homi Bhabha, Edward Said, and Gayatri Spivak, the panel speakers made a sincere but sometimes confused attempt to find cognates from postcolonialism that could usefully address their pedagogic problems and theoretical concerns—an attempt that exemplified not so much the intellectual limitations of my colleagues but rather the shared poverty of our strategies when confronted with the demands of education and the academy in Anglo-America at the turn of the century.

The growing pursuit of relevance and socially responsible theory and pedagogy at a time when racial and class fissures are growing here and elsewhere; when new and often overlapping fields of inquiry (postcolonialism, multiculturalism, race, class, and gender studies) are peddled and exchanged as reigning commodities in the academic marketplace and attacked by conservatives, even as boutique multiculturalism flourishes in the world beyond the academy; when education itself is being subtly annexed into a new world order with indeterminate dimensions and dubious objectives; when boundaries and binaries are under attack by both postmodern theory and transnational economic maneuvers—at such a time, the pressures on the academic corps—particularly in its humane-ities wing—are many. The quest for alliance between postcolonial and composition studies—the former having come to stand in simultaneously for marginality, otherness, resistance, transnationality, and newness—indicates a complex of responses to the circumstances of the moment I have outlined above. This quest might thus be described as an attempt to understand and address otherness in a diversifying population and expanding global market, to capitalize on both the commodity value and the possibilities for ethical investigation offered by postcolonialism, and to explore the concordance and connections among disciplines not traditionally thought of as contiguous. We may learn the most from the potential for failure that is likely to attend this attempt, however, without due vigilance about the limitations and mystifications of postcolonialism.

Before we embark on that catalogue, we need to revisit the ways in which postcolonial studies connects with rhetoric and composition issues. At its most obvious, postcolonialism enters the world of rhetoric and composition in the very person of the third world postcolonial, the authentically ethnic teacher who bears, wittingly or otherwise, the welcome flag of visible diversity. The growing numbers of expatriate, excolonized international academics, the coming of age of a sizable population of immigrants of color in Anglo-America, as well as institutional goals of increasing visible diversity are gradually repopulating the once "color-less" halls of the academy. The presence of these individuals, along with that of a more diverse student body at a time of growing interest in diversity, is at least partly responsible for coloring the rhetoric and composition field in new ways.

Postcolonialism also enters this realm via the composition classroom and by way of culturally diverse readings in the growing number of multicultural texts that routinely circulate among textbook committees and arrive as free examination copies in our mailboxes. The readers will have noted the slippage between postcolonialism and multiculturalism in the preceding proposition, but more on that later. For now, suffice it to say that the postcolonial and the multicultural provide ready grist to the diversity mill. Interest in such matters coexists, to be sure, with resistance to anything non-canonical on the part of some, but by and large, through choice or a sense of obligation to departmental or university diversity requirements, many teachers are apt to be in favor of a more inclusive curriculum.[1] Nudged by, but not always prepared for, the new mandate to educate students in cultural sensitivity, the composition teacher finds a ready ally in the lexicon and concept bank for dealing with otherness, oppression, resistance, and novelty that postcolonial theory has so obligingly provided in the last decade or so. Terms such as orientalism, subaltern, cultural tourism, colonization, neocolonization, monolithic other, difference, alterity, self/other, discourse, power, authority, speaking, agency, and subjectivity (not necessarily unique to postcolonial vocabulary but gathered efficiently under its umbrella) allow the teacher to negotiate the rocky terrain of otherness with some modicum of theoretical guidance and support for teaching and classroom discussion.

It is not only the multicultural text, or the visibly ethnic student, however, that might occasion the deployment of postcolonial theory in the classroom. An interest in the larger question of the goals and effects of schooling might also lead the composition teacher to ponder the connections between the project of education and structures of power, between formal schooling and the cultivation of compliant subjectivity—issues dealt with extensively in postcolonial literature and theory.[2] Increasingly, postcolonial theory deals not only with the impact of colonial education on individual and collective postcolonial identity, but also addresses the politics of education in the Anglo-American academy where many postcolonial critics now find themselves. Such discussions can be very relevant to composition studies, which has been animated by issues of disciplinarity almost from the beginning. Andrea Lunsford and Lisa Ede's essay "Representing Audience," for instance, hints at the possibilities of a connection between their concerns in composition studies and the anxieties voiced by postcolonial critic Chandra Talpade Mohanty. Thinking back on their own education, Lunsford and Ede recollect their "identification with schooling" and the destructive formula of individual success that prevails "throughout our culture, educational institutions, and scholarly disciplines," preventing both the possibility of resistance and the recognition of one's selves as "constructed subjects embedded in multiple discourses" (171, 173). Lunsford and Ede recognize the congruence between this realization and Mohanty's point in "On Race and Voice" that "if complex structural experiences of domination and resistance can be ideologically reformulated as individual behaviors and attitudes, they can be managed while carrying on business as usual" (178). Lunsford and Ede's reflections on the grounds of discursive success and the politics of location find a poignant echo in Mohanty's grim reminder: "the point is not simply that one should have *a voice;* the more crucial question concerns the sort of voice one comes to have as a result of one's location— both as an individual and as a part of collectives" (162). Moreover, the question of disciplinary "success," which Lunsford and Ede broach with insight in the essay, is one that is in turn very crucial to an evaluation of the potential of postcolonialism to deliver the radical critique it is thought to be so eminently capable of. I will return to this topic later.

Clearly, then, it is not only in the immediate scene of the classroom that the common tropes of postcolonialism seem relevant. Composition studies has found commonalities between its concerns and those raised in postcolonial theories. The former's interest in rhetoric, discourse, and power; in the recovery of hitherto silenced voices; in the liberatory possibilities of advanced technologies; and in the relation of the text to the social finds echoes, and often counterparts, in the debates dominant in the latter. As Susan J. Jarratt argues, "questions about speech and representation concern not only postcolonial theorists generating them but indigenous U.S. intellectuals as well. As U.S. intellectuals heighten their sense of a global context for academic work, we ask ourselves the same questions: How should histories and analyses of [. . .] literatures and rhetorics be conducted? Who can do this work? Who can speak for whom? How should we voice differences?" ("In Excess" 224). Indeed, in the chair's address to the 1995 CCCC meeting, Jacqueline Jones Royster pointed to the challenges of a new century and concluded that "much [. . .] depends on the ways we talk and listen and talk again in crossing boundaries and creating, or not, the common ground of engagement" (40). She notes that "from moments of challenge like this one, I realize that we do not have a paradigm that really allows for what scholars in cultural and postcolonial studies (Anzaldúa, Spivak, Mohanty, Bhabha) have called hybrid people—people who either have the capacity by right of history and development, or who might have created the capacity by right of history and development, to move with dexterity across cultural boundaries, to make themselves comfortable, and to make sense amid the chaos of difference" (37).

Recent global situations—large-scale worldwide migration and a new and confusing economic order—have required us to reevaluate traditional categories and relations. At a time when "two percent of the world's population no longer lives in the country in which they were born" (Mohanty, "Defining Genealogies" 351), and global movements of labor, capital, and culture confound our sense of the world, Royster recognizes that postcolonialism offers a way of theorizing the chaos meaningfully: as I have argued elsewhere, "the hybrid, the exiled, the dislocated, the multilocated—the 'postcolonials' in many metropolitan definitions of postcoloniality—have stepped nimbly into the breaches and the flows of the new economic and cultural order, occasioning and creating a theory formulated from myriad strands and schools of thought to explain and exemplify a plexus of disconcerting complexity" ("Introduction" 9). Postcolonial theory's facility in engaging questions of transnationality and hybridity combined with its engagement with poststructuralism, its rearticulation of the questions of power and knowledge, and its persistent challenge to western modes of thought have all contributed to its success in the academy and to an interest in its relevance to other disciplines.

Turning to postcolonialism and composition studies in particular, we might say that both have a vested interest in examining issues of authority and power as sources of psychological and social conflict. Both are, moreover, committed to a vision of theory and teaching as intervention and to addressing the persistently problematic dichotomy between theory and practice. It is thus not surprising that references to Said's formulations of power and discourse or Spivak's discussions on supplementarity, otherness, catachresis, and strategic essentialism now routinely appear in discussions on histories of classical rhetoric, on questions of agency, and various other issues in rhetoric and composition.[3] The considerable and indeed growing interest in Spivak's ideas is admittedly attributable not only to her status as a postcolonial critic but to her standing as a theorist of some repute in the areas of feminism, deconstruction, and Marxism as well. Her position in these areas, however, is almost always refracted through the prism of "difference," by now the hallmark of the postcolonial. Discussions on pedagogy and classroom techniques now include, as a matter of course, citations from postcolonial theorists or discussions of postcolonial texts, and it does not seem strange to find within the pages of a journal such as *JAC: A Journal of Composition Theory* an interview with Spivak, the (most) "highly commodified distinguished professor" in the field (86).[4]

It is already clear that postcolonial concepts and strategies can be very à propos to rhetoric and composition. In dealing with the question of audience, for instance, Lata Mani's notion of multiple mediations can be valuable in exploring questions of positionality and location. In response to audience considerations with regard to her work on *Sati*, Mani's recourse to multiple mediations as a strategy is instructive in its sensitivity to the complex rhetoric of theory: that it is not only a when, but a where (38). The emphasis on the situated nature of her theory in variant contexts—in India, in the United States, in Britain—and the demand for expedient narrative, tonal, and positional strategies to cope with widely divergent audience reactions to the same topic can provide a valuable matrix for those teaching writing or theorizing the art and the economics of writing in different situations. Apart from his careful theorization of the concept of hybridity, Bhabha's formulations of mimicry as a "discourse of ambivalence" that constructs *"a subject of difference that is almost the same, but not quite"* might be seen as useful in many ways (*Location* 86): for those studying the rhetoric of public discourse, the politics of basic writing classrooms, the production of educated or institutionalized subjectivity, or the production of discourse in any of several situations where power conjoins with the production of knowledge but remains ambiguated by its own contradictions. The notion of subaltern, first appearing in the work of Antonio Gramsci and later popularized in postcolonial discourse, is also one that has seemed useful to many and already appears frequently in rhetoric and composition studies. It has served various roles in these discussions: to identify marginal student populations, to describe resistive modes of agency, and to tackle the difficulty of locating agency in the subaltern. On the topic of representation, which arises variously—in the context of the classroom, in the curriculum, in the faculty, in textual productions—postcolonial critics provide very useful taxonomies and discussions.[5] Ashcroft, Griffiths, and Tiffin's *The Empire Writes Back* contains several discussions on language use—the relation of standard English to its variants, the possibilities for resistance articulated through the abrogation of standard language, critical interventions through the insertion of vernacular words or through a regrammatization of the standard language—topics that would be of obvious interest to compositionists. In essays and in fiction, Salman Rushdie provides both a theory and a praxis of inspired and radical uses of language. These "short takes" on some of the central issues in postcolonialism, admittedly suggestive, should indicate the prospects for further possibilities of its collaboration with composition studies.

But rather than continue to propose further possible applications for composition studies—and it would not be difficult to spin out the narrative further in this direction—I will leave readers with a sense of the possibilities and return to the discordant note sounded in my introduction. I focus on the limitations of postcolonialism for the purposes of composition studies and the dangers of the decontextualized, desituated use of concepts. It is not my intention to wag a finger at those who "misuse" postcolonial concepts. Indeed, there is much potential for a useful contract between postcolonial and composition studies, and it would be both presumptuous and dangerous to mandate "correct" pedagogic and theoretical applications. My intent is to point readers to the fissures within the theoretical constructs of postcolonialism as it has come to be articulated within multiculturalism and transnationalism, and to warn against their unreflective deployment. As such, this essay calls for a reappraisal, or at least a moment of clarity, before further explorations into the productive employment of postcolonial concepts in composition theory. Ultimately, it is with a full sense of the conflicts within postcolonial studies that composition theory can engage it to make its most meaningful interventions.

I have argued elsewhere that postcolonialism emerges in "an environment of institutional sanction for counter-narratives [. . .] notwithstanding its potential for challenging the system, it ultimately participates in a system of selections and elisions that replicate the technologies of power it is charged with exposing" ("Marginally" 278). The contained radicalism of constructs such as the postcolonial, authorized by institutional sanction, and altogether too suspiciously welcome in the academy, should give those in composition studies more than a moment of pause. Many of the problems with postcolonialism are tied to definitional and analytic imprecision. Progressively more abstract and impossible to define, postcolonialism succeeds not only despite, but perhaps because of, its ambiguities and contradictions.[6] Arif Dirlik has gone so far as to charge that "postcolonial, rather than a description of anything, is a discourse that seeks to constitute the world in the self-image of intellectuals who view themselves (or have come to view themselves) as postcolonial intellectuals" (339). It appeals "because it disguises the power relations that shape a seemingly shapeless world and contributes to a conceptualization of that world that both consolidates and subverts the possibilities of resistance" (356). Although I cannot subscribe to the entirety of Dirlik's arguments,[7] he alerts us to some of the problems in the field. In fact, in recent years, his has not been the only voice expressing discontent.[8] Most fundamentally, his and other expressions of unease oblige one to ask, yet again, *what* is the postcolonial (for this neologistic noun has come to acquire life along with the expected "postcolonialism")?

So what *is* the postcolonial? The postcolonial is a time, a space, the emblematically philosophic rupture with European modernity; it is a moment, a movement, a method, a message, a mirage, a misnomer because the colonial moment repeats and, yes, it is an alias and an alibi. Its many figurations and transmogrifications are akin to a gymnastic triumph of sorts. It is the condition of independence from colonization, of the relay into neocolonialism, of the vagaries of transnationalism. It is the possibility for resistance and a symptom of its failure. It is a word for the margin, an alias for the marginal; it is the dematerialized vanishing marginal stripped of reference, of history itself. If it is impossible to reign in these disjointed perambulations, it is because the postcolonial has been increasingly difficult to contain within dictionary definitions.[9]

In its literal sense, postcolonialism might be defined, according to Gauri Viswanathan, as "a study of the cultural interaction between colonizing powers and the societies they colonized, and the traces that this interaction left on the literature, arts, and human sciences of both societies" ("Pedagogical" 54). The project of research suggested in the literal definition would entail the study of specific cultures, histories, and cultural productions in the postcolonial phase with a full sense of their context. Such an examination would require that one attempt to understand, to use a phrase that recurs in composition studies, "the deeply situated nature" of the power relations being studied. Such a study would focus less on naming and identifying oppressor/oppressed and other binaries and more on uncovering the dynamics of relations. It would dwell on the complexities of power relations, on power and resistance as multiply located, and on both being examined in specific historical and material contexts. This continues to be the methodology of many historians, notably in the Subaltern Studies group, and has been considered a far more useful mode of scholarship in third world feminist circles than the despecified and monolithic characterization of third world women as hapless victims. Scholars who subscribe to this vision of postcolonialism argue for a definition of the world "in *relational* terms" and for due attention to "our different, often conflictual, locations and histories" (Mohanty, "Introduction" 2, 4).

In its more popular sense in the Anglo-American academy, however, the term and the concept invoke less the kind of scholarship described above than a general attribute of marginality, albeit radical. It is in this sense that the term has come to dominate the discussion on postcolonialism in metropolitan circles. Viewed as an "*attitude* or position" ("Pedagogical" 54), the postcolonial becomes a very slippery configuration indeed, making itself susceptible to a wide array of interpretations and laying itself open to the charge of ahistoricism. Used thus, the lessons of postcolonialism are abstracted from their contexts and brought into discussions of marginality and victimage in domestic debates on diversity. To be postcolonial in this manner is to be marginal (yet somehow eliding the fact that the postcolonial is theoretically validated and authorized within the academy).

Much of the postcolonial theory and a great deal of the literature that circulates in the Western academy is produced by critics and writers who are resident in the West and who, despite their grounding in its universities, seem to float in some "other" space between it and the marginal worlds to which they can trace an origin or connection. I am not suggesting, by the way, that this location should be grounds for its dismissal or that the postcolony is necessarily a more authentic source of information, but rather that it is the disavowal of location in the reception of the postcolonial that leads to its use as a dehistoricized category. The use of postcolonial as a generic term for the "other" within the Anglo-American academy is puzzling when one considers that there are specific groups that might be said to have suffered specific types of oppression in the history of these nations, that there are specific contexts in the present moment when power relations favor some over others, and none of them would fit the strict literal definition of postcoloniality. Why, then, should the term have gained such ready currency in contexts for which it was, at least originally, not intended?

Rather than insist on definitional purity, one would do better to ask, instead, in what ways *is* the term being used? Why this explosion of articles, conferences, and academic activity professing the postcolonial? If the post-colonial is a radical, resistive mode of investigation, should one assume from this proliferation that institutional appetite for discomfort is at an all-time high? I am reminded here of Spivak's forceful rejoinder in a 1993 interview in response to my comment about the need for multicultural texts: "You say there is a demand for multiculturalism. I have to find out who the hell is demanding this from me? Why the hell is there such a need?" ("Transna-tionality" 88). The status and demand for the postcolonial should prompt the same questions. It would behoove us to remember that given the sys-tematicity of the institution, new forms of knowledge and perception are usually guaranteed a place only when they are introduced on institutional terms. Ella Shohat's experience in a multicultural international studies com-mittee at CUNY illuminates the ironies surrounding the success of post-colonialism: "In response to our proposal," she recounts, "the generally conservative members of the college curriculum committee strongly resis-ted any language invoking issues such as 'imperialism and third worldist critique,' 'neocolonialism and resisting cultural practices,' and the 'geopol-itics of cultural exchange.' They were visibly relieved, however," she con-tinues, "at the sight of the word 'postcolonial'" ("Notes" 99). If Shohat's anecdote alerts us to "postcolonial" as diversionary, let us not be afraid to pursue this uncomfortable suggestion. The alliance between market consid-erations and the explosion of interest in matters postcolonial, an enterprise that straddles global and local concerns while locating its address to/in the West, is not one that any of us can afford to ignore. The "success" of post-colonialism in the academic marketplace should thus cause at least as much suspicion as it does satisfaction. While it may legitimately represent a mode of transgressive investigation into the operations of power and enable us to grapple productively with the confusions of a world in flux, it is a presence that should warn us of absences, a voice that should alert us to silences. If the work of postcolonialism goes some way toward undoing certain rela-tions of power, it also functions as an alibi for other avenues of exploration where the task may be a good bit more challenging, the possibilities for in-tervention yet remote.

Postcolonialism as an alibi is certainly a problem for those in postcolo-nial studies, but it should alarm those in composition studies as well. The nexus of postcolonialism and multiculturalism, the often unreflective slip-page, should alert us to the role both have come to play—often through the engines of the composition classroom—within transnationalism. The enlistment of postcolonial texts within a liberal multiculturalist agenda is not without contradiction. If the purpose is to sensitize students to other cultures, there is certainly value in exposing them to a variety of cultural expressions. If it is also, as one assumes, to prepare them for dealing with difference in their own contexts, the postcolonial can actually serve as a distraction. It is the displacement of the local context, of local concerns, and of local struggles by the postcolonial on the one hand and the re-christening of local others with the abstract and historically voided category of postcolonial that concerns me. The net impact of the use of postcolonial literature in this fashion is to present the other as always beyond the local shores rather than in our very midst and to privilege the notion of distant difference instead of examining the complex ways in which *difference and marginality are produced in particular contexts rather than being inherent by virtue of category.*

In a similar fashion, "multicultural" usually (and euphemistically) means a generic name for the other by virtue of race, gender, sexuality, or physical ability, although the term itself would suggest a pluralism that ought not, at least conceptually, to exclude white culture.[10] Too, while it is not entirely clear what is meant by the term culturally diverse, the diversity invoked is usually suggestive of some position of inferiority, marginality, or lack of access to resources more readily available to the mainstream.[11] I am dwelling at perhaps unnecessary length on a point that should be clear by now: the naming of the margin in euphemistic terms is a way of reducing discomfort and diverting attention away from precisely those problems of marginality, otherness, and of historical particulars that should be addressed. The resistive and radical potential of multiculturalism which is submerged within liberal dialogue on the subject, however, assumes a menacing face in conservative discussions that see it as a potent threat to Western civilization.[12] In this discourse, one might recognize what could have been a salutary threat so well "contained" by the liberal deployment of multiculturalism. But given the demonization of multiculturalism in the conservative media, the postcolonial can serve as a safer way of "doing multiculturalism" because its threats are even more efficiently managed and contained. The theoretical sophistication of postcolonialism and its links with elite (and largely Western) movements like poststructuralism and postmodernism, and its often conveniently abstract nature, reinforce its place within the academy while deferring attention to the operations of power and resistance in specific contexts.

Very commonly the site chosen by administrators for the transmission of ideas of tolerance, respect, and diversity, the composition classroom is saddled with many of these problems. It is important, then, that the dynamics of the functioning of the postcolonial text within the multicultural diversity project be investigated. For a variety of reasons, often practical rather than necessarily dubious, the kind of postcolonial text likely to enter the classroom, the publishing industry, and the scholarly engines in the Anglo-American academy is apt to be allowed entry on the basis of the ability to "play up squarely on the green summer pitches of the Imperium in its neo-colonial phase." (Slemon and Tiffin xiii). Such texts (and, some would argue, much of the theory as well) are invariably vectored toward the metropolitan center which continues to serve as the organizing fulcrum of postcolonial studies. The capacity of such texts to be radical and interruptive is already contained by other criteria for selection. Rather than ungenerously charge editors and publishers with insidious motives, however, as some readers might reasonably assume at this point, I would submit that a complex of market and "intelligibility" considerations predetermine the selection of particular sorts of texts. The kind of literature usually introduced thus invokes either a dehistoricized, multi-located transnationalism or a culture that is geographically distant and events that may be far removed in time from the current context. I do not mean to suggest that there is no value in studying texts that emerge within a "foreign" context or belong to an older period—the scholarly pursuit of the productions and histories of distant cultures is a staple of educational systems—but to underline the danger of using such texts to fulfill diversity requirements ostensibly intended to sensitize students not only to other cultures but also to the others within. Moreover, there is little evidence to suggest that these texts or multicultural readings produced within Anglo-America, for that matter, have been successful in promoting greater tolerance and understanding, or even preparation for a diversifying global market. While they may legitimately provoke interest in "marginal" cultures for some students, they also have the potential to further reinforce stereotypical attitudes and may function as rationalizations and alibis for a lack of genuine investigation into other cultures or into a complex understanding of the operation of power.

But, once again, if the potential and problems of postcolonialism are evident in the classroom, they are also present elsewhere. Here I will begin by exhuming the problem of abstract generalizations to concoct what Henry Giroux calls in reference to the use of Paulo Freire's work in the West, "a recipe for all times" ("Paulo Friere" 200), alerting us to a general tendency, facilitated, no doubt, by the definitional ambiguities of the term "postcolonial," to apply the term in any situation where a (sometimes resistive) marginality is sought to be signified. Such naming of the other ensures that the other remains nameless, the other's specificity and history thus being erased. The lack of material particulars in such deployment of postcolonial concepts renders the discussion virtually immaterial for the purposes of a radical critique. The concepts of subalternity, colonization, and postcoloniality can thus all be mobilized for initiating useful discussion, but their value is curtailed if they are left to function as generic shorthand.

The displacing and proxy function of postcolonialism within Anglo-American politics is a matter that should concern us. Viswanathan warns that the "'postcolonial' becomes a kind of replacement for other literatures, like Asian or African American without really dealing with the political challenges imposed by the other constituencies or other literatures" ("Pedagogical" 58). Moreover, regardless of the other problems with affirmative action—most notably, its contentment with token hires and its failure to address the root causes of those who continue to have poor preparation for and access into the mainstream—one of the most troubling is the recruitment of metropolitan imports from the elite ranks of erstwhile colonies in the name of affirmative hiring. Notwithstanding that such individuals may suffer real (or perceived) racism in the West, this kind of interruption in a trajectory intended to address problems of long historical standing within Anglo-America further obfuscates the controversy over affirmative action. In the leveling mechanisms of liberal multiculturalism and affirmative action, *all* the others would seem to exist on the same plane. bell hooks points out that "the current popularity of post-colonial discourse that implicated solely the West often obscures the colonizing relationship of the East in relation to Africa and other parts of the Third World. We often forget that many Third World nationals bring to this country the same kind of contempt and disrespect for blackness that is most frequently associated with white western imperialism" ("Third World" 270).

The lumping of all the others into one contourless, indefinable category privileges their difference from the mainstream while denying their sameness with it at any level or their differences from each other in crucial ways. The flattening of postcoloniality into a "condition" of the moment obscures the economic and social particulars of the postcolony as well as Anglo-America, while creating a liminal zone of otherness that diverts attention from the fact that the others in Anglo-America do not all exist on the same terms. In effect, the easy recourse to postcolonial tropes and concepts dehistoricizes the local struggle and prevents the development of specific strategies to cope with the particularities of the moment, whether in the classroom or in theory.

The use of postcolonial materials *must* be marked by a high degree of vigilance if it is to have any value at all other than to further careerism and a shallow interest in interdisciplinarity. Without discouraging the quest for concordance and intertextual referencing between postcolonial and composition studies, practitioners should explore possibilities together with limitations. I will detail below some reservations about familiar postcolonial concepts in the hope that other such terms are also brought under scrutiny.

If the concept of hybridity is useful in undoing binaries and approaching the complexities of transnationalism, as many would find in composition studies, it also tends to avoid the question of location because it suggests a zone of nowhereness and a people afloat in a weightless ether of ahistoricity. The association of the concept of hybridity with transnational figures such as Bhabha and Rushdie also tends to privilege transnational hybridity arising from an encounter with Western culture rather than allowing us to recognize the ways in which all cultures are complex and hybrid because they are diverse *internally* and not only for the purposes of oppositional figuration in a dialogue with Western discourse. The confusions of transnationalism and globalization, moreover, predispose us to attribute a diachronic flux and dynamism to cultures being produced by global movements *of the present* and *toward the West*—and to relegate the cultures of the postcolony and the "stationary" local to a state of synchronic stasis.

Royster recognizes, quite appropriately, that the concept of hybridity can be a tool to help us meet the challenges of our times. But the visible success of border-crossers like Bhabha and Rushdie can also create a dangerous illusion about the dexterity and comfort of "hybrid people." The scores of underclass immigrants in Anglo-America and illegal border crossers not only cannot "make themselves comfortable" with the same ease that other postcolonials have but also know that border crossing can be dangerous and potentially fatal. The race- and class-segregated nature of our cities, moreover, should also alert us to the intransigent borders within, rather than the more glamorous cultural borders that metropolitan postcolonial celebrities invoke. Lastly, because of the overvaluation of hybridity and transnational border crossing, the usual invocation of hybridity rarely addresses the issue of literal hybridity, that is, the plight of racial hybrids in a black-and-white culture.

Another concept fraught with the potential for misconstruction is that of subalternity. Certainly, it allows us to enter into discussion of a "general attribute of subordination [. . .] expressed in terms of class, caste, age, gender and office or in any other way" (Guha 35). The term subaltern can become meaningless, however, when it becomes overused. Spivak, in fact, complains that "it has become a kind of buzzword for any group that wants something that it does not have" ("Subaltern" 290). If the quest for subaltern voices predisposes us to listen to (and for) the texts that are available and invite such a naming, however, we would do little more than initiate a roll call, a ready identification of whoever approximates our sense of the subaltern and needs to be produced as Exhibit A, B, C, etc. If we were content with "the representation of subaltern voices," and this would appear to be the premise of so many multicultural readers, we would never learn that subalterns and subalternity emerge in the silences and aporias of discourse. We would miss, moreover, the profound significance of Spivak's question, "Can the subaltern speak?"

The notion of subalternity was never intended by the subaltern studies group to be a project of identifying subaltern groups or individuals because the very notion is characterized by "something of a not-speakingness" ("Subaltern" 291). It was, rather, a project requiring painfully careful examinations of history and discourse to uncover failed insurgency, continuously failing resistance, and the modes of such resistance. The recovery of the subaltern subject has thus involved a reading between the lines of texts whose gaps and contradictions must be excavated to suggest the buried resistance of the subaltern. If we are not careful in our usage of this term, we run the risk of turning an attentive historiographic quest into a version of contests for "the worst victim." Anxiety in the Western academy over lost subaltern voices can turn into a frenzied quest for the genuine native, leading to a fetishization of the extreme margin in terms of particularly abject otherness. "Handicaps" in the categories of race, class, sex, sexuality, and physical ability can be turned into formulas for subalternity, supplanting entirely the rhetorical dimensions of the operation of power.

One more postcolonial concept can be linked to the subaltern studies project of attentive examination of discourse and power. The notion of "mimicry," carefully elaborated by Bhabha in *The Location of Culture* provides a way of articulating resistance through the ambivalence of authoritative discourse. His contention is that the colonial discursive system is internally riven, continually producing "its slippage, it excess, its difference" in order to be effective (86). The native thus speaks through the contradictions and ambivalence of a forked colonial discourse. This concept can be useful for those in rhetoric and composition, but there are potential problems of locating agency within the ambivalence of authority. On the one hand, such a strategy would look for resistance within the structures of authoritative discourse; on the other, it would locate resistance only within the structures of a tradition of "speaking" and belittle the many kinds of resistance that *do* take place by implying that it can be found only between the lines. The real challenge, then, is to be critical and wary of our discursive productions while steering away from a tendency to overprivilege representation in textuality and within established regimes of discourse.

The strategic use of postcolonial concepts can be very fruitful indeed in rhetoric and composition studies, and its own agenda and concerns have led to the development of several useful concepts that can, in turn, inform the debates in postcolonial studies or any discipline where the study of rhetoric, power, knowledge, and resistance are of importance. Concepts such as the fundamental idea of "process" exemplified in the work of Janet Emig and Donald Murray and the new interest in social constructionism and postprocess, the notion of the "paralogic" associated with Thomas Kent, the distinction between "audience addressed/audience invoked" developed by Lunsford and Ede, intimations of the need for a new kind of literacy in the "late age of print" associated with Jay Bolter, the many useful reports from composition teachers in the pedagogic battlefield, and the growing and sophisticated discourse on electronics and communication associated with Jay Bolter, Richard Lanham, and Stuart Moulthrop, among others, can provide a conceptual map which is particularly apt for our times because these discussions have come out of a field that might be said to have come of age in the last twenty-five or so years. Additionally, the methods of rhetorical inquiry, well known to those in composition studies, can profoundly impact our understanding of those questions of speaking, listening, and representation that have so bedeviled postcolonial discourse.

This discussion closes in the spirit of collaboration and partnership between postcolonial and composition studies in tackling the challenges of the moment and of the future. If we can agree that the task before us all in a time of cultural chaos and a changing economic landscape is to conceive of a project beyond binaries, of grappling with the challenging proposition that both power and resistance are dispersed and come from everywhere instead of being neatly segregated for our theoretical and pedagogic purposes, then we all need to address in more nuanced ways the abiding issue of differentials and privilege without tokenization, to resist commodification without abandoning ethical investigation, and to agree to a rigorous (self) invigilation in our scholarly pursuits and in the practice of our everyday lives.

Gary A. Olson

ENCOUNTERING THE OTHER

Postcolonial Theory and Composition Scholarship

Theorists of the postmodern have often asserted that now that we have entered what has been termed the postmodern age, ethics is dead and no system or code of moral values can universally regulate human behavior. Those who make such assertions typically point out that prior to modernity, ethics was a product of divine will as invested in and regulated by the social institution of the Church. With the advent of the Enlightenment and the apotheosis of "reason," monitoring and enforcing moral behavior switched from the priests to the philosophers, from the Church to the State. Thus, ethics became a distinctly humanist project. As Zygmunt Bauman points out in *Postmodern Ethics*, ethics as legislated by the philosophers was based on two criteria: *universality*, in that all ethical prescriptions were assumed to be immediately recognized by all human beings as "right" (and therefore obligatory), and *foundational*, in that such prescriptions were well founded in reason and so all rational humans could be expected to follow them (8–9). Of course, postmodern theory has radically challenged the premises of such a concept of ethics, including the notions that distinguishing right from wrong is somehow an inherent capacity, that a system of ethical prescriptions can somehow justly regulate behavior in specific, local contexts, that reason is the most appropriate (or even an adequate) source of ethical behavior, and that prescriptions established prior to specific moral dilemmas can universally and reliably produce proper outcomes independent of local contingencies.

Such critiques of traditional notions of ethics make a great deal of sense, but, unlike Bauman, numerous theorists of the postmodern have unfortunately concluded that there can be no such thing as ethics in a postmodern age. Ethics is a system of values and all systems are undependable and illusory; therefore, no system of ethics can justly and reliably regulate behavior. This position has become almost axiomatic among postmodern theorists. An increasing number of scholars such as Bauman and various feminist theorists such as Luce Irigaray, however, are taking issue with this conclusion. In fact, to many of us, far from being irrelevant, ethics takes on more importance in the postmodern age than ever before. Once we dispense with externally provided ethical structures and once we believe that preestablished prescriptions are inadequate given local contingencies, then the responsibility for ethical behavior falls squarely upon the shoulders of *each individual*. That is, no longer can we conveniently rationalize our behavior by appealing to rules, rule books, priests, or philosophers. Each individual is responsible and accountable for his or her actions—the bulky, impersonal apparatus of official ethics can no longer support, defend, rationalize, or direct our individual choices.[1]

Perhaps the most useful way of conceiving ethics is in the same terms that several postmodern thinkers do: *Ethics is the encounter with the Other.*[2] By definition, all human interactions entail various encounters with an Other, and because we all bring to these interactions our own agendas— our own wishes, desires, needs, motivations—and because these agendas are often in conflict (or at least not in perfect concordance), we are constantly negotiating and renegotiating our interactions. Furthermore, few if any interactions are between equal players; power differentials invariably are at play.[3] Consequently, *how* we interact with an Other—how we balance our own needs, desires, and obligations with those of the Other—is precisely what ethics is about. *How* we effect this balance of needs, desires, and obligations, how we negotiate our encounter with the Other, is a weighty responsibility. Thus, far from being dead, ethics is perhaps more alive than ever, for now we must *actively participate* in our own moral decision making, no longer abdicating our responsibility to external forces.[4]

In many ways, the current trend in composition studies to introduce into the writing class discussion of and writing about issues of gender, race, or "contact zones" is a supremely ethical move, in that it foregrounds interaction with an Other. That is, contemporary composition theory and pedagogy are increasingly more concerned with ethical questions, regardless of whether ethics as a concept is introduced directly into the discussion.[5] This development seems to be a healthy one (even if you do not subscribe to the cognitive-developmental thesis that cognitive and ethical growth are inextricably interwoven) because students are learning to engage the world in substantive ways, to think and write about issues of importance to themselves and others. However, the scholarly examinations of these issues often fall short of presenting the ethical dimension in its fullest complexity. Scholarship on contact zones provides a good example of this shortfall.

Rhetoric and composition scholars have invoked Mary Louise Pratt's concept of contact zone to examine questions of teacher authority in pedagogical situations and to devise multicultural-focused pedagogies.[6] Pratt uses the term to refer to "social spaces where cultures meet, clash, and grapple with each other, often in contexts of highly asymmetrical relations of power, such as colonialism, slavery, or their aftermaths, as they are lived out in many parts of the world today" ("Arts" 34). She further describes the contact zone as a "space in which peoples geographically and historically separated come into contact with each other and establish ongoing relations, usually involving conditions of coercion, radical inequality, and intractable conflict" (*Imperial* 6). Pratt's discussion emerges from a strong postcolonial perspective. Her "Arts of the Contact Zone," the essay that began the conversation about contact zones in composition, draws heavily on the example of a seventeenth century manuscript written by Felipe Guaman Poma de Ayala, an unknown indigenous Andean, written "some forty years after the final fall of the Inca empire to the Spanish" and addressed to the king of Spain.[7] This work, *The First New Chronicle and Good Government*, attempts to re-present the colonized world of Peru from the eyes of the colonized, the Other, rather than, as was traditional, from the official perspective of the colonizer. Pratt uses this example to discuss classroom dynamics from the perspective of contact zones, and throughout the article she relies heavily on postcolonial discourse to construct her argument.

The term *contact zone* is highly evocative. On the one hand, it is an adaptation of the sociolinguistic concept "contact language," "a sort of creole or pidgin that speakers of differing languages develop when forced into communication with one another" ("Negotiating," Harris 31). However, as

Stephen Brown points out, the term *contact* itself carries numerous connotations, being coded with military, historical, anthropological, and psychological meaning. *Contact* is used by the military to describe violent clashes with the Other, the enemy; by historians to describe "not only the dynamics of initial encounters between indigenous peoples and their colonizers, but the epochs preceding those encounters" (as in describing the period of Hawaiian history prior to Captain Cook's "discovery" of the islands as "pre-contact"); by anthropologists to evoke "nostalgic images of an Edenic moment when the native lived in a state of communion with nature, uncorrupted by 'contact' with Western civilization;" and by various theorists to signify "an attempt to reclaim, recolonize, or reterritorialize lost realms of the indigenous self" (2–3). And, of course, the medical community uses the term frequently, as in coming into "contact" with disease-producing bacteria or viruses. Thus, the term *contact* and the concept "contact zone" are imbricated with associations related to an encounter with the Other, especially from a kind of postcolonial perspective.

While Pratt's notion of contact zone has been useful in interrogating how teachers exercise power and authority, especially in the multicultural classroom, some compositionists have tended to deploy it in such a way as to defend a kind of liberal pluralism, thereby subverting attempts to come to terms with the truly colonizing effects of the pedagogical scenario. As Joseph Harris comments, such discussions frequently devolve into a kind of "multicultural bazaar" where students "are not so much brought into conflict with opposing views as placed in a kind of harmless connection with a series of exotic others" ("Negotiating" 33). What's problematic about such a stance is that it undermines the very objective of postcolonial discourse, which is to analyze and articulate the dynamics of systems of domination and oppression, to highlight "difference" as an important, even central, aspect of political relations (be they on the micro or macrolevel), to focus, that is, on the crucial importance of Otherness. The stance taken in much contact zone scholarship effects the opposite: it deemphasizes systems of oppression and attempts to flatten out differences in order to strive for some mythical, elusive harmony.[8]

Now, while my main concern is with how compositionists have used— or, more to the point, diluted—Pratt's concept of contact zone, Pratt herself could be criticized for not fully developing the postcolonial aspects of her work. Harris provides an excellent critique of Pratt in his "Negotiating the Contact Zone." He claims that while Pratt calls for classrooms where the voices of the marginalized get heard, she is vague about how this can be accomplished other than through simply introducing class readings written by authors from diverse cultures. What can we do to truly hear the voices of the subaltern and avoid engaging in cultural and intellectual tourism—an Epcot Center approach to culture that amounts to a process of recolonization? And how can we ensure that diverse *student* voices get heard in the classroom? In the eyes of Harris and others, Pratt undermines her own theory by calling for a kind of unified, utopian community—a "safe house"—where students can articulate differences in a nonthreatening environment. Richard Miller describes the writing generated by such a contact zone as "oddly benign" ("Fault" 390).[9]

While such critiques merit attention, Pratt, working from a strong postcolonial perspective, is at least attempting to interject into the discussion an awareness of how systems of oppression threaten effective pedagogy. She points out, for example, that teacher-pupil language "tends to be described almost entirely from the point of view of the teacher and teaching, not from the point of view of pupils and pupiling (the word doesn't even exist, though the thing certainly does). If a classroom is analyzed as a social world unified and homogenized with respect to the teacher, whatever students do other than what the teacher specifies is invisible or anomalous to the analysis. This can be true in practice as well" ("Arts" 38). The question Pratt is attempting to answer is, "What is the place of unsolicited oppositional discourse, parody, resistance, critique in the imagined classroom?" ("Arts" 39). Yet, these are not the dynamics often investigated in composition scholarship.[10] What is most unfortunate is how contact zone theory, having entered our professional vocabulary, has come to signify a multicultural melting pot approach to pedagogy. We seem to be saying that it's *au courant* to be concerned with cultural representativeness in our pedagogies, so let's introduce the writings of "exotic" others, but let's not be overly concerned with real issues of conflict; let's, instead, paper over difference since we're all the same inside—can't we all get along?

Implicit, then, in the way contact zone is being theorized are serious theoretical and pedagogical dangers. An effective way to elaborate and perhaps even improve such practices is to introduce postcolonial theory into composition theory. Postcolonial theory can illuminate how despite students' attempts to empower themselves by learning to inhabit subject position, and despite our own efforts to facilitate this process, we construct students as Other, reinforcing their position in the margins where it is doubly difficult to gain the kind of empowerment we ostensibly wish to encourage. It also illustrates how colonial impulses come into play between students and teacher as well as between members of different races and ethnic groups, affecting how learning occurs, or doesn't, how students relate to peers and to teachers. And it emphasizes that the exotic readings we assign are often more than simply examples of different kinds of "art;" frequently, they are vocal acts of resistance against the kinds of oppression and even treachery perpetuated by the West. I'm positing, then, that postcolonial theory, given its rigorous concern with encounters with the Other, can reinvigorate our theorizing of contact zones as well as present substantive implications for composition theory and pedagogy.

The literature of postcolonial theory is especially relevant to our own scholarship specifically because it is so frequently concerned with articulating the interactions of discourse, ideology, and authority—interactions that compositionists have been analyzing for well over a decade. For example, those postcolonial theorists most concerned with the ideological power of discourse, such as Gayatri Spivak, are particularly useful. In "Can the Subaltern Speak?" Spivak argues that despite well-intentioned efforts to give voice to the subaltern, there is little possibility for recovering the subaltern voice, in that hegemonic discourse constitutes and disarticulates the subaltern. This "epistemic violence" is a means by which the oppressed subject, through a process of internalizing the discourse of the master, learns to construct his or her identity *as Other*, to rewrite the self as the object of imperialism. Spivak concludes that "For the 'true' subaltern group, whose identity is its difference, there is no unrepresentable subaltern subject that can know and speak itself" (285).

Discussions such as Spivak's are relevant to our own theorizing about whether we as teachers of discourse can help students take on subject position, to have agency in their own worlds, and they also shed light on questions of the balance of power and authority in the classroom. While it would be a stretch, if not a kind of violence, to liken the college student to a Third World subaltern, postcolonial discussions of hegemonic discourse and power dynamics in relation to the latter can nonetheless illuminate similar dynamics in our classes and can do so in a much more powerful and useful way than the current liberal version of contact zones and utopic safe houses.

As another example, consider the work of Homi Bhabha. In "Signs Taken for Wonders," Bhabha explores how the colonizer uses "the book" as an instrument of control of colonized peoples because it carries with it a logocentric and "civilizing" power that displaces the subaltern's authority of experience. The subaltern copes with the colonizer's presence through imitation and mimicry, an ambivalent position involving the attempt both to become like the oppressor and to resist the imperial presence.[11] The colonized at once adopt the master discourse and simultaneously rewrite it in their own key, imitating while parodying, appropriating while subverting. Such subtle misappropriation of the dominant discourse is thus an act of resistance, both against the Word of the oppressor—the logos, law, language —and against the power over the oppressed that the Word authorizes.[12]

The colonial space, then, is agonistic, oppositional; yet, according to Bhabha, resistance is "never entirely on the outside or implacably oppositional. It is a pressure, and a presence, that acts constantly, if unevenly, along the boundary of authorization" (152). In fact, such resistance is just as effective as (if not more so than) more overt forms in that it works imperceptibly from within the heart of colonial authority: its discourse. In "Problems in Current Theories of Colonial Discourse" Benita Parry calls this "a textual insurrection against the discourse of colonial authority" (42). She also notes: "The argument is not that the colonized possesses colonial power, but that its fracturing of the colonialist text by re-articulating it in broken English, perverts the meaning and message of the English book ('insignia of colonial authority and signifier of colonial desire and discipline'), and therefore makes an absolute exercise of power impossible" (42). Unlike Spivak, then, Bhabha believes that the subaltern *can* speak, can adopt subject position, but does so in indirect ways, through a kind of "sly civility." The subaltern does not escape hegemonic discourse, but speaks from within it, turning it on itself. And in this very act of resistance, colonial power is diminished, altered, and thus ambivalent, limited, never complete, never entirely successful.

What is especially valuable about work like Bhabha's is that it often addresses concerns similar to our own and does so rigorously and from a fresh perspective. It sheds light on several lines of scholarly inquiry in compo-

sition, from those concerning the power of our classroom texts to indoctrinate students, often through students' own complicity, into particular
ideological perspectives, to the numerous recent discussions of the nature
of resistance; from debates about the uses and misuses of teachers' authority in the classroom, to debates over whether our role as composition
teachers is to replace students' home discourse with "official" academic discourse or to empower students to move in and out of multiple discourses
with facility.

If in theorizing about contact zones and about the power dynamics of
pedagogical scenarios, we are serious about attempting to comprehend
how power operates in our classrooms on both political and psychological
levels, then postcolonial theory may be able to enrich our understanding of
as well as our own discourse about these subjects. For example, Abdul Jan-
Mohamed has much to say about the intricacies of power relations, and
while his discussions deal specifically with colonial domination, they are
also relevant to how domination works in lesser contexts, such as in our
classrooms. In "The Economy of Manichean Allegory," for instance, he explores how the imperialist uses difference—racial, social, cultural, linguistic
—as the basis or rationale for domination. Assuming that the Other is "ir-
remediably different" provides less incentive for the imperialist to adopt or
try to understand such alterity than to retreat "to the security of his own
cultural perspective" (65). In fact, there is considerable psychological pressure to avoid coming to terms with alterity: "Genuine and thorough comprehension of Otherness is possible only if the self can somehow negate or
at least severely bracket the values, assumptions, and ideology of his culture. [. . .] However, this entails in practice the virtually impossible task of
negating one's very being, precisely because one's culture is what formed
that being" (65). Furthermore, the colonial site provides the perfect opportunity to satisfy a deep emotional need to dominate: "If every desire is at
base a desire to impose oneself on another and to be recognized by the
Other, then the colonial situation provides an ideal context for the fulfill-
ment of that drive" (66). What's at play here, according to JanMohamed's
Lacanian analysis, is that in the very act of domination, the one who dominates is able "to compel the Other's recognition of him and, in the process,
allow his own identity to become deeply dependent on his position as
a master" (66). Thus, the imperialist's own identity and "narcissistic self-
recognition" are dependent on the Other, on the power imbalance that

constitutes the relationship. Once such a relationship of dominance and submissiveness is constituted, the one who dominates derives "affective pleasure" from the perceived moral superiority over the Other, further perpetuating and even intensifying the need and rationale to dominate, to "civilize," and thus to exploit. Once the relationship has arrived at this point, the move from paternalism to hatred seems effortless.

Of course, compositionists, many drawing on the work of Freire, have long been concerned with examining how systems of domination are manifest in pedagogical situations. Most notable is the debate over whether teachers should relinquish part or all of their classroom authority in order to help students gain subject position, some level of agency and autonomy both in their discourse and in their pedagogical interactions.[13] Another related debate concerns the extent to which the teachers' role is to indoctrinate students, to champion their own particular perspectives to the exclusion of other viewpoints—some scholars insisting that teachers are ethically bound to adopt a so-called objective stance, others arguing that such a stance is impossible. All such discussions involving teacher authority are germane to recent work on contact zones and to the ethical obligations of instructors.[14] The work of such theorists as JanMohamed, however, can contribute substantially to these discussions and may even encourage us to interrogate the extent to which we may use difference as a tool of control; the extent to which we may then ignore difference and retreat to the comfort of our own perspectives; and the extent to which we as teachers derive affective pleasure from our positions of authority over students, constructing our identity, at least in part, from our position as master over the uncivilized. All such questions may well help us come to terms with the deeply ethical content of our work as teachers, with how we encounter Otherness.

These brief sketches of some of the postcolonial work of Spivak, Bhabha, and JanMohamed are necessarily cursory, incomplete, and even somewhat reductive, but they are meant to be suggestive, to draw attention to a rich avenue of inquiry that can contribute substantially to our own scholarship, especially that related to deeply ethical concerns such as encounters with Otherness, as contact zone theory attempts. There are many other postcolonialists we can draw on. Edward Said illustrates how we construct an Other to define *ourselves*. That is, Otherness is defined by those in the center and is defined over and against those doing the defining. In a way, defining Others (students? members of other social, ethnic, or racial groups?) as different is a strategy of self-definition, in that by holding up to ourselves a "contrasting image, idea, personality, experience" we thereby carve out what we are not and, thus, what we are (*Orientalism* 2). Sara Suleri, by unpacking the "peculiar intimacy" of the colonized and colonizer, can help us avoid unsophisticated notions of alterity that construct Otherness as a simple center/margin binary—a project Freire was concerned with as early as *Pedagogy of the Oppressed*. After all, comments S. P. Mohanty, "Just how other, we need to force ourselves to indicate, is the Other?" (58). Certainly, a nuanced notion of Other is necessary if our theorizing of contact zones is to be truly useful. And Linda Hutcheon can contribute to our debates about how feminist theory can illuminate questions of agency and subjectivity despite postmodern deconstructions of the notion of subjectivity: "The current poststructuralist/postmodern challenges to the coherent, autonomous subject have to be put on hold in feminist and postcolonial discourses, for both must work first to assert and affirm a denied or alienated subjectivity: those radical postmodern challenges are in many ways the luxury of the dominant order which can afford to challenge that which it securely possesses" (168). These and other theorists of the postcolonial can provide substantial insight into the various discursive practices that we examine in composition as well as give us a conceptual vocabulary for better interrogating our encounters with Otherness in the contact zone.

Furthermore, postcolonial theory is even relevant to our own purposes on a more general level. Much of our work has involved drawing on postmodern discourses to articulate discursive practices, and postcolonial theory has numerous affinities with postmodern theory: both find value in oppositionality, in deconstructing master narratives, in interrogating systems of representation, in determining the availability of agency in discourse, in understanding power dynamics, in examining the role of ideology in the construction of self—and these very projects are central to much recent scholarship in composition. Engaging the postcolonial can help us further such projects in substantive ways.[15]

In short, then, the trend in composition scholarship to interrogate how gender, race, ethnicity, and power relationships manifest themselves in discursive practices is in effect a move toward the ethical, toward understanding the encounter with the Other. However, if discussions such as those about contact zones are to contribute fully to this effort, it is incumbent upon us not to allow a weak multiculturalism or an ineffectual liberal pluralism to diminish that effort. Turning difference into a multicultural bazaar and avoiding the thorny problems of conflict even while saying we valorize it only serve to conceal the underlying power dynamics of discursive practices. As Min-Zhan Lu writes, the field is finally taking seriously two notions of writing: "the sense that the writer writes at a site of conflict rather than 'comfortably inside or powerlessly outside the academy'" ("Writing" 20) "and a definition of 'innovative writing' as cutting across rather than confining itself within boundaries of race, class, gender, and disciplinary differences" ("Conflict" 888). It is important not to undercut these efforts with a "residual distrust of conflict and struggle" (910). As Susan Jarratt, paraphrasing Kathleen Weiler, says, "Recognizing the inevitability of conflict is not grounds for despair but the starting point for creating a consciousness in students and teachers through which the inequalities generating those con-flicts can be acknowledged and transformed" (119). Postcolonial theory, if we allow it, will give us the conceptual vocabulary we need to encounter the Other, both in our scholarship and in our classrooms.

R. Mark Hall and Mary Rosner

PRATT AND PRATFALLS

Revisioning Contact Zones

> The status of a statement depends on later statements.
>
> *Bruno Latour,* Science in Action, 27

In *Science in Action*, Bruno Latour describes a number of examples that show how a hypothesis or speculation becomes either fact (i.e., science) or curiosity. He calls fact "ready-made" science—as in the sense of already made: it is black boxed, certain, unproblematic, and stable, and it provides a foundation for future work. He refers to speculation as "science in the making" or "science in action:" it is "rich, confusing, ambiguous, and fascinating," and its future is uncertain (15). Later in the book, Latour complicates the definition of "black boxed" he has attached to ready-made science, suggesting that he used the term "both too much and too loosely to mean either a well-established fact or an unproblematic object" (131). Instead, he redefines the black box as an actively rhetorical agent. It is "the assembly of disorderly and unreliable allies [. . .] slowly turned into something that closely resembles an organized whole" that can be useful in controlling the behavior of others (130–31).

This journey that Latour describes toward becoming black boxed— either his first explanation that moves from speculation or his second that moves from apparent incoherence—may be a useful way to think about the making of knowledge in general. And so we began to wonder whether Latour might help us follow the journey a concept in composition and rhetoric might take as it moves toward being black boxed. The concept in question had its beginnings in work by Mary Louise Pratt and her notion of "contact zones."[1] Pratt herself has written about these zones in different contexts and in different ways. They have also been described in various texts—for instance, in reviews of her book and in journal articles about composition classrooms.

If, as Latour claims, "The fate of what we say and make is in later users' hands" (29) as they challenge, adopt, alter, or ignore an original idea, then it is important to note what happens to an original idea like "contact zones" in those "later users' hands." In following the path of this term, we found that "black boxing"—stabilizing and taming—may not be advisable. After all, the meaning of "contact zone" is undergoing change, and Pratt herself continues to evolve her explanation of the term. Whatever else it means, it seems best characterized as a process that is ongoing, unstable, and resistant to simple explanations, something like Latour's "rich, confusing, ambiguous [. . .] fascinating" and uncertain "science-in-the-making." And although stipulating a single definition for contact zones may be useful in reducing some of that ambiguity by making the term reflect an organized and single meaning, black boxing it in that way may invite us to use the term uncritically, to idealize it and ignore its limitations.

Pratt's Contact Zones

Three of Pratt's texts illustrate some of the changes affecting her definition of contact zone. "Arts of the Contact Zone," published in MLA's *Profession 91* and reprinted in Bartholomae and Petrosky's *Ways of Reading*; her book *Imperial Eyes*, published in 1992; and a second essay, "Criticism in the Contact Zone" in *Critical Theory, Cultural Politics, and Latin American Narrative*, published in 1993, illustrate the evolution of this term.

Profession publishes articles "on current intellectual, curricular, and professional issues" (inside front cover) important to university teachers. The particular issue that includes Pratt's essay is said to be filled with texts "about complexities, contradictions, conflicts, and the usefulness of ambiguity"

(Franklin 1). In "Arts of the Contact Zone," Pratt writes: "I use this term to refer to social spaces where cultures meet, clash, and grapple with each other, often in contexts of highly asymmetrical relations of power, such as colonialism, slavery, or their aftermaths as they are lived out in many parts of the world today. Eventually I [. . .] use this term to reconsider the models of community that many of us rely on in teaching and theorizing and that are under challenge today" (34). Products of these clashing cultures often take the form of complex and critical texts, which, Pratt says, can lead to "miscomprehension, incomprehension, dead letters, unread masterpieces, absolute heterogeneity of meaning" (37). She cites as examples of these texts a long critical letter written by a seventeenth-century Incan that never reached its audience; homework, written by her fourth-grade son, critical of the assignment it responds to; a course for a new "western civilization" requirement at Stanford; and passing references to slave narratives and early published writing by Chicanas. Pratt argues that the potential frustrations from these texts are outweighed by two potential benefits: exploding the myth of community, which wrongly suggests that everyone is equal in important ways; and making a place for those who have long been silenced, giving them "the experience of seeing the world described with [them] in it [. . . and] exhilarating moments of wonder and revelation, mutual understanding, and new wisdom" (39). She explicitly commends multicultural university courses when they function like contact zones.

It is unfortunate that an essay directly critical of the effects of power imbalances does not include the voices Pratt's story silences. The students in the western civilization class who, she says, experience joys and pains; the teacher of her son who, she says, does not acknowledge his criticisms; and the seventeenth-century Spanish who apparently brutalized the Incas are not heard in "Arts of the Contact Zone."

Imperial Eyes, published in 1992, is described by its publisher as a work intended for "readers interested in issues of colonialism and post-colonialism; in nineteenth-century British and Latin American literature; and in theories of discourse and knowledge" (*Imperial Eyes* i). Distinguished by a broader scope than "Arts of the Contact Zone," its specific attention to analyzing travel writing as literature, and its argument that all texts are ideological, *Imperial Eyes* defines contact zones as "social spaces where disparate cultures meet, clash, and grapple with each other, often in highly asymmetrical relations of domination and subordination—like colonialism, slavery, or their aftermaths as they are lived out across the globe today. [. . . T]he space of colonial encounters, the space in which peoples geographically and historically separated come into contact with one another and establish ongoing relations usually involving conditions of coercion, radical inequality and intractable conflict" (4, 6). Using examples of eighteenth- and nineteenth-century scientific and travel texts written by Europeans, Pratt shows how they typically represent stories that justify their domination of South America and Africa.

Critical Theory, Cultural Politics, and Latin American Narrative aims "to test an eclectic array of works in Latin American narrative literature" against poststructuralist theory and to redress "the relative absence of reciprocal dialogue and direct interaction between First World (North American) criticism and theory and Third World (Latin American) culture and literature" (Bell 5). In her essay in this collection, Pratt uses "contact zone" as a frame for examining Spanish American literature written by women in the nineteenth and twentieth centuries. Rejecting a critical approach to literature that would "bleach out" conflicts and differences between the so-called first and third worlds, she draws attention to literature representing zones of "differences and hierarchies [. . .] produced *in and through contact* across [. . .] lines [of difference, hierarchy, and unshared or conflicting assumptions . . . These lines are] borderlands, sites of ongoing critical and inventive interaction with the dominant culture, as permeable contact zones across which significations move in many directions" (88–89). Pratt privileges an approach to literature that examines how texts engage with and transgress "official categories" (101).

Bringing the three definitions in contact with each other, we begin to notice the changes Pratt has made so far in revising her work:

Changes in the context for contact zones: from far-reaching public social acts—colonialism, slavery, "education"—to literature and literary critics.

Changes in the relations among those in the contact zones: from "relations of power" to "relations of domination and subordination" to relations of "difference, hierarchy, and unshared or conflicting assumptions."

Changes in the specific nature of the relations: "meet, clash, and grapple with each other," to "meet, clash, and grapple with each other [. . . in] conditions of coercion, radical inequality and intractable conflict" to "ongoing critical and inventive interaction [by means of] permeable contact [. . .] across which significances move in many directions."

An aggressive meeting denoted by "clash" and "grapple" becomes even more aggressive and undeniably negative with its "conditions of coercion," "radical inequality," and "intractable conflict." But in the most recent of the three texts, Pratt transforms aggression into the promise of "inventive inter-action." These revisions show Pratt herself grappling with her meanings and—because we've done this tracing—we grapple with them as well. As a result, we cannot understand contact zones as a single, tidy, black-boxed term.

There are other arguments against using contact zones as if it had the stability of a black box. We can, for instance, look at the multiple interpre-tations of contact zone revealed in scholarly reviews.

Reviews of Imperial Eyes

Soon after its publication, *Imperial Eyes* was reviewed in specialized jour-nals in history, geography, sociology, cultural studies, and literature.[2] Dis-agreements among these reviews were often dramatic. For *The Journal of Imperial and Commonwealth History*, Pratt's cover is evidence to her lack of reflectiveness: "The cover of *Imperial Eyes* really says it all. There, an Andean '*stilletero*' carries a European in a makeshift chair on his back across the mountains in the rain. The porter looks down submissively at his footing, the Imperial Eyes look back at the unfolding view. It is a powerful image whose obvious implications—to late twentieth-century eyes at least—this study never questions. So, although the assumptions of every travel writer are suspiciously unmasked, those of Mary Louise Pratt remain self-evidently true" (Carroll 157). But for *Victorian Studies*, the cover functions as a sign of Pratt's complexity: "The cover illustration of Mary Louise Pratt's *Imperial Eyes*, taken from a travel account of the 1870s, shows a booted European adventurer crossing the Andes while seated in a chair strapped to the back of 'a barefooted Indian.' It thus dramatically introduces the complexly inter-woven dichotomies of culture and nature, colonizer and colonized, observer and observed that structure Pratt's thoughtful and illuminating discussion of the relation of Europe and 'the rest of the world.'" (Ritvo 498–99). According to these two scholars, you *can* tell a book by its cover—though this cover apparently tells of very different books.

At issue is more than critical disagreements among reviewers. As the mock multiple-choice quiz presented here demonstrates, reviews suggest not only some of the different assumptions and values of these disciplines, but also certain shared criteria that complicate easy distinctions we might be tempted to make among them and their readings of Pratt.

If we bring reviews into contact with each other, "clashing and grappling" so to speak, then we can recognize how we often privilege the reviews of our own discipline and how—because of the context that reveals varied assumptions, hierarchies, values—that privileging must be tentative. If we bring reviews from within the same discipline together, we are again invited to notice that the most persuasive and most powerful reflect our own specific and partial interests rather than unproblematic evaluations. For instance, reviews from three literary journals agreed in finding much to praise about Pratt's book—its clarity and critical precision, its style and scope, its balance and originality—suggesting that in this discipline, *Imperial Eyes* and its contact perspective may be on the road to "theory in the making," as Latour might say: "By themselves, a statement, a piece of machinery, a process are lost. By looking only at them and their internal properties, you cannot decide if they are true or false, efficient or wasteful, costly or cheap, strong or frail. These characteristics are only gained through *incorporation* into other statements, processes, and pieces of machinery" (29). Yet all the reviewers see a slightly different text that is potentially useful in different ways.

The journal *World Literature Written in English*, from the University of Singapore, calls itself the journal that students, teachers, and researchers "turn to when they want to learn about alternative writing, writing that has been marginalised by a mainstream dominated by England and the United States." Its review finds *Imperial Eyes* "useful not only for unpacking the important issues inherent in transcultural writing but also for pushing at the boundaries of existing theories and methodologies of post-coloniality" (Couling 125).

Research in African Literatures, published by Indiana University in collaboration with the Ohio State University, "invites scholarly contributions on all aspects of the oral and written literatures of Africa" (inside front cover).

DIRECTIONS: Choose the journal on the right from which the *Imperial Eyes* review excerpt on the left comes. You can use the same journal more than once; some journals may not be used at all.

REVIEWS

1. Equates male with evil, possessive desire.

2. Does not include any African writers in its consideration of transculturation.

3. Seems too often like a one-way process of culture change [in its description of transculturation].

4. Juxtaposes sources that have conventionally been separated by provenance.

5. [Unmasks] assumptions of every travel writer [but Pratt herself].

6. Listens carefully to voices that have often been neglected.

7. [Tends] to take the texts out of context.

8. [Sees] gender as an important variable in the construction of colonial and imperial discourses.

9. [Insists] on relations between "discoverers" and "discovered."

10. Implies a certain uniformity throughout large regions of global periphery.

11. Sketches out the way that all those involved in imperialism created potential subject positions for themselves and others in a process of bricolage.

12. Tells a fascinating story of the interrelations of European politics, science, exploration, abolition, trade, and travel discourse around the turn of the nineteenth century.

13. Illustrate[s] the many different voices in which relations of domination and submission can speak.

14. Devote[s . . .] informed and disciplined energy to the demystification of "innocence."

15. Runs into some rough water, especially the choppy seas of crossdisciplinary analysis.

16. Suggests both the possibilities of a vocabulary increasingly shared across disciplinary lines and the limitations of that kind of thinking.

JOURNALS

American Ethnologist

Annals of the Association of American Geographers

Eighteenth-Century Studies

Eighteenth-Century Life

Feminist Review

Journal of Historical Geography

Journal of Imperial and Commonwealth History

Journal of Modern History

Novel

Research in African Literatures

Victorian Studies

World Literature Written in English

The review suggests that *Imperial Eyes* clears the way for further work in, for example, "Victorian women's narratives in which innocence is constituted in relation to older, imperial, male rhetorics of conquest" (Blake 156).

From Brown University, the journal *Novel* publishes scholarly texts that "deal with larger issues of genre, history, or theory" rather than "close readings of single texts" ("Attention" 2). Its review notes that Pratt's argument "in challenging Europe's representation of itself as a '*sui generis* entit[y],' [. . .] enables a rethinking of similarly represented [and long accepted] categories like 'Romanticism' and 'Literature'" (Reitz 365).

If, as Latour suggests, "the status of a statement depends on later statements," it's fair to say that the status of Pratt's work for literature specialists has been affected by how well these reviewers have responded to it. To determine how its meaning has been affected as well, we need to look not only at the way the different journals perceive the usefulness of *Imperial Eyes* but also at the ways reviewers explain Pratt and her specialized terms.

In *Imperial Eyes*, Pratt tells us that she chose the term contact zone carefully to complicate previous discussions of the imperializer and the imperialized—in fact, to avoid the opposition and fixedness we just articulated by using those two terms. She tells us that she intended the term "to invoke the spatial and temporal *copresence* of subjects," "to foreground the *interactive, improvisational*, dimensions of colonial encounters," to emphasize "how subjects are constituted in and by their relations to each other," to treat "the relations among colonizers and colonized [. . .] not in terms of separatedness [. . .] but in terms of *copresence, interaction, interlocking* understandings and practices, often within radically asymmetrical relations of power" (7 emphasis added). Her definition consciously evokes the interrelatedness and interconnectedness of conflicting groups to invite her readers to complicate their ideas of "colonial frontier," "colonist," and "colonized" —ideas that are already black boxed.

Yet reviewers consistently simplify her complex term.[3] And they just as consistently accept it. Latour tells us, "You make [a statement] more of a fact if you insert it as a closed, obvious, firm, and packaged premise," and each of the reviews does that (25). But their versions of contact zone are not the same versions, and the differences complicate the term so that even while it goes unchallenged, its meaning is not pinned down. And while writers could simply stipulate a single meaning and limit the term in ways that may seem useful for some purpose—in Latour's terms, for creating and controlling allies in an argument—a single definition of contact zones can be problematic in other ways.

"Contact" in Rhetoric and Composition

Three journal articles from rhetoric and composition continue this journey toward becoming black boxed. Our readings suggest that black boxing—organizing and controlling—may not be a desirable end for Pratt's contact zone, which seems to us best characterized as a process that is itself always in the making. Just six years after the publication of "Arts of the Contact Zone," however, Joseph Harris's history of the discipline and critique of Pratt's "Negotiating the Contact Zone" shows how others in composition have proclaimed Pratt the 1990s "patron theorist of composition" (117), a label that suggests to us the certainty and stability of a black box.

In "Contact Zones and English Studies," Patricia Bizzell helps Pratt achieve the "patron theorist of composition" status by applying the idea of a contact zone to our discipline at large, arguing that in response to multiculturalism, English studies ought to undergo a radical reorganization based on the image of the contact zone. Bizzell suggests that "we organize English studies not in terms of literary or chronological periods, nor essentialized racial or gender categories, but rather in terms of historically defined contact zones, moments when different groups within the society contend for the power to interpret what is going on" (4). By defining the "contact zone" as an environment that promotes "productive dialogue," Bizzell glosses over the perils of the contact zone, including—as Pratt herself reminds us—"miscomprehension, incomprehension, dead letters, unread masterpieces, absolute heterogeneity of meaning" ("Arts" 37). While Pratt sets contact zones in opposition to utopian ideas of community, for Bizzell contact zones become alternative utopias where difference, not homogeneity, and discord, not agreement, are idealized.

Overstating its potential for cultural mediation and ignoring the inherent violence suggested by Pratt's image is one danger of the uncritical adoption of a contact-zone perspective. Pratt herself warns against this: "No one [is] excluded, and no one [is] safe" in the contact zone ("Arts" 39). Like others who have poached from Pratt, Bizzell ignores Pratt's comparing the cultural clashes in the contact zone to those that occur amid slavery and colonialism. Bizzell puts too much faith in negotiation. "We would, in effect, be reading all the texts as brought to the contact zone," she argues, "for the purpose of communicating across boundaries" ("Contact" 4). But how much mediation can take place where colonialism and slavery exist? How appropriate is the comparison of slavery and colonialism to English studies—or to our classrooms? These are questions that, in an eagerness to adopt and black box Pratt's image, many have not yet asked.

Wolff's "Teaching in the Contact Zone: The Myth of Safe Houses"

Some rhetoric and composition scholars have begun to ask these questions. Rather than simply appropriate Pratt's image wholesale, Janice Wolff, for example, examines how her understanding of the contact zone influences her construction of the classroom, and how her reading of the classroom shapes her understanding and deployment of Pratt's ideas. In particular, she challenges Pratt's notion of "safe houses." In Pratt's words, "Where there are legacies of subordination, groups need places for healing and mutual recognition, safe houses in which to construct shared understandings, knowledges, claims on the world that they can then bring into the contact zone" ("Arts" 40). Wolff begins the semester attempting to model her classroom after Pratt's "'safe house' for learning, an environment that would encourage knowledge making and risk taking" (Wolff 317). But herein lies the rub: "Teaching in the contact zone can be fraught with danger, and sometimes establishing a 'safe house' is little more than a myth. For each exhilaration, there seems to be a corresponding downward spiral. Using the contact zone theory as a screen through which to read [. . .] was one thing, but realizing that the metaphor of the contact zone was also active upon my own classroom itself was daunting" (325). Wolff makes this discovery one day in class when she and her students are discussing the differences between print and oral cultures. She aligns herself with print, her students with orality. When her students reject this false dichotomy, Wolff comes to recognize that "in the very telling of contact-zone theory, I had centered myself and relegated students once more to the borders of knowledge making" (326). "Students," she realizes, "recognize marginalization when they see it, and perhaps not even classrooms that want to be 'safe houses' can be very safe, either for students or for teachers" (326).

Wolff concludes that a democratic pedagogy requires teachers to read their own theories critically. Like Bartholomae and Petrosky, she urges us "to read against the grain, to read critically, to turn back [. . .] *against* [theories], to ask questions [that might] come as a surprise, to look for the limits of [theories], to provide alternate readings [. . .] to find examples that challenge [theories], to engage [theories] in [. . .] dialogue" (11). This, we would argue, is exactly what Pratt's idea of the contact zone invites: to see it as a useful method of analysis, one which is always in the making, not a stable, tame, and unproblematic ready-made theory. In Wolff's words, "My best advice is to read theory but refuse to privilege it. Read about the 'contact zone,' use it as a metaphor for the classroom, let it inform pedagogy, but always with a Derridean caveat: Use the term under erasure" (326–27).

Wolff's advice is useful, because, as we have suggested, Pratt herself continues to evolve her explanation of the "contact zone," which seems best characterized by multiple, unstable, developing definitions. But even Wolff, who challenges Pratt's usefulness, helps to black box the contact zone by relying on a single definition. In her paraphrase of "Arts of the Contact Zone," Wolff describes contact zones as "imaginary spaces where differing cultures meet. Very often the cultures have different languages and certainly different values, and very often one culture will dominate the other as it privileges itself" (316).

We recognize that we too must tread lightly, for as we argue for destabilizing Pratt's contact zone, we risk suggesting that "unstable" is the "correct" —and thus another black boxed—way to read Pratt's image. Nevertheless, Pratt's own grappling with her definition and the multiple interpretations of contact zone reflected in scholarly reviews do invite us to complicate our understandings of Pratt's concept and to challenge instances of fixedness.

Miller's "Fault Lines in the Contact Zone"

Like Wolff, Richard Miller not only challenges but also extends the usefulness of Pratt's contact zone. Yet he too helps package this concept by relying solely on a partial reading of Pratt's early definition in "Arts of the Contact Zone": "where cultures meet, clash, and grapple with each other, often in contexts of highly asymmetrical relations of power" (390). Miller finds Pratt's image a "promising" way to imagine the classroom, but he points out that the examples she offers of the kind of writing produced in the contact zone are "oddly benign," hardly the sort of clashing and grappling Pratt herself advocates (390). How, Miller wonders, should teachers respond to "unsolicited oppositional discourse, parody, resistance, critique" that we find downright offensive or frightening? He asks, "What 'Arts of the Contact Zone' are going to help us learn how to read and respond [. . .] when the kind of racist, sexist, and homophobic sentiments now signified by the term 'hate speech' surface in our classrooms?" (391).

With the example of a student's essay called "Queers, Bums, and Magic," which recounts an incident of gay bashing and the beating of a homeless person, Miller explores several possible answers. One response might be to remove the offending student from class. Another might be to read the essay under the assumption that the violence and hatred depicted there are fictional, responding not to the content, but only to the surface features of the text. But silencing or ignoring transgressive discourse, Miller points out, fosters neither contact nor learning. "Reinventing the classroom as a contact zone is a potentially powerful pedagogical invention," he argues, "only so long as it involves resisting the temptation either to silence or to celebrate the voices that seek to oppose, critique, and/or parody the work of constructing knowledge in the classroom" (407).

A third option—and Miller's own choice—is to make the offending essay available, alongside legal definitions of hate speech, for the entire class to discuss. The goal in this case "involves articulating, investigating, and questioning the affiliated cultural forces that underwrite the ways of thinking that find expression in this student's essay" (397). Miller's approach invites not only the consideration of the cultural conflicts that produce hate speech, but also how and why this discourse is regulated. Importantly, Miller recognizes the possibility that even in this case, negotiation or reconciliation may not take place. Cultural mediation is a possibility, but it is not guaranteed—or even necessarily a desirable outcome in Pratt's contact zone. Unlike Bizzell and others who have overemphasized the possibility of negotiation, Miller understands that the potential of a contact perspective rests upon its ability to raise critical awareness about the consequences of contact. Nevertheless, we're left wondering about the student writer of "Queers, Bums, and Magic." What is the view of the contact zone Miller imagines for *him?* How are he and his text shaped and appropriated by Miller?

We began by looking at the different ways Pratt has written about the contact zone and also how her concept has been interpreted in book reviews. We wondered whether Latour might help us follow the journey that the contact zone has taken as it has moved toward being black boxed by users in rhetoric and composition. If Latour is right that "the fate of what we say and make is in later users' hands" as they challenge, adopt, alter, or ignore an original idea, then Pratt's contact zone seems most promising to us when users resist the neat and tidy package of Latour's black box when that box remains open to critical inspection, when the contact zone is evoked as a "rich, confusing, ambiguous [. . .] fascinating" and "uncertain" method of analysis, or speculative instrument, rather than a static theory (15).

As a method of analysis, Pratt's contact zone helps teachers and scholars in various disciplines to achieve a heightened sensitivity to those written and spoken interactions in which, as Pratt puts it, participants "are from different classes or cultures, or one party is exercising authority and another is submitting to it or questioning it" ("Arts" 34). But what we've not yet adequately examined is the metaphor of the contact zone itself, which turns on a troubling contradiction: the image of contact is at odds with its definitions. "Contact zones," Pratt says in "Arts of the Contact Zone," are "social spaces where cultures meet, clash, and grapple." But contact suggests a benign or even genial relationship, not a violent battle. Contact denotes a state of being in or coming into close association or connection. Contact also suggests touching or unity. This interpretation is just the opposite of the breach, break, rupture, or split that results from the clashing and grappling that Pratt imagines.

On the one hand, clashing and battling point to what Catherine Lamb labels a commonsense view of power: "the ability to affect what happens to someone else" ("Less" 100). On the other hand, "contact" suggests for Lamb a friendly, supportive meeting, one characterized by power, "not as a quality to exercise on others, but as something which can energize, enabling competence and thus reducing hierarchy" ("Beyond" 199). As a result of this contradiction between Pratt's image and her definition, those who have deployed it have done so with considerable latitude. While some emphasize the *differences* among ideas and opinions, others stress the unity they expect to achieve through *negotiation* of these differences. What we need to do is to reflect more critically upon the contradictions inherent in Pratt's contact zone and the consequences that result from evoking it for particular purposes. This includes, of course, our own purposes in this essay. By bringing the various meanings and interpretations of Pratt's contact zone into contact with each other, to what extent do we exercise power over—and possibly even distort—the ideas of others, and to what extent do we help to energize and enable a productive conversation about Pratt's concept?

What's more, stories of contact zones are so far told only from the perspective of teachers, not students. If we are to continue to use Pratt's metaphor to describe our classrooms, then we need to find ways to give voice to students, to better understand how they view the construction of their classrooms as contact zones. After all, what might seem like productive contact to us might seem like little more than unproductive conflict to them. The result may be only seeming negotiation or accommodation that merely masks deeper divisions. If we are to realize the full potential of Pratt's contact-zone perspective, then we must ask ourselves what potential dangers may result from constructing our classrooms—or our disciplines—this way. Elevated to the status of high theory, might contact zones become simply another system of domination, an unproblematic black box?

Finally, the popularity of Pratt's image reminds us that as academics we privilege difference and the adversarial discourses that result from it— what Jane Tompkins calls "fighting words." But Pratt's image may be problematic for those who, like Lamb, seek to enact a feminist pedagogy with an emphasis on "cooperation, collaboration, shared leadership, and integration of the cognitive and affective" ("Beyond" 195). The antagonism suggested by "clashing and grappling" may invite us to consider alternatives to "contact zones," such as Lorraine Code's notion of "rhetorical spaces," which she defines as "fictive but not fanciful or fixed locations, whose (tacit, rarely spoken) territorial imperatives structure and limit the kinds of utterances that can be voiced within them with a reasonable expectation of [. . .] being heard, understood, taken seriously" (ix–x). In the contact zone, we and our students may become energized by a moment of clashing and grappling, what Tompkins calls "a moment of righteous ecstasy" (590). As a site of conflict, a place where people of unequal power come together, the contact zone offers a rich opportunity for critical reflection. In Tompkins's words, "It's the moment to look out for, the moment whose content and whose consequences need to be examined" (590). Rather than privilege contact blindly, we need to do more to examine what actually takes place *at the point of contact*, perhaps thinking of it as both spatially and climatologically, as Code does, asking questions "not merely about whether it is possible to say just anything at all, indifferently, in the discursive spaces that epistemology calls its own, but about the conditions for flourishing there" (4). This might help move us toward a more reflective use of the "contact zone" as a thinking device in the making, with all its attendant strengths and weaknesses.

Susan C. Jarratt

BESIDE OURSELVES

Rhetoric and Representation in Postcolonial Feminist Writing

The value of postcolonial theory for teachers of writing arises in part from its focus on the rhetorical situation of intellectual work applied to the question of difference. By pointing out that academic traditions of Western universities are built on several centuries of economic and cultural imperialism, this theory demands that scholars and teachers of literature and literacies ask rhetorical questions, the answers to which had been for many years assumed: who speaks? on behalf of whom? who is listening? and how? It interrogates the assumption of any group identification and more specifically the relationship of the single "I" to a collective "we" (see Anderson, Mohanty, Roof and Wiegman[1]).

My aim in this essay is to address the problem of speaking for others by looking at how "others" speak. Employing the figures of metaphor and metonymy, I analyze the ways three postcolonial feminists open up the workings of representation—of the self, groups, and audiences—such that participants are no longer disposed in the classical rhetorical position, a single subject facing an audience, but rather "beside themselves." This colloquial expression calls to mind situations of deep emotional turmoil—worry, anger, or maybe grief. Perhaps it means that, in times of intense emotional distress, one loses bodily or mental integrity and manufactures another version of oneself to express or absorb the pain. My appropriation of the expression bears some relation to its everyday use, in the sense that oppressed groups experience the pain of self-distancing or alienation (Fanon). As a rhetorician, though, I'm interested in the way an experience of suffering is turned into a tool of language: an artful, rhetorical practice of self-multiplication used by speakers in response to their historical, rhetorical, and institutional circumstances. I'm also interested in the way a painful image of self-division could be transformed into a hopeful vision of collectivity. Tracing representational strategies of postcolonial feminist rhetoric might offer ways for composition teachers and students to imagine that scene—a difficult task in a culture that values individualism so highly. This essay contributes to that project in three ways: by analyzing changes in concepts of *ethos* and audience under the historical conditions of postcoloniality, by describing complex processes of writing the self, and by attending to the ways teachers and students in U.S. universities "read" (about) formerly colonized people.

Figuring Structures of Relation

How can differences be imagined? In what forms of relation? Rhetoric is useful for addressing these questions because it gives names to figures that structure relations in language and in the material world. Any choice of a figure is a discursive act that also simultaneously configures a material relationship of power and difference. One of the ways postcolonial theory has heightened attention to the politics of representation is to point out that exercises of domination occur not only in the sphere of politics proper but also through cultural practices. They insist on the dual functions of rhetoric as both political and figurative representation.[2] Gayatri Spivak, in her now-canonical essay "Can the Subaltern Speak?," warns First World intellectuals about the danger of obscuring their own acts of discursive imperialism in the process of facily "representing" the interests of apparently silent subjects of oppression. She makes her point historically and philologically, using Marx's essay on the mid-nineteenth-century coup d'état of Louis Bonaparte, who came to "represent" a peasant class politically through an exercise of executive power without their having any consciousness of themselves as a class, i.e., without participating in an imaginative or political construction of themselves as a class (Marx 602, 608). The typical translation of two different German words *(Vertretung* and *Darstellung)* into a single English word, *representation,* emblemizes for Spivak the danger of collapsing these two distinct processes: the first, a political or legal process of standing for members of a constituency group; the second, a symbolic process of creating images of such groups (Spivak "Subaltern" 276; see also Landry and MacLean 198). She associates these two forms of representation with two kinds of rhetoric, persuasion and trope, graphically captured in the analogies of "proxy" and "portrait"—arguing that in her historical example of Bonaparte the former assumes or enacts the latter: "The event of representation as [a political process . . .] behaves like a[n imaging], taking its place in the gap between the formation of a (descriptive) class and the nonformation of a (transformative) class" (Spivak 277). In other words, when someone uses power over others to represent them politically—to act for them—there is an unavoidable, concomitant symbolic process underway: the represented group is sketched, painted, and described in a particular way through that process. And this description may or may not "represent" them in ways they themselves would endorse.

The reason Spivak writes "nonformation" is to emphasize that "identity" as a class does not take place naturally (at what she calls "ground level consciousness"), but rather must be constructed through acts of political agency and *self*-description (Spivak 277–78). One cannot assume a class identity for the French peasants Bonaparte forcibly represented in the absence of their own representations of themselves or of acts on their behalf as a class. The backlash against feminism in the United States (and other countries as well) offers a contemporary example of processes of "nonformation" and transformation. Many women on university campuses reject feminism— that is, reject being identified as a politicized class, "women"—because they believe they haven't had a hand in constructing the symbolic representations of the class. In women's studies classes, female students actually read and discuss the works of feminists (as opposed to absorbing uncritically the grotesque caricatures offered on talk radio and other popular media). As they talk and write about the ways their self-identification fits with or differs from the representations they read, a process of class formation/transformation takes place, creating a locally grounded understanding of the class "women." Some will actually go forward to act out of that class consciousness (in campus activism, volunteer work, or career choices). Inevitably, their subsequent actions as women on behalf of other women will recreate the gap between political agency and self-description.[3]

Discovering the workings of these two forms of representation at any site, the interwoven operations of imaging—textual descriptions of otherness—and political representation—entailing identification of or with a group—is the work of teachers and students of language practices. Rhetoric mobilizes an interaction between representation (political) and re-presentation (cultural), possibly enabling the transformative practices Marx found missing in the nineteenth-century French peasants: that is, driving the movement from descriptive to transformative class, or at least calling attention to where and by whom groups are described. Some postcolonial feminists have been particularly useful in activating rhetoric in these two senses, and an analysis of their work in these terms might advance the argument over identity politics, helping to delineate with more care and refinement the bases on which identities are constructed, claimed, and linked with others. This framework might serve the ethical aim of "recognizing the responsibility for linking" (Faigley 237).

My method is to use rhetorical figures—metaphor and metonymy—to analyze the ways postcolonial feminist writing calls attention to these dual processes of representation: political and pictorial. In this analysis, metaphor is a figure of substitution: one thing or person standing in for another, and in the process, obscuring some particularities of what it represents.[4] A metaphoric style of representation occurs any time a speaker or writer functions as a spokesperson for a particular category of people—workers, women, voters in a particular constituency—the partiality of the single member standing in for the whole. Consider an example of a critic using this definition of metaphor to distinguish autobiography from *testimonio:* "In rhetorical terms, whose political consequences may be evident, there is a fundamental difference here between the *metaphor* of autobiography and heroic narrative in general, which assumes an identity-by-substituting one (superior) signifier for another (I for we, leader for follower, Christ for the faithful), and *metonymy*, a lateral move of identification-through-relationship, which acknowledges the possible differences among 'us' as components of a centerless whole" (Sommer 61).

Metonymy, on the other hand, as the passage above suggests, creates a chain of associations. It configures a relationship based on contiguity and context (Jakobson 79, 83, 90–91; Irigaray; Brady). The example of metonymy provided by Jakobson has an eerie resonance for postcolonial history. A hut may metonymically be associated with "thatched roof," "family of twelve," or "burnt by the army," each association creating a narrative or contextualized understanding of the word without displacing or blocking out the word itself. Applying metonymy to identity politics suggests that differences can be spoken of not in terms of exclusive categories but rather as places, descriptions, or narratives of relation. The writings of Gayatri Spivak and Trinh T. Minh-ha offer eloquent illustrations of what I see as a metonymic process of subject construction. Each simultaneously makes visible the intellectual work of theorizing and gives voice to varieties of otherness, placing themselves not at the head of some silent group of followers but rather beside themselves. But in so doing, they unavoidably participate in a metaphoric process of representing "others," thus enacting a tension between these two modes. After analyzing rhetorics of linkage and spatial location in the texts of Spivak and Minh-ha, I turn to a very different text. The 1983 testimonio of Rigoberta Menchú,[5] a Quiché Indian peasant and peace activist, arose from the midst of the Guatemalan civil war, a situation calling forth different strategies of representation from those used by postcolonial feminist academics writing within the context of the U.S. academy.[6]

Immigrant Academics as Metonymic Subjects

The first two subjects are both professional "representers" engaged in literary criticism and cultural critique (Spivak) and in documentary filmmaking, ethnography, and cultural theory (Minh-ha). These feminist theorists are hypersensitive to the constructed nature of the discourse of personal experience yet, nonetheless, acknowledge the need for the representation of others—to give others a vocal and visible presence. They both meet this need through the production of what Spivak terms "counter-sentences" by subjects of imperialism: alternatives to re-presentations—images of the "other"—produced from within dominant cultures. Such counter-sentences come into being through the strategic placement and voicing of narrative, but both Trinh and Spivak seek to avoid speaking for the other through displacement and indirection. Unlike the "Third World intellectuals" in metropolitan universities described by Ahmad, who "materially represent the undifferentiated colonized Other [. . .] without much examining of their

own presence in that institution" (92), Minh-ha and Spivak figure themselves with an awareness of their placement within systems of privilege
and draw attention to the modes of production and consumption of their
academic work.

Cultural critic Gayatri Spivak is an upper-caste Indian, an economic
immigrant from Calcutta, who has studied and taught in English departments in U.S. universities since the early sixties. This biographical sentence
introduces Spivak to those who don't know her work, but by consolidating
her into a unified, coherent subject, it works against the grain of her own
rhetoric. In the second half of the "Subaltern" essay, Spivak calls into question the desire of First World intellectuals for an authentic native voice
when that desire is directed toward people like her.[7] Spivak is at pains to
point out her difference from that Other. She complicates the illusion of a
single "native voice" by delineating various positions among Indians under
British occupation. Setting off a silent underclass from those in closer contact
with their colonizers, Spivak uses as her prime example colonial subjects
whose agency and voice had the least possibility of being heard—Indian
widows who became victims of *sati*, sacrificial burning—to demonstrate
how many of the historically colonized had in fact no legitimate platform
from which to speak (297–308; see also Mani). Spivak argues that this situation is a problem not only for First World intellectuals but for diasporic
postcolonial academics as well in their own production of knowledge about
their homelands. Her conclusion is that a postcolonial intellectual cannot
speak *for* these unrepresented groups but only *to* them in an imagined conversation across class lines and historical distances (295). The emphasis here
is on "imagined," for of course Spivak assumes no possibility of reaching
the present-day remnants of this group through the rarified discourses of
Western academies.[8] Rather, she uses this formulation to displace the representative potential of her own voice, opening a space for others. "Speaking to" might be construed as a movement from the metaphoric to the
metonymic. Instead of substituting one voice for another, the speaker adds
another voice to the parallel strands of discourse, a voice without its own
clear origin. Her writings stand alongside other accounts and the person
herself who continues to regenerate a speaking subject.

The ethical implications of Spivak's performance lie in its difference
from a rhetoric of substitution on the one hand, and on the other, from
what Chandra Mohanty calls a "Western, postmodernist notion of agency

and consciousness which often announces the splintering of the subject, and privileges multiplicity in the abstract" ("Introduction" 37). Spivak's performance should be understood as an ethical practice of seeking to displace any fixed sense of knowledge of the "other" that a Western listener might be tempted to grasp through an encounter with an elite, immigrant academic. When "card-carrying hegemonic" listeners listen for someone speaking as an Indian, a Third World woman speaking as a Third World woman, Spivak asserts, ignorance of a complex history is covered over with a fabricated homogeneity ("Alterity" 270). Within her chosen area of literary and cultural studies[9], Spivak puts before a Western audience a multitude of postcolonial subjects —the Indian widow of 1829, the sixteen-year-old member of an Indian independence group who committed suicide in Calcutta in 1926, the women workers in today's Export Processing Zones—along with her own "selves."

Indeed, it seems that part of Spivak's strategy for multiplying others is achieved through the manufacture of more and more versions of herself. She has experienced an amazing degree of public scrutiny, and it is interesting to examinine how she has negotiated her self-constitution through that process. *The Post-Colonial Critic*, a series of interviews, collects and multiplies the many versions of this "highly commodified academic," as she ironically calls herself (Rooney, "Word" 130). In an interview with Ellen Rooney, she acknowledges complaints that "Spivak talks too much about herself" ("Word" 130). Though this focus on the self might suggest the seduction of "representativeness," it might also be read as a continuing attempt to disperse the representative Indian in the U.S. academy.

Spivak is meticulous about her own processes of self-identification. Refusing several of the available options for self-representation—unmediated accounts of experience, the philosophical voice from nowhere, and the hollow echoes of the now-dead "author"—Spivak instead practices "deidentification [. . .] a claiming of an identity from a text that comes from somewhere else"[10] ("Word" 130). Resisting the Western academy's attempt to hear from her the voice of the native, she differentiates "talking about oneself" from a process of "graphing one's bio" such that it becomes representative of certain histories ("Word" 130). In this formulation, the text represents, not the self. This process of contexture and displacement begins when Spivak identifies herself with contingent and polemical labels—"woman," "literary critic," "Asian intellectual," "Non-Resident Indian." She then reveals the persistence of imperialist and sexist attitudes by recounting situations when one or another of those labels provoked conflict or effected marginalization in public forums. But instead of grounding these claims in authenticity, Spivak practices what she calls a reactive strategy, adopting different identities at different times to create a consciousness of the hazards of fixity and substitution. She seems to be saying: If you take me to be a feminist, I'll show how I'm not the same as Western feminists. If you take me for an Indian, I'll explain elite immigrant privilege. If you define me as anti-institutional, I'll show you the disciplinarian. Spivak consistently cannot be found where she is sought. She signals the relatively minimal significance of color and former colonial status (those markers of difference through which she appears as the representative Indian) through references to her high caste status, the historical moment within which her immigration took place (the early 60s brain drain of Indians to United Kingdom and United States), and the benefits accruing to her as the product of a British education from American academics' Anglophilia. In specifying the geographical, economic, and class locations of her background and academic formation, she engages in the project Ahmad calls "periodizing:" connecting academic practices with modes of production and larger historical movements, rather than assuming their distance from the material world (36).

In introductory passages contextualizing the essays in her latest book, *Outside in the Teaching Machine*, Spivak reflects on her positions in relation to other women (see especially 121–29, 141–46). Returning to early writing enables her to place positions side by side in a narrative sequence: "When I wrote 'French Feminism in an International Frame' my assigned subject-position was actually determined by my moment in the United States and dominated my apparent choice of a postcolonial position. [. . .] Now it seems to me that the radical element of the postcolonial bourgeoisie must most specifically learn to negotiate with the structure of enabling violence that produced her" (145). Spivak now seeks to negotiate "white feminism" rather than simply resisting it; she seeks not "to neglect the postcolonial's particular generalization in the vaster common space of woman" (145). Throughout these passages she rearticulates the problematic of representation: "It is obvious that these positions [feminism, European Enlightenment, nationhood, etc.], logically defined, swirl in the inaccessible intimacy of the everyday, giving hue to being. To fix it in paint is to efface as much as to disclose" (144–45).

It is through a carefully crafted rhetoric that Spivak revises her early position.[11] Sometimes tortured, almost always tortuous, her prose seems at times almost to parody classical philosophical argument. Deeply engaged with the most traditional philosophical issues, Spivak's prose is full of "lurches": unconventional word use (e.g., "to operate" as a conceptual process), abrupt transitions, unexpected juxtaposition of subjects. Whereas most academic readers are accustomed to the Aristotelian format—state your case and prove it—Spivak seems to work laterally, moving from case to case, point to point, rarely offering examples.[12] Despite all her efforts, we see an operation of substitution emerging when Toril Moi suggests that Spivak's texts might be representative of "an enactment of the violent clash of discourses experienced by the subject in exile" (20). Although her writing at first seems radically different from the *écriture féminine* of French feminists, I find common elements: along with deep engagements with the canonical male texts of Western culture, there is "a courageous effort to explode linear sequentiality, a deliberate desire to enact the decentering of the subject and its discourses" (Moi 21). Simultaneous with the pretense of what Catherine Clément calls "democratic transmission" (Cixous and Clément)—the implicit agreement with a reader that she seeks to communicate—we find at times "a text where the connections are so elusive as to become private" (Moi 20). I've seen some of the same patterns in the writing of female students: a struggle under the burden of a masculine literary heritage, a movement from public communication into the realm of private codes, a breakdown in the conventional structures of argument. I'm suggesting not that these textual features be celebrated as expressions of a gendered essence, nor praised as the curious idiosyncrasies of a brilliant thinker, but rather be read as symptoms—textual traces of a strained encounter with multiple forms of dominance. Within Spivak's meticulous and principled renunciation of a representation of substitution, her highly artful theory and practice of metonymic association with others, I find an informing if painful case of writing difference.

Trinh T. Minh-ha claims writing without equivocation as the defining act for "Third World women," a phrase she chooses despite its anachronistic assumption of a tripartite division of world powers and the risk of homogenization. From the jacket of her first book, *Woman, Native, Other: Writing Postcoloniality and Feminism*, we learn that she is a writer, filmmaker, composer, and academic. But, despite the fact that her text is full of first person pronouns both singular and plural, her one moment of specific self-definition is delayed until late in the book and displaced into third person: "From jagged transitions between the headless and bottomless storytelling, what is exposed in this text is the inscription and de-scription of a non-unitary female subject of color through her engagement, therefore also disengagement, with master discourses" (43). The self she creates in her text is figured by the broken mirror. It destroys a pure relation of "I to I" (23), but does not cease reflecting: "here reality is not reconstituted, it is put into pieces so as to allow another world to rebuild (keep on unbuilding and re-building) itself with its debris" (23). The subject is dispersed throughout her text, yet Minh-ha speaks at times with complete presence, easily adopting the role of "writing woman" (as opposed to "written woman") and using conventions of the "priest-god scheme" (her version of the critique of the author). Her discussion of commitment, responsibility, and guilt capture Minh-ha as a most consolidated subject: "In a sense, committed writers are the ones who write both to awaken to the consciousness of their guilt and to give their readers a guilty conscience. Bound to one another by an awareness of their guilt, writer and reader may thus assess their positions, engaging themselves wholly in their situations and carrying their weight into the weight of their communities, the weight of the world" (10–11). For those on the margin, Minh-ha suggests, constructing a "we" implies a responsibility for representation. While Spivak only goes so far as to speak of "un-learning privilege," Minh-ha foregrounds the ethical entailments of her representative status.

At other moments she delights in the multiplicity of voices in writing, dividing herself into subject and object through a play of pronouns: "writing [. . .] is an ongoing practice that is concerned not with inserting a 'me' into language, but with creating an opening where the 'me' disappears while 'I' endlessly come and go" (35). She then breaks the boundary of that "i": "Taking in any voice that goes through me, I/i will answer every time someone says: I. One woman within another, eternally" (37). Pronouns are powerful tools for Minh-ha, who doubles the "I" in upper and lower case, privileging the subject case (but multiple) "I" over the object "me." This mix of modes—metaphoric and metonymic—stymies attempts to categorize her and enacts her point that "woman can only redefine while being defined by language" (44).

Minh-ha's most effective strategy for moving between metaphoric and metonymic subjectivities is her frequent use of a broad ironic tone. In the following passage, she sarcastically rejects the position of authenticity, mimicking (but at the same time using) a voice of unreflective autobiography: "I am so much that nothing can enter me or pass through me. I struggle, I resist, and I am filled with my own self. [Here the tone shifts.] The 'personal' may liberate as it may enslave" (35). On the same issue, she asks: "How do you inscribe difference without bursting into a series of euphoric narcissistic accounts of yourself and your own kind?" Minh-ha wants to find her way between "navel-gazing and navel-erasing" (28).

Minh-ha is sensitive to the current seductions of fashionable otherness in academic circles, devoting the better part of a chapter to what she terms the "special" Third World woman issue. Parodying the title of a special issue of an academic journal, she points out how both the Western audience and the iconized postcolonial are complicit in dealing with otherness *as* a special issue: "Specialness as a soporific soothes, anaesthetizes my sense of justice; it is, to the wo/man of ambition, as effective a drug of psychological self-intoxication as alcohol is to the exiles of society" (88). The admonition is to be more sensitive to the systems of authorization, as well as the (very Western) myth of authenticity.

For Minh-ha, the relation to the collective is highly textualized but still there. Again we hear her mimicking one of the familiar voices of the American collective: "A writing *for* the people, *by* the people, and *from* the people is, literally, a multipolar reflecting reflection that remains free from the conditions of subjectivity and objectivity and yet reveals them both. I write to show myself showing people who show me my own showing. I-You: not one, not two" (22, emphasis in original). I hear in this passage a bold refiguration of the "subject," involving the group in its formation and complicating visibility as it is theorized in classical Western systems of representation.

Minh-ha is more at ease than Spivak in making common cause across differences. She accepts the alliance of nonwhite U.S. minorities with citizens of the older nonaligned nations who made up the original Third World group. She finds more threat in the colonialist creed of divide and conquer than she does in the threat of obscuring differences when such pacts are made. The radical dispersion of self through writing coexists in this text with a voice of collective solidarity. This coexistence in the rhetorical scene is articulated metonymically: "The process of differentiation [. . .] continues, and speaking nearby or together with certainly differs from speaking for and about" (101). "Difference does not annul identity. It is beyond and alongside identity" (104).

What strikes me as most apt in the specifically *post*colonial rhetoric of these two feminists is the tension between metonymic and metaphoric representation—between a poststructural dispersal of subjectivity and an ethical commitment to analyzing communication in terms of the material realities of speakers and listeners. Postcolonial feminists dare to commit theoretical inconsistency, deploying a pragmatic rhetoric that suits their multiple locations. The principled resistance to the temptation to speak for India, for Vietnam, for women is joined with the principled impulse to put the voice of the "other" in play in First World academic discourse. When we hear Spivak's speaking to (rather than for or about) and Minh-ha's speaking alongside, we hear an attempt to move between the two poles in the double session of representation.

For both writers, the metonymic operation of speaking alongside is not divided sharply from a rhetoric of substitution; they coexist, operating simultaneously. Practices of political representation cannot avoid the enactment of symbolic representation, the constant process of creating and recreating public images of difference. Actually appearing through symbolic representation entails access to public forums gained through (loosely defined) political processes. Both these writers are fully aware of their representational function: they *do* speak for the other. But they simultaneously recast images and frustrate any simple process of representation. As postcolonial subjects located in the metropolitan academic scene, both choose a complex construction of subjectivity in an ethical response to the exigencies of that placement.

These choices are consummately rhetorical, revealing a disruption of conventional assumptions about ethos and audience. Unlike the classical scenario, wherein the speaker constructs an ethos in relation to an audience —assuming it to be a group of which he was a member—the habitus of the postcolonial feminist is not shared by a Western academic audience.[13] The aim of this rhetoric is to open the distance between writer and audience rather than close it. Lunsford and Ede suggest a similar distancing in a recent self-critique of their earlier essay on audience, pointing out the "exclusionary tendencies of the rhetorical tradition" (174) in its assumption that the rhetor (and in their case, the student writer) would unproblematically seek to mold herself to the audience at hand. I believe these postcolonial feminist restructurings of ethos and audience might be helpful to teachers of writing and rhetoric. First, they illustrate through their elaboration of difference the power relations and assumptions about social similarity inherent in the classical model. Next, they might help us in developing strategies for our own speaking and writing that avoid reproducing unproblematically those older models, based on the assumption that speaker and audience *will* unquestionably share knowledge, goals, and habits. Finally, they might help us as we read student writing about the self to discover how students resist or refigure ethos and audience to characterize their own relations to the academy. I'm not suggesting that students will consciously employ the complex tactics I've outlined in the writings of the two academic postcolonial feminists but rather that we might use Spivak's and Minh-ha's rhetorical gestures as guides for reading traces or symptoms of texts from students writing their own relations to institutional power. Imagining students capable of inscribing multiple selves could be an important reading posture for teachers concerned with subject construction in a postcolonial era.

I've proposed ways that the writings of Spivak and Minh-ha might contribute to rhetorical theory and to the reading practices of writing teachers.[14] The third subject of my analysis occupies a substantially different position in relation to composition studies in that (1) she was not a writer[15] and (2) her published account has appeared on reading lists for undergraduates across the country. As winner of the 1993 Nobel Peace Prize, Rigoberta Menchú has gained international recognition as a spokesperson for her people. Given her chosen status as representative "other," her rhetorical task would appear to be quite different from that of the other postcolonial immigrant intellectuals analyzed.

A Revolutionary Subject

In the 1983 English translation of Guatemalan Indian Rigoberta Menchú's testimonio, the construction of a subject appears in high relief from the opening lines: "My name is Rigoberta Menchú. I am twenty-three years old. This is my testimony. I didn't learn it from a book and I didn't learn it alone. I'd like to stress that it's not only *my* life, it's also the testimony of my people.

It's hard for me to remember everything that's happened to me in my life since there have been many very bad times but, yes, moments of joy as well. The important thing is that what has happened to me has happened to many other people too: My story is the story of all poor Guatemalans. My personal experience is the reality of a whole people" (1). There appears to be no hesitation here to claim representative status—no hedging about subject positions or the problem of speaking for others. Menchú tells the story of Indian peasants deprived of land, freedom, and life by an oligarchic government using the army to suppress any attempts by the Indians to seek justice and stop exploitive land grabs and cruel labor practices.[16] Literary critics identify a distinctive articulation of the speaking subject as a feature of the genre, testimonio. John Beverly's persuasive analysis places these accounts within the context of struggles for national autonomy: they are "novel or novella-length narratives told in the first person by a narrator who is also the real protagonist or witness of the events she or he recounts" (*Literature*, 70). The claim of representation is at the center of these texts: "the situation of the narrator in testimonio must be representative (in both the mimetic and the legal-political senses) of a larger social class or group." Indeed, there is "an insistence on and affirmation of the authority of the subject" (Beverly *Against* 74, 76).

Neither the "deliverers," compilers, nor the critics of testimonio, however, are naive about the processes of textual construction involved in the production of these accounts. Barbara Harlow, whose book *Resistance Literature* brings a number of these texts to the attention of Western readers, makes note of the ideological complexity of resistance organizations and national liberation movements (29). The involvement of a First World intelligentsia in the collection of material complicates the question of authenticity further. Elizabeth Burgos-Debray, the compiler of Menchú's testimonio and a Venezuelan social scientist living in Paris, documents the ways she shaped and changed the oral account. In a recent visit to Miami University, Menchú spoke about the caution she exercised in shaping her account for Burgos-Debray. This caution involved presenting herself as a particular kind of subject, as well as withholding information about the Indian resistance fighters still at war in Guatemala at the time she was working for peace in Europe and Mexico.

Even though they acknowledge these mediations in the collection and production of testimonios, however, critics generally place more importance on the commonality of political goals between compiler and testifier. Beverly, for example, offers Margaret Randall, who assisted women in Cuba and Nicaragua through workshops in writing popular histories, and Nawal al-Saadawi, whose work with women in an Egyptian prison eventually led to the testimonial novel *Woman at Point Zero*, as examples of politically committed testimonio compilers ("Margin" 15, n. 8; 17, n. 11; see also Harlow). These relationships are forged out of "mutuality in struggle against a common system of oppression." The compiling of the testimony under these conditions is specifically not, Beverly argues, "a reenactment of the anthropological function of the colonial or subaltern 'native informant'" ("Margin" 21).

The testimonio still offers interpretive challenges on the issue of representation, even if they aren't exactly the same as those created by the particular national, educational, and class circumstances of the immigrant academic feminists.[17] For both Spivak and Trinh, the denial of authenticity is a necessary position for the diasporic intellectual, one that forces the First World academic to notice the difference between another academic and a suppressed history of colonization. For Menchú, the claim to authority—to the truth of her lived experience—is central to her project. There still remains a question about how to interpret the representational force of the strongly asserted "I" in the testimonio and how to understand the relationship with the reader. Does this mode of representation constitute a rhetoric of substitution?

Interpreters of testimonio answer that question by changing the terms. In the material and historical circumstances of a revolutionary struggle, the idea of one speaker "blocking out" another, as though subjects were individual, strongly differentiated units, gives way to the exigencies of communicating as a collective. The elite intellectual postcolonial feminists, working within a Western discourse tradition, needed to take apart individual subjectivity from the inside; Menchú, on the other hand, comes out of a completely different set, a strongly communal Indian village culture. Despite the use of first person in Menchú's title, Lynda Marín notes that testimonios are marked by the "self-professed eschewal of the first person singular subject" in favor of a collective "we" (52).[18] Though these authors do specify their personal conditions, those details are less significant than the group struggle against state coercion. Their primary aim is getting out the reality of their collective experience to a metropolitan reading public, bringing to light experiences and events hidden in large measure from First World

media. Doris Sommer, in an elegant reading of Menchú's continual reference to secrets about the community that cannot be revealed, claims that
this strategy "defends us [First World readers] from any illusions of complete or stable knowledge, and therefore from the desire to replace one apparently limited speaker for another more totalizing one" (57). Sommer
goes on say that Menchú "takes care not to substitute her community in a
totalizing gesture. Instead, her singularity achieves its identity as an extension of the collective. The singular represents the plural, not because it re-
places or subsumes the group, but because the speaker is a distinguishable
part of the whole" (60–61). It is worth noting that Sommer's purpose in analyzing Menchú is to distinguish the genre of testimonio from standard
Western autobiography, a centuries-old locus for individuality: "Where au-
tobiographies nurture an illusion of singularity, assuming they can stand *in*
for others, testimonies stand *up* among them" (61). John Beverly similarly
attempts to redefine the terms through which subjectivity is expressed:
"testimonio constitutes an affirmation of the individual self *in a collective
mode*" ("Margin" 17). The oral delivery of testimonio and the political context of collective struggle combine to disperse concepts of "author" and
"individual," and along with them, the problem of speaking for others as a
gesture of substitution.

Looking at the testimonio from a rhetorical rather than a literary perspective actually makes it easier to imagine this shift. When we examined
the postcolonial academic writers, the analysis was framed in terms of writing style. But for an orally produced text, the rhetorical category of ethos
is more suitable. Sommer acknowledges the value of a shift to rhetoric:
"while the autobiography strains to produce a personal and distinctive *style*
as part of the individuation process, the testimonial strives to preserve or
to renew an interpersonal *rhetoric*" (Sommer 65). The ethos/audience relation was redefined above for Asian postcolonial feminists to indicate a difference and distance between rhetor and audience. In the case of Menchú,
ethos marks the intense solidarity among members of the revolutionary
group, as well as a powerfully rhetorical relationship to First World readers.

Whereas the first two writers needed to disperse their subjectivity and
representativeness for Western readers, Menchú, as a subject of a nation
still in struggle, has a much stronger interest—indeed, a life-or-death need,
to engage the audience. Written for a metropolitan public, the testimonio
creates a complicity with its readers, "involv[ing] their identification—by
engaging their standards of ethics and justice in a speech-act situation that

requires response" (Beverly, *Against* 78). The rhetoric of reading testimonio is cast as a movement from identification to persuasion, or "complicity." Sommer uses that term to spell out the psychological dynamics of subject-formation and audience address in the public event of testimonio:

> When the narrator talks about her*self* to *you,* she implies both the existing relationship to other representative selves in the community, and potential relationships that extend her community through the text. She calls us in, interpellates us as readers who identify with the narrator's project and, by extension, with the political community to which she belongs. The appeal does not produce only admiration for the ego-ideal, of the type we might feel for an autobiographer who impresses us precisely with her difference from other women, nor the consequent yearning to be (like) her and so to deny her and our distinctiveness. Rather, the testimonial produces complicity. Even if the reader cannot identify with the writer enough to imagine taking her place, the map of possible identifications through the text spreads out laterally. (65)

In this lateral spread, the represented community, testifier, and readers are found beside themselves.

Reading Menchú against the two Asian feminists enables us to see a reversal of the movement from descriptive to transformative class. We are to understand from Menchú that the class she represents is solidly constituted, already engaged in political action. Her task is to create that group as a descriptive class—to bring the Mayan Indians of Central America into view for a U.S. and Western European public. Because the two poles in the double session of representation are so closely connected for her group, there is a strong justification for the representational strategy she uses. Her goal is exactly the opposite of Spivak's: not "deidentification" but identification. My goal in making this contrast is not to value one mode of representation over another. It is, rather, to develop more supple instruments for recognizing and responding to diverse subjects in the absence of stable criteria for doing so. It has become standard for feminists (and others) to complain of poststructuralist theory that it robs nondominant groups of subjectivity before they've ever had a chance to have it. Gregory S. Jay raises a question about the terms of this dilemma: "It is not clear how the widely challenged classical schemas of representation can be replaced by a different representative system if there is no agreement about the 'unit' or basic element grounding the claim to representation [in the Enlightenment, the individual]" (15). Perhaps the rhetorical materials at use here might give us a way to describe subjectivities as something more multiple and diverse than "units," to discuss the question in terms less simply binary than presence or absence of a subject.

Pedagogy

The political reason we need something more complex than poststructural or postmodern critiques of the subject concerns the ways such arguments "travel." Criticisms of a representation of substitution—of "authentic voice" literature that claims to speak for others—from within nondominant groups line up disturbingly with the derision of a right-wing dogmatist like Dinesh D'Souza, who uses the evidence of Rigoberta Menchú's differences from the Indians she represents as an excuse to dismiss her as a *"seemingly* authentic Third World source" (72 emphasis added). That Menchú was able to move from the position of silenced subaltern to vocal victim of oppression provides D'Souza the opportunity to dismiss the account of her experience, to hear her instead as a mouthpiece for "Marxist and feminist views," and to focus his critical energies on the travesty of her displacement of Western classics in the Stanford University canon.

The difference between John Beverly's reading of Menchú as an organizer, organic intellectual, and "foreign agent" to the West—that is, as specifically not "the subaltern"—and D'Souza's reading is that the former is doing a sympathetic reading of representational strategies. The latter rejects Menchú's account in favor of silence, that is, he disqualifies her representative status to silence her. D'Souza's response recalls a stance I've encountered in some students who find reports from the margins so disturbing that their very claim to be heard is called into question (see Lu, "Reading"). This reaction takes shape as the skepticism on the part of an autonomous knower toward any truth claim: the response of a Kantian subject who, in rejecting the authority of teacher and text, overcomes "tutelage," the barrier to ascendance into full personhood, a rejection made all the easier if that narrative in some way calls into question the status of that very subject. Is it possible to distinguish between a silencing skepticism and a nuanced reading of representation?

It is our responsibility as teachers to try to mark out that difference. Through our choices of texts and every word we say about them we in-

evitably represent others to our students. Choosing different reading strategies for different texts is an exercise of power, but then Rigoberta Menchú
is not Louis Bonaparte and neither are "we," teachers of language and literature in U.S. universities. Every pedagogical moment is a complex fusion
of re-presentation, exercises of executive power, and transformation of consciousness. If we enter into that process relying solely on what Linda Alcoff
calls the "retreat" response—claiming to speak only from our own narrow
positions—we not only blind ourselves to the multiple functions of pedagogical discourse, but also lose opportunities for political effectivity (17–19).

Many of us believe that we have remade the teaching scene to avoid
careless abuses of power. But we can't control the processes of representation—of metaphorical substitution. As those in nondominant positions
well know, their voices are often heard as *the* voice of women, African-
Americans, or lesbians despite disclaimers or qualifications. If as teachers
and scholars we retreated from the risk of representation, punctiliously refusing any occasion of speaking for others ourselves and vigilantly pointing out any instance of metaphoric substitution in others, we would avoid
making a theoretical error. But, as Alcoff points out, "the desire to find an
absolute means to avoid making errors comes perhaps not from a desire to
advance collective goals but a desire for personal mastery, to establish a
privileged discursive position wherein one cannot be undermined or challenged and thus is master of the situation" (22).

What is it we recognize? What parts of the whole do we "read?" What
forms the links in the chains of association that lead us to act? Can we
transform the modes of visibility through our teaching? Who is the "we"
in these questions? By locating texts, including our own, in their different
geopolitical contexts, teachers in U.S. universities can practice modes of
writing and reading that allow us (students and teachers) to move collectively across the axes of metaphor/metonymy rather than speech/silence.
And by enabling our students to write multiple versions of themselves informed by a knowledge of rhetoric in its political and figurative functions,
we may give them access to their own experiences of conjunction and disjunction, of association and substitution. In doing this, we might more fully
inhabit the meanings of the prefix to both figures, *meta*—which, in the poetic language of the Greek lexicon, places us "beside, alongside, among, in
common with, with the help and favor of, in the midst of" others.

Martin Behr

POSTCOLONIAL TRANSFORMATIONS
IN CANADIAN INUIT TESTIMONIO

New genre theories offer valuable insights into how theories of writing that inform composition studies, especially pragmatic theories about writing as social action, are responsive to important issues in contemporary postcolonial studies. Such issues pertain to subjectivity, ethnicity, class, gender, and race. This is so because the new genre theories explain the discursive features of a genre functionally, as standard rhetorical responses to recurring types of rhetorical situations.

Testimonio, until recently almost exclusively associated with Latin America, is a notable genre in postcolonial analysis where colonized writers and critics have appropriated features of the imperial discourse to articulate their subject positions in the global arena. According to Bill Ashcroft, testimonio functions as a "strategy of transformation" in which "the colonized culture interpolates the dominant discourse in order to transform it in ways that release the representation of local realities" (18). This interpolation is typically that of a collective form of autobiographical witnessing. With testimonio, the narrator "speaks for, or in the name of, a community or group" (Beverley, "The Margin" 95). In fact, in Latin America, testimonio "has played an important role in developing international human rights, solidarity movements, and liberation struggles" (Gelles 16).

The emphasis of genre analysis on the functional operation of recurrent, diachronic patterns in testimonio helps explain why this genre emerged, and how it renders a means of responding to a recurrent type of rhetorical situation. A key concept within the new genre theories that helps illuminate how these recurring situations evoke similar responses is Lloyed Bitzer's idea of *exigence*. For Bitzer, "an exigence is some kind of imperfection marked by urgency" that, through discourse, is "capable of positive modification" (67). Testimonio is exemplary of such positive modification because it emerges from postcolonial exigencies that give voice to silenced peoples. Such exigencies amount to "an *invitation* to create and present discourse" (9). The invitation "is for a *fitting* response, one which is appropriate" (Brinton 236). The *form* of response must thus be understood in terms of what, exactly, the particular discourse is supposed to achieve; it must be viewed in terms of the *social actions* the writer is trying to effect in the world.

This is why Carolyn Miller contends that "a rhetorically sound definition of genre must be centered not on the form of discourse but on the action it is used to accomplish" (151). When viewed in this way, a genre "becomes more than a formal entity; it becomes pragmatic and fully rhetorical, a point of connection between intention and effect" (153). But this does *not* mean that the situations that confront writers *determine* the forms of discourse through which they voice their responses. Rather, writers take certain "*decisions* to make salient or not to make salient these situations" (Vatz 158). Genres are formed *in response* to writers' perceptions of readers' expectations and to perceived exigent qualities of the rhetorical situation. As Kathleen Hall Jamieson argues, "the proper response to an unprecedented rhetorical situation grows not merely from the situation but also from antecedent rhetorical forms" ("Generic" 163).

Although the cultural context in Canada is less explicitly oppressive than most postcolonial situations in Latin America, a similar situation here serves as an explanation for the emergence of *I, Nuligak*—the first book-length testimonio by a Canadian Eskimo. In this northern Canadian context, the exigent situation has evoked a fitting response on the part of the principal narrator, Nuligak, who articulates how he and his people, the Kitigariukmeut tribe of the Mackenzie Delta, were dispossessed of their native traditions and lands by whites. Nuligak's discourse functions to voice what would otherwise remain a silent, indigenous Canadian underclass; he tells readers that "the young Inuit are learning the white man's way of life and our own is fading away" (160).

Roxanne Rimstead provides some critical insight into the nature of this unjust social situation by contending that in Canada "many oral histories of muted cultural subjects testify powerfully to the reality of the oppression of concrete subjects, marginalized and mistreated due to differences rooted in class, ethnicity, race, gender, poverty, sexual orientation, age, region, physical handicaps, and so on" (147). Nuligak's 1930 condemnation of his people's recently acquired dependency on the white capitalist fur trade and the Hudson's Bay Company (H.B.C.) is a good example of fitting response needed to contest the unacceptable social conditions that Rimstead describes. He testifies that "the H.B.C. clerk gave us a mere seven dollars for the best fur. The Inuit had nothing to eat" (156). Their situation was such that the Kitigariukmeut could not even buy new cartridges for their guns at the Hudson's Bay store in Baillie because "it is the H.B.C. custom to ignore you when you become poor" (Nuligak 158). The social action of Nuligak's discourse functions as a strategy of transformation because its context evokes certain substantive patterns, attitudes that call for the recognition of basic human rights and collective social struggle. Hence, the recurrent situation—both in Latin America and in northern Canada—"seems to 'invite' discourse of a certain type" (C. Miller 157). When fashioned into a genre, this discourse becomes "*formed* matter (which becomes meaningful in relation to contexts)" (Coe, "An Apology" 16, 20). Therefore, form implies a "strategy" of response, an "attitude" (Burke, "The Philosophy" 296–97) because many of the literary features of a genre like testimonio are recurrent; they have an a priori existence, and "insofar as a form is socially shared, adopting the form involves adopting, at least to some extent, the community's attitude" (Coe 19). And while the social situation in which the form is used incorporates certain attitudes, the genre also is formed out of other elements: antecedent substantive and stylistic features, which that situation evokes, patterns that originate from both within and without Inuit culture. This is to say that "it is sometimes rhetorical genres and not rhetorical situations that are decisively formative. [. . .] In an unprecedented rhetorical situation, a rhetor will draw on past experiences and on the genres formed by others in response to similar situations" (Jamieson, "Antecedent" 406, 408).

With Canadian Inuit testimonio in general and with *I, Nuligak* in particular, these antecedent patterns consist of Western autobiographical and ethnographic literary conventions, as well as recurrent themes, topics and dramas from literate and preliterate Inuit culture: images of traditional and contemporary hunting practices, starvation, climatic variation, topography, contact with Europeans, political and social change, and a highly developed oral tradition embodied in myth, legend, and song. According to Mikhail Bakhtin, such discourse constitutes a "hybridization" of narrative forms, which he defines as "a mixture of two social languages" within one discursive genre, an "encounter" between "two different linguistic consciousnesses" (358). Kathleen Hall Jamieson and Karlyn Kohrs Campbell similarly argue that a genre is unified by a "constellation" of forms that appear in other discourses; what makes a genre unique is "the recurrence of the forms *together* in constellation" ("Form" 20). Once formed as a genre, these patterns "may be energized or actualized as a strategic response to a situation" (Jamieson, "Rhetorical" 146).

Patterns of Literary Collaboration

A great deal of this discursive hybridization in *I, Nuligak* emerges out of collaborative literary initiatives. This collaboration pertains to the principal narrator, Nuligak, whose discourse often contains antecedents from Inuit intellectual culture, and his Western collaborator/translator, Maurice Metayer, whose terms of reference are usually ethnographic. Together in constellation, these divergent patterns inform readers of the adverse social changes the Kitigariukmeut faced with the recent arrival of Europeans, during the early to middle twentieth century. What emerges are images of widespread starvation, epidemics, a declining game population, the loss of language, custom, and religion, and a reliance on white people's technologies and habits, such as drinking. However, "this does not mean [. . .] that the situation 'controlled' the response" (Vatz 160). Readers must keep in mind that, among other antecedent genres, autobiography, ethnography, and the Inuit oral tradition also have conditioned the responses that are voiced in *I, Nuligak* and other, later versions of Canadian Inuit testimonio. Another consideration is that the Inuit writer "is responsible for what he chooses to make salient" (Vatz 158).

The postcolonial situations made salient in *I, Nuligak* are evidently ones that are negotiated between Nuligak and Metayer. This raises important questions about authorship. With Latin American testimonio, such collaboration usually has involved a class of left or liberal-minded intellectuals or professionals—literate, university–educated people who partially align themselves with, and thereby help give a voice to, those underprivileged groups in society who are voiceless. According to John Beverley, such agents assume a relative autonomy to illiterate or partially literate subaltern subjects when they commit themselves to the production of their testimonios. He contends that "[t]estimonio gives voice in literature to a previously voiceless and anonymous collective popular subject [. . .] but in such a way that the intellectual or professional [. . .] is interpolated as being part of, and dependent on, this collective subject without at the same time losing his or her identity as an intellectual" ("The Margin" 76). Whether or not Metayer's role is that of an intellectual is debatable. However, this is irrelevant because Beverley's narrow formulation of the concept "intellectual" is specific to the Latin American postcolonial situation, where illiterate or partially literate activists relate their lives of political resistance to engaged intellectuals (Rimstead 146). It is therefore possible that Beverley's heightened expectations for the political and cultural potential of the teller-writer relationship depend partly on his idealist construction of it within a narrow genre of works (146).

What is relevant is that the relative autonomy of such agents—whatever they are called—helps to vocalize what would otherwise remain silent within most postcolonial contexts. This challenges Philippe Lejeune's contention that the compilers of such discourse are the authors of the subject's autobiography. According to Lejeune, the author of texts such as testimonio and collaborative autobiography is the collaborator, the person who "tries to capture in writing the voice, the autobiographical discourse *of those who do not write*" (196). As a result: "[t]heir story takes its value, in the eyes of the reader, from the fact that they belong (that they *are perceived* as belonging) to a culture other than his own, a culture defined by the exclusion of writing. [. . .] All merit in [the subject's] story is a merit added by writing, or rather by the new network of communication into which the mediator introduces him" (196). This new discursive network, however, is really "a doubly authored text, with the editor's voice and the storyteller's voice together making the narrative" (Davies 6). The editorial role is one of choosing to make salient certain situations, which often means that "attempts are made to be faithful to the *voice* and *words* [. . .] of the narrator" (10). This is certainly the case with Nuligak's testimonio, because Metayer states in his introduction that he translated Nuligak's text "idea for idea, faithful to tone and colour [and that] at times, although rarely, [he] altered the order of sentences in order to clarify what was said, but this was never done when such a change might in any way have altered the sense" (9).

A more useful way, then, to make sense of the testimonio genre is to not make indeterminate claims about authorship; it is better to examine what this genre does by assessing how its ordering principles motivate certain social acts and attitudes. This involves a consideration of how the genre is active rather than passive, dynamic rather than static, since its discursive features emerge from disparate and, at times, competing intentions of authorial subjects and their collaborators, not to mention the expectations of readers. The genre, in other words, amounts to "a socially standard rhetorical strategy for addressing a [particular] type of situation, for attempting to evoke a desired type of response" (Coe, "Genre" 2).

Recurrent Patterns of Ethnography

To respond to his situation and to motivate readers' responses, Metayer repeatedly forms his discourse as footnoted ethnographic descriptions and comments, which purportedly explain the cultural significance of Nuligak's writing. Ironically, these recurrent patterns establish Metayer as the authority on the meaning of the text. This restricts Nuligak's testimonio from functioning as a strategy of transformation for a northern Canadian postcolonial situation. In fact, the urgency of the Kitigariukmeut people's situation is often debunked by competing motives contained in Metayer's footnotes.

Metayer voices these attitudes omnisciently. His omniscient rhetorical perspective is part of a larger ensemble of recurrent patterns that have formed what is often called ethnographic realism. According to George Marcus and Dick Cushman, ethnographic realism is a term borrowed from nineteenth century fiction that "seeks to represent the reality of a whole world or form of life. [. . .] In fact, what gives the ethnographer authority and the text a pervasive sense of concrete reality is the writer's claim to represent a world as only one who has known it first hand can, which thus forges an intimate link between ethnographic writing and fieldwork" (29).

A discursive emphasis on the real is the catalyst behind Metayer's conversation with what he assumes is an ostensibly Western audience, since he consistently contextualizes and provides (frequently inappropriate) ethnographic background information on Nuligak's testimony. For example, when Nuligak tells his readers that stone *kudlik* lamps were used to cook food such as bear, seal, or the *ugiuk* (the big bearded seal) and that it was only fish that they ate frozen (39), in the footnote that follows Metayer states that "our narrator does not mention caribou, probably because that year they lived from the sea and did not hunt the caribou of the steppes. As a matter of fact, fish and caribou are the only food the Eskimo will eat raw or frozen. The Cape Bathurst Inuit and those of the Kitigariukmeut used to hang the caribou meat and eat it when both high and frozen" (39). The terms "probably," "that year," and "as a matter of fact" name typical situations in ethnographic discourse. According to Kenneth Burke, such words "size up" these situations; they amount to "*strategies* for dealing with *situations*" (*The Philosophy* 293, 296). This is because the terms used by writers label and characterize situations, inviting readers to respond in a manner consistent with that characterization.

The strategy couched in the terminology that Metayer uses to describe Nuligak's situation is premised on what George Lakoff and Mark Johnson call a theory of purely objective truth, which stems from Enlightenment philosophy. Here, it is appropriate to assume that absolute truth is attainable and that it is possible to give an account of it (182). However, the idea of a purely objective truth is problematic because "[i]n making a statement, we make a choice of categories because we have some reason for focusing on certain properties and downplaying others. [. . .] Since the truth of a statement depends on whether the categories employed in the statement fit, the truth of a statement will always be relative to the way the category is understood for our purposes in a given context" (163, 164). By invoking categories characteristic of ethnographic discourse, Metayer sizes up Nuligak's situation, focusing readers' attention on a purely objective kind of truth; the situations he describes he designates as facts. *Ethnography as description* is the label Martyn Hammersley uses to name this pattern, which emerges "when the *production* of understanding and the *construction* of the text are hidden to form an account that purports to present what is described simply 'as it appeared'; this being treated, with more or less conviction, as 'how it is'" (23).

Descriptive ethnography is the pattern that appears when Metayer tells his readers that Nuligak's "original manuscript is somewhat like a mate's log [. . . where] the most interesting *facts* of an eventful life are re-

lated" (10 emphasis added). This attitude of objectivity in Metayer's discourse is even more telling when he contests Nuligak's competing orientation by informing readers that his references to Inuit legends "are *only* the
projection in folk-tale form of what *in reality* must very often have been the
life of the 'poor little orphan.' Nuligak was just such an orphan, and the ad-
ventures of his life closely parallel the Eskimo legends" (10–11 emphasis
added). Much of the social action of *I, Nuligak* is governed by a Western
ethnographic perspective that is quite antithetical to the rhetorical motives
of the native subject. Perhaps this is why Arnold Krupat argues that, with
what he terms bicultural composite compositions, readers are confronted
with a textualized equivalent of a "frontier" where two cultures meet, but
not in a reciprocally equal manner (31–33).

The frontier perspective that Krupat describes recurs in Nuligak's testimonio when he recounts that, as a young boy, he and his grandmother
travelled on a cargo boat and reached the Kitigariuit settlement, where, he
says, "We were invited to eat with the people, for they already killed white
whales. We feasted on *maktak*" (27). In Metayer's footnote, readers are informed that "*Maktak*, the skin of the whale, is eaten either cooked or raw.
Raw the Eskimo prefers it when it smells high. Only Eskimo palates seem
to relish maktak in this state. However, cooked white whale skin is delicious.
It is prepared rather like pig's feet or calf's head, and tastes somewhat the
same" (27). The form and substance of Metayer's and Nuligak's discourses
become fused as a genre. But as Krupat contends, this fusion is hierarchical, not reciprocal. While the substance, "the semantic value of discourse,"
is the "common aspects of experience that are being symbolized," the form
is often antecedent in that it "shapes the responses of the reader or listener"
(C. Miller 320). Thus, with emergent genres like Canadian Inuit testimonio,
form will sometimes occupy a privileged position within the hierarchical
relationship that form and substance have with one another. This is certainly true with *I, Nuligak*, because the attitudes of Western ethnography
contained in Metayer's discourse evoke a response in which his point of view
is represented as what Marcus and Cushman call the *native point of view*. This
involves "presenting material as if it were, or faithfully represented, [as] the
point of view of its cultural subject[s] rather than [the ethnographer's] own
cultural reference" (34). This native point of view is evoked when Metayer
sizes up Nuligak's situation; he tells readers that only the Eskimos will eat
maktak when it is raw and high and that they prefer it this way. His choice

of words suggests that the Eskimo, unlike his civilized Western counterpart, enjoys consuming tainted, spoiled meat. Thus, by voicing his own "epistemological shock or surprise in [Nuligak's] narrative," Metayer moves his readers "toward a particular stance in relation to cultural difference" (Marcus and Cushman 47).

This sort of epistemological self-reflection is sustained when Metayer compares the taste of cooked white whale skin with that of pig's feet and calf's head. His comparison furnishes a didactic rationale common to ethnographic genres that, Marcus and Cushman contend, represents "difference, and especially difference that pertains to native subjectivity" (49). They argue that this provides "very strong rhetorical support for making the native practices and meanings, set off from our own, seem authentically their own, rather than just the work of the ethnographic writer's imaginative bricolage from the knowledge he has acquired from another form of life" (49). Such imaginative bricolage facilitates Metayer in instructing readers to consider the habits of the Inuit from his culture's point of view, since he suggests that cooked white whale meat is much more palatable than its raw competitor. The social action of his discourse conveys the idea that the eating habits of Westerners are superior to those of the Inuit.

This attitude resurfaces when Metayer comments on Nuligak's reference to "the Krangmalit tribe on the shore of the wide, deep bay called Prince Albert Sound" (41). In defining the Krangmalit Inuit as "the people east of us," Metayer claims that "[b]y this name the Eskimos of the Mackenzie Delta designate roughly all the tribes between Ballie Island and Gjoa Haven. [. . .] Often a slightly depreciatory sense is understood, for the western tribes consider themselves more 'civilized' than the eastern. The Krangmalit are comparative dullards in their eyes" (41). As the preceding conversation indicates, it is really Metayer's position that the western tribes consider themselves more civilized than the eastern ones. His claim gives ethnographic authority to his own voice, thus undermining the motives implicit in Nuligak's testimonio acts. As Jeanette Ireland remarks, the term "civilized" symbolizes an attitude that permeates ethnographical and anthropological studies of Inuit culture, one that has also influenced "government measures to educate and integrate 'native, aboriginal, indigenous' people into the modern social organization, since it assumes that there is a uniform pattern of cultural evolution, all societies passing through the same stages of 'primitive' collective to a *civilized*, modern society with differen-

tiated classes and social institutions" (98 emphasis added). When this Western "civilized" attitude recurs in genres like Canadian Inuit testimonio, it significantly brings into question whose exigencies the genre actually responds
to—those of the native subjects, or those of the Western collaborators?

Patterns of Inuit Intellectual Culture

Canadian Inuit testimonio makes salient the attitudes of two disparate cultures; the authority of the Western collaborator is not the only voice per-
meating the genre. This appears evident when Nuligak evokes references
to the Inuit oral tradition to describe his social status as *the poor little orphan
boy*. According to Robin McGrath, Nuligak's orphan-boy references allude
to the Inuit legend of the orphan boy Kaujjarjuk. McGrath notes that Kaujjarjuk "is a sort of male Cinderella who is homeless and dependent on unkind people for support," who later on in life encounters "a powerful spirit
who helps him become strong" ("Oral" 161). Kaujjarjuk eventually becomes
a legendary hero by single-handedly killing three polar bears, and then
taking revenge against those who have been unkind to him. In *I, Nuligak*,
this revenge takes the form of the protagonist becoming more successful
than his rivals: "I was very proud to be the champion of the young men with
whom I was living," Nuligak tells his readers (107). Agreeing with James
McNeill's analysis of the Kaujjarjuk legend, McGrath concludes: "The auto-
biographer, writing at the end of his life, may in looking back see the mythic
structure of his life, but it is possible to see, also, how he may have imposed
that structure on his life either while living it or retrospectively. [. . .] It may
be that the legends were projections of the reality, but the parallels to the
Kaujjarjuk myth in *I, Nuligak* suggest that in this case at least the reality as
Nuligak reports it is a projection of the legend" (*Canadian* 105). Whether
the legend is a projection of the reality or whether the reality is a projection
of the legend is irrelevant, since what is at issue is how the recurrent situation evokes the recurrent pattern. That is, how the Kaujjarjuk legend *functions* as part of the social action of the text, as a strategy to transform the
situation of the Kitigariukmeut people. The Kitigariukmeut Inuit were
starving and many children were orphaned and left to fend for themselves.
When a contemporary circumstance such as this is explained through references to mythic or legendary entities from the past, these entities perform
a *real* social function in terms of their rhetorical effects. As Dell Hymes ar-

gues, "myths have only partly to do with the past [. . . because they] are a dialogue between past, present, and future" (164). He says that in accordance with the received tradition, present circumstance, and projected need of the culture that uses a myth, this myth will change. In fact, *"it must change, if it is to be coherent with experience"* (165).

In testifying that even at the age of six he "never forgot what he saw [because he . . .] was the poor little orphan boy, begging here and there to live, most aware of what was going on around [him]" (24), Nuligak refers to a received Inuit tradition to transform a contemporary situation. Then, as a young adult who has gained a measure of wealth and social status in his tribe by becoming a successful hunter, but who nonetheless remembers his earlier years of hunger, begging, and poverty, he informs his readers that "to this day [he] cannot eat in the morning, because he was the poor little orphan boy" (51). His reference to the Kaujjarjuk legend helps to explain the lasting effects his poverty has had upon him. The traditional meaning of the legend is altered in that it now makes his *own* experience coherent to the reader. Finally, as an elder who is once again poor and hungry, Nuligak recalls that "once upon a time, [he] had been the poor little orphan boy" (158). This time the pattern informs readers about how very little has changed for the Kitigariukmeut. Such references to the Inuit oral tradition recurring in Nuligak's testimonio thus "reveal the extraordinary capacity of indigenous and indiginized forms to appropriate and reform the powerful discursive practices of the colonizer" (Ashcroft, "Modernity's" 22).

Nuligak's recurrent references to the Kaujjarjuk legend can also be viewed as instances of what Burke, borrowing from Bronislaw Malinowski, terms "addressed" discourse, which includes terminology that conveys phenomena such as myth, legend, magic, and witchcraft. It is necessary to recognize such terminology's rhetorical function, a function that Burke argues is by nature a realistic one, even though it "may be quite far from the kind of realism found in strictly 'scientific realism'" (*Rhetoric* 44). In other words, the discourse of the supernatural, like the discourse of ethnographic realism, should be viewed in rhetorical terms "that bear upon the *persuasive* aspects of language, the function of language as *addressed*, as directed or roundabout appeal to real or ideal audiences, without or within" (43–44). With *I, Nuligak*, this addressed discourse appeals to both an Inuit and a non-Inuit readership. This is evidenced through the voices of the native subject and his Western collaborator, whose discourses oscillate between Western ethnographic and Inuit worldviews. This epistemic dualism is evoked when

Nuligak recalls the reported speech of Naoyavak, his grandmother's brother, who relates a "strange but true" story in which "the people from Booth Island said they discovered a dead whale stranded somewhere on the shore of Franklin Bay. It was buried in snow. The *Krangmalit* Eskimos ate of it— until the day when, clearing the snow, they discovered that the whale wore a belt. A whale wears no belt. It was a giant! His skin was as coarse as that of a whale. They had eaten of the *inukpak*, and they died!" (43).

What is important is not whether or not Naoyavak's testimony ver- ifies the existence of giants who wear belts but the symbolic action of this discourse—that is, how this story is addressed to a particular readership through typified terms of reference that readers consider fitting to the sit- uation. Nuligak makes numerous statements describing exactly what the situation among his people was like at this time. With the recent arrival of the white man's economy, diseases, and plunderous hunting practices, "the Kitigariuit people fell ill and many of them died" (27). So in relating his ac- count of this tragic situation, the persuasive *function* of myth is to Nuligak "neither a fictitious story, nor an account of a dead past; it is a statement of a bigger reality still partially alive. It is alive in that its precedent, its law, its moral, still rule the social life of the natives" (Malinowski 58). But because *I, Nuligak* is a hybrid genre that appeals to a Western-Inuit audience, there are two competing sets of attitudes at work. And this is precisely why it is also fitting for Metayer to contest Nuligak's mythical evocations, since he tells readers that "what was meant by the 'belt' around the whale I do not know, but the people were probably poisoned by the spoiled meat" (43). What Metayer is essentially saying is that Nuligak's appeals to tradition are irrational and that the truth of the so-called phenomenon is best explained through Western ethnographic terms of discourse. However, Metayer is overlooking the fact that the Eskimo stories from the Inuit oral tradition recurring in Nuligak's testimonio "explain the world views of the Inuit who, though they may have forgotten the legends themselves, still react to everyday situations according to the values embodied by those old beliefs" (McGrath, *Canadian* 77).

Rather than recognizing how Nuligak's references to Inuit legends are addressed to readers in ways McGrath describes, Metayer accounts for the presence of such patterns by invoking attitudes of Western ethnography. He contends that such stories merely "mingle fantasy and the fantastic with the *real*, making it most difficult to draw a line between the two" (62 em- phasis added). Hence, it appears that the exigency that has motivated

Metayer to write has also induced him to address only Western readers, as he consistently ignores the perspective held by the other audience of Nuligak's testimonio—the Inuit readership.

This same attitude is exhibited when Metayer dismisses Nuligak's accounts of witchcraft performed by Inuit shamans, the *angatkot*. Readers are told that the angatkot acted as intermediaries between the spirit world and the Inuit. Metayer contends that "they often resorted to coarse quackery and exploited the credulity of their compatriots [. . . but were] sincere men who really believed in their superhuman powers" (59). But this so-called quackery served a *real* social function as a form of addressed discourse "involving ways of identification that contribute variously to social cohesion" (Burke, *Rhetoric* 44). Hence, what matters is not what witch magic is believed to be (that is, if it is real according to the precepts of ethnographic realism), but how it functions within a society, how it affects people acting together in a social environment (Ireland, "Ideology" 101). The recurrent references to the powers of angatkot in Nuligak's testimonio serve as a *strategy of transformation* for the deteriorating social situation of the Kitigariukmeut Inuit during the early twentieth century.

A similar situation is well described by Edmond Carpenter in "Witch-fear among the Aivilik Eskimos." Carpenter contends that witch fear among the Aivilik dates back to only the 1930s when, as a result of their contact with white people, their survival became threatened by tuberculosis and a declining food supply. Witch fear, argues Carpenter, was therefore neither a normal nor an aboriginal phenomenon in Aivilik society. It came into existence through a belief in "the potential malevolence of other people reflecting great insecurity in interpersonal relations" (56). In other words, witch fear emerged in response to the exigencies of a once contemporary situation. As a result, "[n]atural and mystical causation came to exist side by side, offering a dual, though not conflicting, interpretation. [. . .] Today in those fields where whites do not, or cannot, offer the Aivilik a natural explanation, only one interpretation is made. We might call it a mystical interpretation, but to the Aivilik it is merely *the* interpretation" (60).

The Aivilik Inuit thus used and incorporated elements of their traditional intellectual culture to respond to changes brought about by the arrival of Europeans. Since a similar situation recurred among the Kitigariukmeut Inuit, this explains why a natural explanation is untenable in Nuligak's testimonio, so the discourse being *addressed* to readers is a mythical one that functions to explain an otherwise unexplainable event. In relating the crises that his people were facing at this time, Nuligak testifies: "We did not have any more to eat. We were unable to hunt seal in the crevasses because the ice was not opening. The Inuit appealed to the angatkot" (60). Nuligak then relates an account of the rituals performed by the angatkot in a darkened igloo, where strange voices and the beating of wings were heard. When the *kudlik* lamps were re-lit one of the angatkot's bodies was black with soot. And the very next day, "the ice opened in large crevasses and the Inuit killed many seals" (60). The references to the angakot appearing in Nuligak's testimonio indicate that a great deal of the social action of his text is voiced through references to Inuit intellectual culture and is *addressed* to both Inuit and non-Inuit readers. His testimony is fitting in that it serves as a solution for the desperate situation faced by the Kitigariukmeut Inuit. As Carpenter observes, natural and mystical causation exist in unison, a constellation of patterns informing the acts of a genre.

The preceding account of recurrent patterns in Canadian Inuit testimonio explains how the new genre theories within contemporary composition studies can productively inform theories and issues associated with postcolonial studies. New genre theories consider how and why features of Western genres such as autobiography and ethnography are used by native and other subaltern subjects in ways that help them transform their postcolonial realities. Testimonio is clearly a genre within postcolonial inquiry that epitomizes how these subjects use features of Western genres to relate collective experiences of colonization and marginalization. The new genre theories elucidate how rhetorically effective such strategies of transformation are because they account for how the patterns of a genre motivate readers' attitudes and responses. This seems particularly useful for postcolonial analysis, since it deals with how subjects make strategic attempts to control the representation of reality.

This effort is well illustrated in *I, Nuligak*, where the native subject interpolates aspects of "the dominant discourse in order to transform [them] in ways that release the representation of local realities" (Ashcroft "Modernity's" 18.) His autobiographical acts amount to "the insertion of an oppressed postcolonial reality into the master discourse of literature and history" (21). Yet by invoking references to Inuit intellectual culture, Nuligak adopts the Western autobiographical form without adopting its colonial attitudes.

Aneil Rallin

(IM)MIGRANT CROSSINGS

I did not choose the note form consciously; a combination of things drew me
to it. An urgency for one thing. I also felt incompetent to construct an essay in
which I would describe the intimacies, fears, and lies I wrote of in "Speechlessness." I felt my thoughts, things that I had held within for a lifetime, tra-
versed so wide a terrain, had so many stops and starts, apparent non sequiturs,
that an essay—with its cold-blooded dependence on logical construction,
which I had mastered practically against my will—could not work. My subject
could not respond to that form, which would have contradicted the idea of
speechlessness. This tender approach to myself within the confines and inter-
ruptions of a forty-hour-a-week job and against a history of forced fluency was
the beginning of a journey into speech.

Michelle Cliff, "A Journey Into Speech" 58

I am writing these words in San Diego, on the border between Mexico and
the United States of America, the border that Gloria Anzaldúa calls the
"1,950-mile-long open wound" (*Borderlands* 2).

What are the stories behind the body? What is the text that the body
would write? The ruptures do not always leave visible marks. The wounds
heal, then rupture again. The wounds do not heal completely.

I am four maybe. I watch a man undress. He is beautiful. I long to reach out and touch his pubic hair. I don't. I know even then that that desire is transgressive, dangerous.

The students in my ESL classes are hesitant, nervous, reluctant to speak. They fear I will read their indecision with the English language, their pauses, as signs of ignorance. I work hard to convince them that I insist on asking them to speak not to mock their English-speaking abilities but because I believe they have valuable insights to share.

In a public lynching of students, the trustees of the City University of New York approve a measure relegating "remedial" courses to the community colleges. Students unable to pass an entrance exam are deemed not to be adequately prepared for the university and must be refused access. Students who have limited reading and writing skills, as determined by a single test, are not seen as having any potential or promise and must be denied entrance to the university.

I do not know how to, cannot, will not erase myself when I walk into the classroom. As someone from the Third World and queer, I am aware particularly of the dangers of keeping silent. As a teacher I have to constantly ask myself not only whom my primary responsibility is to, but also what my primary allegiance is to. My instinct dictates that my primary allegiance in any classroom is to my colored students, my queer students, my working-class students, my disenfranchised students, but then I immediately think of the colored Republican students and caution myself against assuming this essentialist position. As a teacher, my main goal is to radicalize my students.

The working conditions of part-time faculty across universities in the United States are very different from the working conditions of tenured and tenure-track faculty. Many part-time faculty are not even given one-year contracts and must work without health benefits. Universities can give all their employees benefits regardless of how many courses they teach or what kind of contract they have, but they choose not to. They argue that it would cost a great deal to give all employees health benefits. But even if it costs a great deal, shouldn't the university have an ethical obligation to give all employees health benefits in a country where the right to health care is not given to all people?

In this city where I am often (mis)taken for Mexican, Spanish-speaking women and men who don't speak English ask me if I speak Spanish, ask me for directions, ask me for help. I look at the people who speak to me in Spanish in embarrassment (they seem embarrassed, I am embarrassed) and I say, "No hablo español." I feel ashamed, feel as if I betray them by not speaking the language of this city whose soul has been crippled, mutilated by the English-only legislation of California. It is in this divided city that I am trying to write. I am here on a visit. Because I speak English I can count on navigating my way through the city with assurance. But people who live here and speak only Spanish cannot.

The professionalization of gayness requires certain performances and productions of the self.

At the queers-of-color meeting the talk invariably turns to how we must be authentic to our people.

I sought the note form consciously. Constant migrations and relocations have made me realize that the narratives I construct have to do with images and dispatches. The images and dispatches are signifiers of place, of location. I think of history as experiential. I construct my narratives around these clues to center myself. My marginal experiences are central to my existence.

Locating myself in the classroom, re/presenting myself as having a traveling history, a worldview, a personality, collides in many ways with my training, which encouraged me to erase myself when I walk into the classroom.

The soul of the university, the site of public education, is being crippled, mutilated by writing assessment that is used as a gatekeeping device to limit student access to higher education. Writing assessment is used to deny students the right to enter the university, the site of education to which they belong. Is there any doubt which students will be turned away? The decree of the university is to punish and to exclude, to separate those who are prepared from those who are not. Those whose English language skills are inadequate, those whose racial and ethnic backgrounds are not white and/or middle class, those who are second-language users of English, those who have not mastered standard English discursive practices, will be denied entrance.

This is not a coincidence or a side-effect of an otherwise benign system but a direct and calculated result. The economic order and the U.S. system of governance depend on keeping a large number of people barred from entering the gates of the state, the city, the university.

Manage, oversee, regulate, supervise, command, govern, rule, dominate, domineer, master, overpower, contain, rein, repress, restrict, subdue, authority, charge, command, dominion, jurisdiction, power, check, curb, suppressant, corner, monopolize, aplomb, composure, self-control.

To distract myself momentarily from my apprehensions about certain powers of the state, I pamper myself with a visit to the hairdresser. The person who usually cuts my hair is away and the person who cuts my hair instead asks where I am from. I tell him what part of the city I live in, but he is not satisfied with my response, for he has already assumed that I am not really from here. He tries again. He asks where I lived before living here. I tell him I lived in Ohio. But you are not from Ohio, he says. I tell him I am from there as much as anywhere else. He says I am teasing him and he wants to know where I am really from. I tell him that having lived in many different parts of the world, I am not sure how to answer his question. He says where you are born is where you are from. I don't argue with the simplicity of his logic and tell him that I spent the formative years of my childhood in Bombay, India. My "foreignness" established in the first five minutes of our meeting, he is satisfied and proceeds to tell me how lucky we are to be living in the United States where people don't have to struggle to survive. I don't have the energy to argue with his assumption that all people in the Third World struggle to survive, but I can't stop myself from pointing out that the homeless who have been stripped of their rights to claim public space in the city are not lucky.

In writing, it is crucial to negotiate with the question raised by Jacqueline Royster: "How do we translate listening into language and action, into the creation of an appropriate response?" ("First Voice" 38). Listening involves moving from seeing and observing and hearing to witnessing and testifying and acting.

The homeless routinely charged by the police for endangering public safety are not lucky. No, the homeless are certainly not fortunate to be living in the United States of America.

Radical teachers not only process received knowledge but they actively transform knowledge.

The dualism of self and other reinstates dominant racist ideologies and preserves the arrangements of white hegemony.

The institution of learning models the state. It is built on inequities and on the insatiability of those who hold the power to hang onto it. The university is not the kind, just, egalitarian space that many of its citizens believe it to be. Even members of the institution committed to the rights of all peoples in their intellectual pursuits are not committed to granting the same rights to all the people who inhabit the university.

An item on the evening news is presented without comment and doesn't lead to public outrage: the state of California awards one billion dollars to the Border Patrol to make "our" borders safer. A week later, the *Los Angeles Times* reports that as many as seven million people in California do not have health insurance.

Every semester, I overhear conversations among composition teachers in the hallways. The teachers complain about their ESL students. They don't believe they should have to teach students unable to speak and write standard American English fluently. They don't believe ESL students belong in their classes.

I wonder who among us hasn't fumbled with language? I also wonder why they believe that the ability of students to speak a language fluently is a warranty that their writing will be articulate, will not be a struggle. I speak fluently but I grapple with language, with words, every time I write.

A paragraph from Gayatri Spivak leaps out at me: "May I not forget to question: what is it to assume that one already knows the meaning of words; something is taught by others and something is learned by me—seems to point at three different generalizations for this resistant reader's subject position: ethnic in the U.S., racial in Britain, negotiating for decolonized space. These are generalizations that now seem good for teaching and learning in classes, lecture hall. They will not travel, directly, of course, to all situations of struggle in all the three arenas, as some of us, impatient with the grounding uncertainty of teaching, talking, writing, seem to quickly presume" ("Post-Colonial" 144).

An edict that takes effect in Philadelphia on the first day of the new year forbids the homeless from the streets of Center City, the city's recently gentrified commercial and cultural nucleus. The injunction establishes into law the city's agenda to push the homeless out of sight, outside the borders of the city's limits. In this city that calls itself "the city of brotherly love" (perhaps appropriately since there is no place for sisterly love here), the homeless are prohibited from claiming even public spaces as their own.

Gayness gets conflated with whiteness and dominant formulations of gay are both white and middle-class in this consumerist society where revolution has come to signify a new deodorant or household appliance. The predominant struggle of gay and lesbian activists is for gay men and lesbians to be allowed to serve in the military and for institutional space in racist, sexist, classist, ablist institutions. My white friend, the activist, wants to know why I refuse to support the March on Washington. I wonder why I am supposed to support a movement uncritical of the armed forces and the police, who are accountable for the deaths of thousands of colored and poor bodies? As a queer, I am expected to focus exclusively on "queer" issues and to make separations between sexual oppression and race and economic exploitation, even though the majority of queers are working-class women of color.

On the evening news, an upper-middle-class white woman is being interviewed after alerting the INS to the presence of suspected illegal immigrants. She says she saw shadows running across her backyard and immediately knew that the suspects must be illegal immigrants because they were running. She is asked if she felt threatened or if she felt she was in any danger. She says she didn't but claims it was her duty to call the police. She is commended by the news reporter for being a good citizen, for having acted bravely and responsibly.

In thinking about the responsibilities of teachers, I find myself returning to a question Adrienne Rich poses: "How can we connect the process of learning to write well with the student's own reality and not teach her/him how to write acceptable lies in standard English?" (239).

For me, that is still the central question, one of my main concerns in charting a pedagogy that is antiracist, antisexist, antihomophobic, and antinationalistic. The emphasis on the "student's own reality" invokes many possibilities. Students and teachers have a responsibility to think about and through our most immediate location, our selves. However, thinking only about one's self can lead to paralysis, insensibility, immobility, solipsism. The "student's own reality" could easily become an excuse for students and teachers not to engage with anything that they are not familiar or comfortable with. But the phrase is useful in a wider sense—starting with but moving beyond local worlds, making connections, and constantly negotiating with the global in terms of accountability, responsibility, action. Learning does not take place in a vacuum. It is situated within specific histories and geographies.

The summer of 2003 has already seen over a hundred border crossers die of heat and exhaustion.

In this city bruised and partitioned, I sit surrounded by my notes. I write in fragments, little bits at a time. I write on scraps of colored paper (the backs of discarded fliers), bits torn from newspapers and magazines, train tickets, movie stubs, paper napkins from cafés. I sit surrounded by my many writings on this collection of assorted papers. These word fragments on these bits of paper represent a trajectory of sorts. I must confess that I am not always interested in thoughts that connect perfectly. My mind disconnects. It makes sense in strange and idiosyncratic ways. I like that strangeness and the idiosyncrasies of my mind, of other people's minds. I am trying to push my words together, my notes, my fragments. I am trying to weave them together and in weaving make some sense of the moment of these writings. These notes are my effort at making sense. In and through these notes, I am attempting to pit ideas and thoughts against each other to question what it means to be an academic and a "citizen" in this country.

The academy and the state legislature depend upon creating divisions between the different ranks of people who teach in the university. The private academy is not interested in breaking these distinctions either. There are different payscales for the same classes. A part-timer typically earns between eighteen hundred and three thousand dollars for a first-year composition class while a full-time faculty member rarely earns less than thirty-two thousand a year. In fact, in fields like English and history, nearly half of the part-time faculty are in the category of those earning less than two thousand dollars per course ("Summary"). Why aren't part-time faculty offered equitable wages? And why haven't all tenured and tenure-track faculty made this issue of inequitable wages their struggle? How can part-time and tenured or tenure-track faculty be equal colleagues when part-time faculty make so much less in terms of remuneration than tenured or tenure-track faculty? Part-time faculty are hired to teach the same classes as tenured and tenure-track faculty but are clearly not deemed worthy of receiving wages equal to those of full-time faculty members. Who makes these decisions? Are only the management and administration to be implicated for this tiered state of affairs? What about the role of tenured and tenure-track faculty in perpetuating and maintaining such an unjust state of affairs?

I find on a notecard a couple of lines (but no citation) that I have jotted down from Marlene Nourbese Philip: "The imagination [. . .] is both free and unfree. Free in that it can wander wheresoever it wishes, unfree in that it is profoundly affected and shaped by the societies in which we live."

While desire itself may transcend place, the enactment of desire/s is certainly constantly bound to, connected with, space. Place constructs desire/s and may therefore inhibit the performativity of certain/other desires.

If part-time workers are the migrant laborers of the academy, the janitors and cleaners are the invisible laborers who toil at all odd hours to dis-
infect and deodorize the physical space of the academy so that those of us
who teach and do research can do the mental work, the real work, of the
academy. But even among academic workers, the hierarchies flourish and
the borders grow wider.

The side of the border that I am on offers me some privileges at the
same time as it constructs me as "other," as "alien."

But who are my people? Learning that I am from Bombay, a queer colored colleague tells me he is pleased that the renaming of Bombay has
finally returned the city to its people. He does not seem to be concerned
that imbricated in this renaming are the desires of Hindu fundamentalists
who would mark all that is not Hindu as other, as alien.

I am a visitor. I am given the designation of Visiting Assistant Professor. My position is full-time as opposed to part-time, and I am given some
of the benefits awarded to tenured and tenure-track faculty. I am somewhere in between the part-time faculty and the tenured and tenure-track
faculty. Like the part-time faculty, I have been hired to teach what are increasingly coming to be known as the service courses—courses that prepare students for other supposedly more rigorous courses, the real courses
taught by tenured and tenure-track faculty. The director of the program I
am hired to teach in tells me that they are interested only in my teaching
and my teaching evaluations, not in my scholarship. He tells me the main
criteria used to determine whom the program will rehire are the teaching
evaluations. The teaching evaluations are standardized forms devised by
those in charge of the program. They include questions such as "Did the
class meet regularly?" "How many papers were you asked to write?" "How
many papers were you asked to revise?" "How many conferences did you
have with your instructor?" The questions are not designed to provide teachers with feedback that will be useful to them but to monitor the classes, to
see if we, those who are transient workers in the academy and the graduate
students who provide cheap labor, are doing what we are supposed to be
doing in our classes. We are not trusted to teach our own classes satisfac-
torily.

Where is the evidence that students whose reading and writing abilities do not measure up to certain standards (that in any case reflect biases against students of certain racial and ethnic backgrounds) are incapable of analysis, innovation, promise in the university? The gates of the university are being closed to students who cannot pass a test. Their potential is unrecognized, their merit disregarded.

I am visiting the bruised city from across the country. I am allowed to do so (no questions asked, no official procedures to follow, no papers to file) despite my status as an "alien," a designation given to me by the INS, but people who live a few miles away on the other side of the border cannot even enter without papers, without legal documents that are hard to acquire, especially if one lives on the wrong side of the border.

Viewpoints, perspectives from various locations around the globe abet in decentering, recentering, negotiating, renegotiating the borders, boundaries.

Zoe Wicomb: "Setting an agenda that bans certain subjects and prescribes others seems foolish, since it can generate only two categories of writers: the obedient, who will slavishly follow the agenda, and the disobedient, who will avoid it as a matter of principle" (15).

Returning to Philadelphia, I mull over what responsibility means for someone like me, an "alien," who has lived in the U.S. for ten years and who has been given the charge of educating its citizenry but who has been conferred none of the rights that citizens of the state are usually granted.

A white lesbian colleague of mine tells me she is sick and tired of her students not making gay issues the center of their lives. I tell her I am sick and tired of white queers not making race a central issue of their lives.

Regulate writing. Regulate desire. Regulate taste. Regulate the boundaries. If there are no regulations there will be chaos.

Transnational economic structures and politics affect us all in different ways. Glancing at a discarded newspaper during a bus ride, I note that the entire country of Namibia uses a miniscule amount of the energy consumed in Las Vegas in a single day.

I like the struggles that come with belonging in the margins and do not want to become assimilated into the center.

Elspeth Probyn: "In creating our own centers and our own locals, we tend to forget that our center displaces others into peripheries of our making" (n.pag.).

Othering is a national and international pastime. For the moment, I forget the pleasures of othering, of being othered. It's a complicated business.

At San Diego State University, the largest university within the California State University system, the largest public university system in North America, there are 973 full-time faculty and 836 part-time faculty ("Headcount"). Part-time faculty are responsible for teaching at least 40 percent of all classes taught. Many other campuses within the California State University system of twenty-two campuses do worse. In the fall of 2000, there were more part-time faculty than full-time faculty at seven campuses, and almost as many part-time faculty as full-time faculty on five campuses ("Headcount"). These numbers are not unusual at universities across the United States.

The politics of everyday life are different for those entitled to space from those who have to struggle for it daily.

At San Diego State University, no tenured or tenure-track faculty teach the first year composition course offered by the Department of Rhetoric and Writing Studies. First year composition is taught almost entirely by part-time faculty and teaching assistants. This, too, is not unusual at universities across the United States.

I tell another queer white friend who is a U.S. citizen that he will never have to face what I have to face at airports around the world. He doesn't understand. He wants to know what connections I am trying to make.

Colonialism robs not only the psyche of the colonized but also robs people of basic human rights. Basic human rights are tied to constructs like political territory. In the U.S. territory, the responsibility of the state is to its citizens. But even here, not all citizens are seen as worthy of the charge and responsibility of the state.

Chandra Mohanty: "Teaching practices must combat the pressures of professionalization, normalization, and standardization, the very pressures of expectation that implicitly aim to manage and discipline pedagogies so that teacher behaviors are predictable (and perhaps controllable) across the board" ("On Race" 153).

Since I am an "alien," my right to teach is dependent on the INS granting me the authorization to accept employment with a specific employer within the United States for a specific period of time. I am required to attain permission from the INS to change employers. My movements are thus controlled by the INS, who may at any point deny my application for reemployment for any reason.

But he says, "We have to have rules and regulations. Otherwise, our classes will be out of control."

The response of the responsible United States government to the cries of the divided earth is to issue a series of warnings on television beseeching border crossers to be wary of the heat and the fury of the earth. Do they think the people crossing the borders daily do not know the risks involved? Do they think the people crossing the borders do not know that maintaining the border is a billion dollar industry?

The people were running; therefore, the good citizen assumes they must be dark-skinned and illegal.

The senate agrees to spend fifty million dollars to hire an additional five hundred U.S. Customs Service Inspectors for the U.S.-Mexican border next year. This is not a luxury but a necessity due to increased traffic along the entire Mexican border, says the senator who introduced the measure.

Notions of authenticity are used as traps. I fail all tests of authenticity and refuse to be trapped, colonized by authenticity. I do not want to engage with this obsessive notion, but disengaging is not easy. Colonial and post-colonial fantasies rest on this concept of the "other." They want you / me / us to neatly fit in.

In California, the state projected to be the first in the union to have more people of color than white people, Proposition 187—an initiative making il-legal immigrants ineligible for medical care and high school education—was backed by Governor Pete Wilson and approved by 59 percent of voters in the November 1994 elections.

My department has a meeting to discuss domestic partnership policy in a university that doesn't approve of granting domestic partners benefits. Though several faculty members—notably junior faculty members with-out tenure—argue passionately for institutionalizing domestic partnership policies, there is much resistance and the faculty as a whole votes against the measure. Many argue that even though they are in favor of such a pol-icy, they don't think it is appropriate for the department to go against the wishes of the university we work for. The message is clear: even if we don't believe in the discriminatory mandate set by the university, we should not try to alter or resist the mandate.

Implicit in this decision not to go against the wishes of the university is the yearning to seek the approval of those who are in power.

Deborah Davis: "Of all the aspects of American life that have ever con-cerned me, it is this craving for the respect of people who have sold their own souls that I find most disturbing" (72).

We are told borders are maintained for the sake of order and efficient administration. Without borders there would be chaos. But the desire to maintain the borders reveals our respect for power.

In writing classes, boundaries and borders are erected to maintain so-called standards. And writing teachers who are disproportionately part-time workers are the ones expected to regulate the borders and the boundaries.

Those who are not given full citizenship rights are the ones entrusted with and expected to maintain the borders.

Linda Brodkey: "Composition teachers are not paid to teach writing but to patrol the borders of language and literature" (xii).

If they disobey they can be sent away, banished from ever returning. Part-time faculty must live with the constant trauma of being subject to being fired.

The note form offers no certainty, only uncertainty. It offers no predetermined resolution, no unequivocal results except a questioning of the uses of language, the possibilities of linguistic and intellectual pleasures, the axes of power, and the politics of nation states and institutions.

I present these notes together to create the effect of synchronicity, not equivalence.

The necessity of disturbing, of disrupting, borders and boundaries is an attempt to escape not only from the fixity of European rhetorics of modernism that places you/me/us as "the others" of Western cultures, but also to make room to inhabit multiple positionings.

To rephrase Sunil Gupta, the fixity of European rhetoric does not take into account the wide variety of constituencies for the production and consumption of knowledge on a worldwide scale. It does not explore the reciprocity of language and culture. Writing is not tolerated as a questioning but only as an answer, as something fixed and not as something that is uncertain in its movement, in its ambitions, something that is unfinished.

David Dzaka

RESISTING WRITING

Reflections on the Postcolonial Factor in the Writing Class

I was born and raised in Ghana, the first sub-Saharan nation to gain political independence from Britain. English is the official language in Ghana, and yet it is the second, third, or fourth language for many of us in that country, and indeed in many parts of Africa. My identity as a postcolonial subject raises several questions about my writing development that should be of interest to compositionists: How are my writing difficulties and peculiarities related to my postcolonial background? To what extent are metropolitan writing theories responsive to or interrupted by postcolonial realities?

There is really no agreement on what constitutes the "postcolonial." Padmini Mongia sums up this difficulty when he asks: "Does the term refer to texts or practices, to psychological conditions or to concrete historical processes? Or does it perhaps refer to interaction of all these?" (1). I adopt the definition by Ashcroft, Griffiths, and Tiffin, which characterizes the postcolonial as "all the culture affected by the imperial process from the moment of colonization to the present day" (*The Empire* 2). In this view, the postcolonial presupposes histories of contact, and the interplay of political, economic, and cultural power between the imperial center and the margins. As the history of the present, the postcolonial implicates the past in present constituencies.

Cultural theorists remind us that we speak or write from specific locations. My subjectivity as a writer is embedded in the historic process that turned the Gold Coast into a British colony in the nineteenth century. I learned to read and write according to an instructional paradigm first introduced by the colonial schools and presently maintained with little modification within the national literary ethos. Part of the reason I resist writing can be understood by reference to colonial legacies of writing. I propose an understanding of writing resistance grounded in postcolonial school experiences, and I position my writing within a narrative of the postcolonial school system in Ghana, which has shaped it through a lifetime of specific pedagogical experiences and relationships.

By writing resistance I mean an aversion to writing as a thoughtful process. It is manifested by the extreme disinclination to write anything beyond the routine recording of prescribed information. It is commonly demonstrated in avoidance behavior patterns, such as putting off a writing task as long as possible and trying to complete a draft without taking a second look at it once it is done. For the resisting writer, there is nothing intrinsically exciting or motivating about writing, whether personal or academic. Writing is a distasteful requirement that one faces when one must, not because one has something significant to communicate.

This type of resistance is to be distinguished from writer's block. Every writer, skilled or unskilled, native or non-native, is subject to moments of dryness in the course of shaping thoughts into a text. The type of resistance considered here is a mind-set, an inhibition against writing as a cognitive act. In the sphere of academic writing in particular, resistant writers characteristically produce slim texts, lacking in detail, or wordy texts that are inattentive to precision and clarity of thought and expression. Helen Fox puts it this way: "[This resistance] can cause a student to disagree, sometimes politely, sometimes hotly, with every change the instructor suggests, thus making substantial revision of the draft impossible" (82).

Resistance to writing, like all attitudes, arises, at least in part, from our psychosocial makeup. Although writing resistance is a common occurrence among students from different types of backgrounds, the reasons for its persistence vary from one group to another. For me, perceptions of writing and the interactive processes that characterize writing instruction are key. Language difficulties apart, these modes of thinking, acting, and relating make a world of difference between the confident, effective writer and the resisting one.

Perceptions and relationships are anchored in specific ideological matrices, in my case, in postcolonial conceptions of knowledge and power. I wish to argue that continuities between colonial and postcolonial epistemologies and relationships promoted by the school system qualitatively affect the writing efforts of students who claim such a background. I came to this understanding through reflections on my own development as a writer.

During my elementary and high school years in Ghana, I got the idea from my teachers and classmates that I was a "good writer." They often praised my essays as brilliant, although in retrospect, I can say that they were only decent papers, manifesting a great deal of potential but nothing spectacular. The success I enjoyed as a writer at that time was probably due to the fact that I had developed an early interest in reading that was fast building my vocabulary, grammar, and prose style beyond the expectations of my instructors. Since the emphasis was on correct, informative writing rather than on thoughtfulness and creativity, my papers easily passed as excellent works in comparison to those of my peers, who often had a hard time with basic proficiency, as many second-language learners do.

We did a fair amount of in-class writing, but in rather formal and restrictive circumstances. We were each expected to produce a complete essay at a single sitting, under the policing gaze of the teacher. The system set us in constant competition with one another, ruling out collaboration and teamwork. Everyone worked on his or her own in a vertical, hierarchical relationship with the instructor. I do not remember most of my teachers as friendly listeners or readers. As respondents to our writing, they saw their role mainly in terms of formal evaluators, graders, and critics. Thus, although I did well on most of my writing assignments, thereby earning the recognition and approval of my teachers, I felt very uncomfortable with writing, avoiding it whenever I could.

College did not present me with the writing challenge and stimulation I needed to fine-tune my basic skills. Correctness and formality were still emphasized out of proportion to thoughtfulness. I soon learned that when the college lecturers talked about the need for critical and divergent thinking, they did not mean it. The authority of their perspectives was final. Reality was regarded as fixed, limited to the perspective of the instructor. If something did not exist in his or her conceptual world, it probably did not exist at all. The "good students" were the ones who learned to toe the line of their instructors. There was no room for personal voice, reflection, or creativity. In these circumstances our academic lives became circumscribed by narrow-minded consumption and reproduction of "book knowledge" in the various disciplines.

As a result, my writing process became a rather reductive three-step linear activity. In dealing with an assignment, I researched the required information and then made an outline that I developed into fairly coherent paragraphs. As much as possible I adhered to standard arguments and traditional rhetorical format. There was neither opportunity nor desire to revise first drafts beyond editing for sentence-level errors. Looking back on those years I realize that I probably maintained my reputation as a good writer only because I had a good memory for retaining prescribed information and presenting it in acceptable literary English.

It is not difficult to see the role played by colonial history in constituting my subjectivity along the lines sketched in the foregoing paragraphs. Colonialism operated within a Manichean ideology that polarized reality between the West and the non-West. It was an ideology that constructed natives as benighted savages in need of European civilization. In India, Africa, and elsewhere in the former British Empire, it was, to borrow Kipling's famous words, "the white man's burden" to bring them to the frontiers of Western civilization (See, e.g., Trinh Minh-ha's *Woman, Native, Other* and Frantz Fanon's *The Wretched of the Earth*).

Following Michel Foucault, we have come to associate regimes of representation with power—power to construct, in the case of colonial narratives, the margins in relation to the dominance of the center. As Stuart Hall has observed, such representations have the power to make us "see and experience ourselves as the other" (114). Nowhere is this regime of representation and "othering" better exemplified than in the colonial school system.

Schools emerged in Ghana, as in most of the former European colonies, as part of this hegemonic project. As H. O. A. McWilliam has noted, the curriculum of the early schools set up by missionaries consisted of reading, writing, and arithmetic. As missionary activities expanded and the colonial administration consolidated itself, the curriculum broadened but its core remained firmly rooted in the three R's. Reading and writing were little more than the mechanical decoding and encoding of required information. The curriculum provided the barest minimum of literacy necessary for producing catechists, messengers, and clerks for church and colonial service. Teaching and learning were very formal and prescriptive because it was in the interest of the colonizers that natives unquestioningly assert the Christian message and work as loyal, obedient servants in Her Majesty's administration. One direct outcome of this school system was the establishment of a master-servant relationship between the colonial officer and the native, the priest and parishioner, and the teacher and student. Furthermore, because many natives first encountered the printed word as a Sunday school memory verse taken from the Bible and presented as the word of God, many came to unconsciously associate written communication with unassailable truth. Even today, virtually all school children in Ghana are acquainted with the dictum "book no lie," a playful expression of faith in the immutability and inerrancy of knowledge inscribed in books.

The colonial literacy project, which still informs the present educational system, is an exercise in what Paulo Freire calls "banking education" *(Education)*. In such a system, the instructor represents a body of knowledge essential for civilizing the younger generation and making them fit members of the community. Teaching is therefore reduced to a bipolar process between a knowledgeable individual and an empty vessel who needs to be filled.

This school system reflects an old version of European intellectual tradition that perceives knowledge as universal and fixed, something "there to be passed on." The conception that valorizes school knowledge, in Kwame Appiah's words, as "a body of truth always already given" (78) creates problematic roles for both the instructor and the students. If one stays long enough with this system it stifles originality and creativity since the classroom dynamic conditions the instructor to be a disseminator and the student a passive recipient.

A typical college writing class in Ghana illustrates this point vividly. An instructor in my undergraduate college, whom I will call Dr. Kuma, was the best known and most feared of the writing teachers. He was greatly respected for his diligence, thoroughness, and total commitment to seeing students make progress in their academic work. But he was also feared for his strictness and grimness of approach to teaching. He would stand in front of the class and systematically lecture the students on the essay, paragraph development, unity, cohesion, and coherence. Producing a model essay from an old textbook, he would meticulously show the class how the various elements of rhetoric were realized in the text. On some occasions, he would ask the class to point out the thesis of a passage and to outline the rhetorical constituents of the text. On other occasions, he would ask the class to bring samples of good writing to class for analysis.

His students did a great many grammar exercises. Like many language teachers with no specific training in writing instruction, Dr. Kuma believed that if students could only master the rules of grammar and recognize faulty constructions, they would be able to write good papers. Therefore, he was very fond of error analysis exercises, something most students hated. His favorite was the dangling modifier. "Point out the dangling modifier in this sentence," he would intone, "and say why it is dangling!" Students understandably nicknamed him dangling modifier.

As would be expected, these exercises proved more mystifying than illuminating or liberating to the students. Having done little or no real writing in these writing classes, they missed the opportunity to wrestle with the writing process, to practice generating ideas, drafting, revising, and editing their work. As a result, much of the prodigious effort exerted by both lecturer and student often turned out to be unproductive in real terms, making no positive impact on student writing. Indeed, it might even have produced a negative effect: writing apprehension and resistance to writing. It is no wonder that the college academic community remains stupefied and appalled at the fact that many of their college students write so poorly in spite of the efforts of well meaning, hard working professors like Dr. Kuma.

In a situation where writing is primarily seen as a means for assessing prescribed knowledge rather than the expression of thought, it is not surprising that learners often graduate trapped with all the negative baggage associated with testing. When I was an undergraduate student in Ghana, the school or college exam was the single most important event in the life of the student and the institution. Whether one moved from one level to the next or got the much needed certificate that opened up career opportunities depended almost entirely on success in the two- or three-hour exam taken at designated periods throughout the academic program. The rigid formality with which such exams were conducted sometimes bordered on the ludicrous. At college we took exams in a large room that seated 300 or 400 students in an assembly-line manner. Several proctors policed the room, keeping an eagle eye on us as we agonized over very demanding essay questions. We were told that understanding the questions was part of the examination, and so we could not ask for clarification or use general reference materials such as dictionaries. We nicknamed the examination hall "slaughter house" to convey our sense of the merciless butchering of defenseless creatures that took place in the name of assessment. Testing anxieties in an exam-driven curriculum invariably carried over to writing apprehension.

It is often argued in defense of the Ghanaian system of banking education that professors need to cover a great amount of disciplinary content required for the maintenance of so-called international standards. The problem is compounded by inadequate staffing, large classes, few and expensive books, and little equipment. Writing is still done mainly with the pen, which means that revising and rewriting drafts are much more laborious and time consuming than is the case with the use of a computer. Even though countries like Ghana spend about 35 percent of their national budget on education, such funding can only go so far. It must be admitted that these are practical postcolonial realities that defy easy solutions. The success of writing programs in elementary schools, high schools, and colleges in the Western world greatly depends on adequate funding, availability of qualified personnel, and other supportive resources.

In many cases professors choose the easy way out of these problems by simply dictating lecture notes in class. Certainly this is an unsatisfactory solution. However, what is important is for us to recognize the nature of the solution chosen by these professors: the fact that it is related not only to the dire economic exigencies of the state but also the prevailing colonial mentality that sees the school primarily as the disseminator of information. The failure of the system to create opportunities for interactive learning in an engaged manner naturally results in the reproduction of reticence among students in classroom situations. More specifically, I would suggest that the habit of this intellectual inertia encouraged by this system, when carried on long enough, creates a distaste for writing as a means of holding, interrogating, and exploring ideas independently and analytically.

What is surprising though is the amount of acceptable writing that the system has produced. Thousands of scholars, creative writers—mainly in the academia—as well as professionals in various fields who command good writing come out of this rather restrictive system. One can boast of a decent collection of academic treatises, reports, and creative and journalistic writing comparable in standard to some of the best writing in the noncolonized world. Still, the system I am describing is too exclusionary; its impact on the writing experiences of the ordinary student is one of deep-seated apprehension.

We may blame this system not only for the mediocre writing of most students, but also the prevalence of plagiarism among resisting writers. In my experience both as student and instructor in Ghana, I have observed that many students do not cite sources to lend support to their own ideas or to serve as a basis for contrast and analysis. Often they reproduce material from sources, making them part of their own text without acknowledgment because such material looks good and is well expressed, and so saves them the trouble of thinking through their own arguments carefully.

Pennycook and others have attributed this practice to the influence of societal norms that venerate and valorize traditional wisdom as superior knowledge that must be received unquestioningly. For instance, Pennycook, in a study of a group of Chinese students, noted that they borrowed freely from printed material in circulation that they regarded as the common heritage of the community from which anyone could draw.

By contrast, for the category of the postcolonial students I am writing about, it seems to me that plagiarism might be seen as an act of pure dishonesty, which the perpetrator hopes no one finds out about. It arises from a frantic attempt to avoid the messiness and agonies of the writing process and a characteristic inability to engage in sustained analysis for reasons already noted in the school system. As an instructor in Ghana, I have had, on several occasions, to confront my students with evidence of plagiarizing some text that I happened to recognize. It could get as bad as students lifting chunks of passages from published material into their own writing without any acknowledgment. Sometimes plagiarism was thinly disguised in the form of students' rewording sections of a sentence or a passage that they had borrowed from another source without presenting it as a paraphrase of the original. Often, the students insisted that it was their own work until confronted with the evidence of sources.

In a sense this problem was one of not knowing how to make acceptable use of other writers' ideas in one's own work. It takes a program of interactive reading and writing—in which students are being encouraged to come up with ideas of their own, to think and rethink them, and to set them in relation to ideas from other people—to develop a frame of mind conducive to analytical discourse. Where such deliberate nurturance is lacking, where student responses can be only right or wrong, the intellectual spirit that writing calls for can hardly blossom.

Besides faulty perceptions of knowledge, postcolonial modes of interpersonal relations present yet another kind of difficulty for writing development. The quality of writing relationships is a vital factor in learning to write. Lad Tobin makes this point very succinctly: "writing students succeed when teachers establish productive relationships with—and between —their students. It makes sense, then, for a writing teacher to focus as much on questions of authority and resistance as on invention heuristics and revision strategies, as much on competition and cooperation as on grammar and usage" (6). The deployment of power relations within the postcolonial school system is very disturbing. Students relate to their instructors on the basis of fear and formal respectability. They habitually cower in submission to such an extent that they are never relaxed in the presence of a teacher, nor are they capable of openly questioning their propositions. When we write papers, we do so with the fearsome image of instructors looming in our minds, demanding to be satisfied on their terms.

The instructor's power reflects configurations of power that had structured relations between the colonizer and the colonized in the past, and continues to organize relationships within the postcolonial state. Thus, a nonegalitarian power arrangement can be seen in every aspect of social organization, in the prisons, in government, in business, in school, and at home.

In *Transforming Power: Domination, Empowerment and Education*, Seth Kreisberg offers a very useful conceptualization of power. Kreisberg takes ideas espoused by Starhawk and adapts them to his analysis of classroom relationships. He distinguishes three types of power: power over, power within, and power with. "Power over" is exercised by one in domination of another. It is the way of the colonial and postcolonial state, as well as the way prisons and schools tend to be run. By contrast, "power within" describes the state of being when one begins to understand oneself as a powerful being, as an actor, a subject in history. "Power with" is the point at which one is confident of one's power as a writer or a being in the world, and from that position, forms powerful alliances with other people. In the last case, power is shared between individuals who see themselves as powerful beings in their own rights. An instructor who operates from a position of power over is invariably dominating, and the student becomes an appraised, dehumanized being incapable of exercising free thought, expression, or action.

Writing resistance in the sense I have used the term implies writing without power. That is, the resistant writer feels no personal power within to generate original thought, to confidently weigh it against the ideas of others and draw compelling insights and conclusions on the basis of the power within. Having been the object of the educator's action for a long time, resistant writers cannot speak or write from a subject position that reflects inner power. I unconsciously experienced this powerlessness in writing until I entered the American system.

My writing came under fire in graduate school. At the Manoa campus of the University of Hawaii (UHM), I have undergone a protracted process of rebirth as a writer. The defining moment occurred in one of the first classes I took in composition theory and pedagogy. I came to the class armed with my Walkman recorder ready to tape the lecture. I had assumed, as was the case in Ghana, that the professor would deliver a lecture, refer us to readings, and then assign a writing task sometime later in the semester.

The professor asked us to free write for five minutes about our expectations for the class. As soon as we finished he asked us to do a further ten minutes of free writing, exploring our thoughts about current writing practices in the schools. I felt tense and perplexed. I propped my arm in a writing posture, fidgeted for a while, but wrote nothing. "What is this man about?" I thought. "Won't he give the class a lecture? Will he collect this writing exercise? How will my piece compare with those of my peers? Will this exercise prematurely betray my weaknesses to the professor and to the rest of the class even before I have time to gather my wits and prove my mettle?"

Instead of focusing on generating ideas, I was allowing my background to get in the way of the creative process. In the past, my writing was essentially a test of my knowledge of specific and factual information. How much one knew or was supposed to know was a big issue both for one's image in the class and the prestige of one's family. This was my first class in this new field, and I was sure I did not know anything to write about. The tension ebbed considerably when the professor did not collect our free writing. Later I got to know that free writing was going to be a common feature of our classes and should be seen as an exploratory tool for stimulating thought and critical reflection.

It was not only exploratory writing I was having initial difficulties with. My essays also presented a different kind of demand I found rather stressful. I was confronted with the fifteen-to-twenty-page seminar paper in which my own carefully thought out position on significant issues in my field was critical. Obviously, this was the sort of stimulation I needed in college for my development as a writer, but when it did come I was not ready.

Some of my professors raised concerns about my writing: "What do you think about economy in writing?" "Has anyone talked to you about the slimness of your writing?" "I need to hear more about————." "You move too fast from idea to conclusion." "This is a good deal of history and description, but where is your own contribution?" These are familiar questions about the writing of non-native students in general. Like many of them, I was an impatient writer turning in drafts that could have been improved by close revision for rhetorical effectiveness, detail, and analysis.

As I reflect on this experience two years later, I understand very well what Mina Shaughnessy means when she refers to her nonmainstream students as "strangers in academia" (3). A section of Shaughnessy's students at City College presented a dilemma to the authorities in that, although they were in many respects good college material, they were rather poor writers. Since college work relies substantially on writing, such students were considered out of place by many of their professors. Even though I have studied English since I was six, endured seven years of college writing, and have served as an English instructor for several years back home, I have felt very much disoriented in graduate school, displaced like a fish out of water, like a stranger in academia.

In accounting for the writing resistance of immigrants, Helen Fox emphasizes the unwillingness of such students to adopt Anglo-American writing style for cultural reasons: "whether it is angry or polite, or depressed or panicked, or blithe or uncaring, or devious, or continually confused, resistance to academic writing has one primary function for a writer with different cultural assumptions—to avoid the inevitable changes in personality, outlook, and world view that go hand *in* hand with the new writing style (82)." This may well be the case with, say, Japanese, Chinese, or Russian students who have a long-standing tradition of writing in their own cultures. By contrast, many African, Maori, or Native American cultures are essentially oral in nature. Writing was introduced as part of an imperial process, so the resistance we see among such students must be understood within this specificity. The distinction between oral and written traditions is important because present-day concerns for multiculturalism can mislead us to negotiate with cultural elements that may not be responsible for the writing problem that we are dealing with.

Many postcolonial students, then, have been the victims of misguided literacy practices that arose from their colonial past and still remain in place long after independence. Such practices have ingrained in them bad writing habits and a general apprehension for writing that cannot be reasoned away. Their mind-sets developed over a long period and cannot be changed as easily as one discards worn-out clothes.

If this is the germ of the problem, then the way out might seem deceptively simple. Emphasize process, not product. Give students sufficient time to wrestle with the conditions of a writing assignment, intervening perceptively at appropriate stages in the process until an acceptable product emerges. Make use of peer response and evaluation, journals, and all the latest trappings of process and interactionist models of pedagogy. Although these approaches are certainly more attractive than the earlier pedagogical models prevalent in the postcolonial countries, they may not in and of themselves prove transformative and empowering to the postcolonial student writer. One ready explanation for this situation is that the process/interactionist approaches have been developed and work best in free, open, and democratic societies that cherish notions of individuality, choice, and respect for ideas. By contrast, many postcolonial student writers come from less open societies built on authoritarian, traditional, and postcolonial relationships. It takes quite some time for them to break free both in their thinking and self-expression.

Furthermore, one might ask: How free is free writing? Without a certain minimum standard of linguistic competence in the second language how much free exploration of ideas can we expect as a preliminary drafting activity? When Peter Elbow asserts that the cognitive acts of creating and criticizing can be greatly eased and enhanced by pursuing them one at a time within the recursive processes of free writing, drafting, and revising, such a proposition can work only for postcolonial learners if they have a certain minimum proficiency in English. Where such learners are battling with words to express their ideas and feelings, composing could be a much greater challenge than expressivist pedagogical philosophies seem to indicate.

Some would suggest that these students can first write their drafts in pidgin or their first languages before converting them into standard English as a deliberate revision process. It must be remembered, however, that pidgin and the vernaculars have not been part of the writing tradition in most postcolonial countries. It may seem a strange thing to say that though I speak my first language more fluently than English, I write English much better than I do my first language, because writing in my mother tongue has never been an important part of my schooling experience. Therefore, as a matter of habit and practical necessity, English remains the medium of writing struggles for postcolonial writers like me.

It is crucial to understand that when postcolonial learners exhibit shallowness in their writing, it is not because they are incapable of being expressive, interesting, deep thinkers. Their struggle with writing arises out of a sincere desire to communicate. When they fare badly, it is partly because of their history, a history of miseducation, of misguided pedagogy, of domination and submission.

If my own path to self-invention is anything to go by, the first thing that international students with postcolonial backgrounds need to do about their writing is to understand and develop a sound writing process. This must happen before we can work on improving the content of our writing. It makes a lot of sense for me to know that writing is a generative process, that the more I write, the more ideas I can come up with and the better my writing gets. It is also good to know that I can generate a mess, ignoring mechanics, organization, and style for a moment, and then deliberately reorganize and rewrite with an eye on saying something significant. It is a good feeling to know that I am important and what I say as an individual matters, and so it is worth the extra effort to think deeply about what I do say, and not to short-circuit the thinking process by merely reproducing what others have said.

This process of self-transformation is assisted tremendously by readings that enable me to set up a frame for interrogating my past and to imagine possibilities for reinventing the present. Writers and critical pedagogues like Paulo Freire, Donaldo Macedo, bell hooks, and Henry Giroux have been particularly challenging and persuasive in helping me to see things from a different perspective. For example, Freire's critique of banking education as a distortion of the intellectual vocation, his ideas on critical reflection and dialogic action, and reading the word in relation to the world are profoundly life-changing readings for me. I can identify intimately with them because they speak so compellingly to my postcolonial background. Similarly, I enjoy bell hooks's *engaged pedagogy*, with its emphasis on wholeness and experiencing the pleasure of being on the cutting edge of mind-altering ideas.

Beyond the readings, I find writing about myself even more liberating. I took a class called The Art of the Personal Essay, which featured readings from Montaigne to Richard Rodriguez. Though the readings were enjoyable, what helped me most was the writing workshop we took part in. For several weeks I worked on a full-length essay, combining personal details with the familiar subject of homelessness. At first I was uncomfortable with the idea of self-disclosure, coming from a background where competition rather than collaboration was the norm. I was, however, reassured by the sensitivity, sincerity, and openness of both the instructor and my peers, whose feedback was very supportive. Most liberating of all is the writing of a personal literacy narrative, such as this one. Reflecting freely on one's development as a writer is a therapeutic experience for reinventing oneself that every postcolonial student should try. While I am still far from obtaining the goals I have set for myself as a writer, I am definitely more in control of my writing intellectually and psychologically.

I must admit that the total situation in the postcolonial world is more complex than this essay has space to describe. Globalization has produced multiple tensions, impulses, and influences. The emergence of counterhegemonic formations such as activists for women and children's rights, students' groups, and labor unions means that we are constantly engaged in a struggle to redefine power relations and expectations in various communities. In addition, the influence of print and electronic media emanating from free and democratic societies cannot be underestimated. Every now and then, the activities of insurgents spill over and there is a breakthrough in one small sphere of life. While nothing short of total transformation of society can ensure liberatory practice of education in postcolonial nations, the first significant step can be taken by the two most important individuals in the educational scenario, the teacher and the student, in the privacy of their classroom space.

Jaime Armin Mejía

ARTS OF THE U.S.-MEXICO
CONTACT ZONE

[A] primary goal of our efforts as workers in English studies is to prepare young people to be better participants in democratic economic, political, and cultural arrangements. Our work is to fathom possibilities for language and living heretofore unimagined.

James Berlin

[T]heories about the nature of writing, writing development, the uses of writing, and the process of writing, cannot be said to correspond to external reality broadly if these theories do not account for the experiences of over half of the world's population, the half that can be placed along the bilingual continuum and classified as fluent and functional in two languages.

Guadalupe Valdés

Women across generations didn't go for the word "feminism" because it was a white middle- to upper-class movement. Feminism never quite worked for Chicanas because our struggles were very different in the United States (from those of Anglos). Feminism to me is inclusive of men and women because as much as women have suffered, our men have suffered.

Ana Castillo

The words of Berlin and Valdés highlight both the strengths and weaknesses of composition studies in a postcolonial world. Valdés explicitly challenges all those who look to composition studies as a way to "fathom possibilities for language and living" to realize the extent to which such possibilities have been imagined for over "half the world's people." Along the U.S. side of the U.S.-Mexico border, for instance, the majority of people are Americans of Mexican descent, and most are fluent and functional in English and Spanish, yet their experiences have not been systematically addressed by rhetoric and composition scholars. These bilinguals, though, are not, as many argue, living in a postcolonial world, as the external reality of these people's lives instead reflects what is better described as a form of internal colonialism along the U.S.-Mexico borderlands.

The term "postcolonialism" suggests in part that the colonial powers have left the colonized region and that the formerly colonized have gained some semblance of autonomy. But in the Southwest, the colonizers have not left; they remain and in many parts continue their colonial domination, especially through exclusionary practices in educational institutions like English departments. The reasons whole cohorts of ethnic minority students, like bilinguals in the Southwest, have been left "unimagined" by rhetoric and composition studies are many. But particularly unimagined among this cohort have been Chicanas and the roles they play within clustered extended families of borderland bilinguals, as their roles have arguably worked to create households where collaboration is fostered, a collaboration which, I argue, can extend to the writing practices of bilinguals.

Some of the reasons why borderland bilinguals have been left unimagined shall be examined to show the dynamics of exclusion that have historically existed for ethnic minority groups within this U.S.-Mexico contact zone. Also, reasons shall be shown for how certain groups, like Texas Mexicans, have responded and can respond in a transcultural manner to these exclusionary practices in schools and society. Evidence shall be introduced to show that if given the right culturally-based textual materials to analyze, bilingual and bicultural students from the U.S.-Mexico borderlands can reverse the processes of exclusion many of them have been subjected to in their schooling. People of Mexican origin in the Southwest have a great deal to teach us if we only begin to imagine ourselves living together in an increasingly smaller world, which is making exclusionary practices all the more absurd as technology works to connect people around the globe.

James Berlin reveals how English departments contribute to such exclusion through their institutional practices:

> Thus, the English department both serves an important exclusionary function and mystifies the role it plays in precluding reading and writing practices that might address inequalities in the existing social order. In other words, by excluding reading practices that might discover the political unconscious of literary texts and by refusing to take seriously the production and interpretation of rhetorical texts that address political matters, English studies has served as a powerful conservative force, all the while insisting on its transcendence of the political. The enforcement of this invidious division of the literary from the non-literary has served to entitle those already entitled and to disempower the disempowered, doing so in the name of the sacred literary text. (*Rhetorics* 15)

As Berlin (as well as Susan Miller in *Textual Carnivals* and Lester Faigley in *Fragments of Rationality*) shows, the field of rhetoric and composition, which has focused on teaching non-literary writing, has been placed in the position of a carnivalesque side-show, marginalized from the center: literary studies. And while institutional histories like those of Berlin, Miller, and Faigley help us understand the dynamic that led to marginalizing rhetoric and composition, they fail to show how this dynamic has further left studies of bilingual and bicultural ethnic minority students even farther from the center of English studies.

Other related institutional reasons also account for the exclusion of educational practices which might not have kept studies of bilingual and bicultural students, such as those of Texas Mexicans, so marginalized. One reason involves the national canonization of U.S. literature. In recent years, postmodern theories have forced the center of English studies—literary studies—to reexamine its process of canonizing Anglo-centered literary texts. In this atmosphere, the literature and oral traditions of people of color in the United States have experienced what seems to be an unprecedented revival. Since the advent of the canon wars, however, efforts to maneuver Chicano and Chicana literary texts to the center of English literary studies have not succeeded. This failure to achieve centrality is surely related to the fact that persistent discrimination has kept people of Mexican descent from obtaining the material and educational circumstances necessary for literary production and distribution. Even in the so-called "multicultural readers," the canonization process is at work, as Sandra Jamieson notes: "although the collections of essays used to teach composition appear to have been radically transformed in recent years, the changes are largely superficial because the same mainstream / margin model is operative in them as in earlier texts. While appearing (and in some cases claiming) to represent a resistance to hegemonic culture with its traditional mainstream / margin structure, many of the current wave of "multicultural" projects and texts in fact simply replicate that structure" (2).

Sandra Jamieson states that the "new inclusions remain consistent with the older model in which white men are the producers of academic or 'correct' writings in the terms set out by the text, while white women write less-academic prose about women and 'women's issues,' and people of color write, largely from a child's perspective, narratives about racial victimization" (6). The examples Jamieson cites from the ethnic selections "still demand that the reader adopt a white, middle-class reading-subject position, which is also still generally male" (16). She finds not "one piece by a writer identified as an African American or a Latino / Latina which does not deal in some way with racist victimization" (20). She adds that the subject of these particular ethnic texts is always a child who is "frequently a victim of language or linguistic complexities [. . .] and is thus powerless to prevent the problem, protect him or herself against it, or even, for that matter, understand it with the comprehension of an adult" (20). The use of textbook readers like the ones Jamieson describes illustrates yet another reason why specific cohorts of ethnic minority students with bilingual and bicultural backgrounds have been excluded from studies in the field of rhetoric and composition.

One could search in vain to find significant studies in rhetoric and composition journals discussing particular writing problems and rhetorical situations facing bilinguals, such as Texas Mexican college students. One could expand research to include all Mexican Americans, or more broadly still, Hispanic students, yet one would find little if anything of any significance or relevance to teaching bilingual and bicultural critical literacy. Comparatively, scholarly attention given to African Americans in rhetoric and composition studies, as well as in all of English studies, dwarfs studies about Hispanic American groups and their use of two languages. Some studies in rhetoric and composition today examine rhetorical aspects of African American texts such as slave narratives and African American oral traditions such as sermons, playing the dozens, or rap, to name just a few. Yet no comparable studies exist for Mexican American texts or oral traditions, leading many to believe they don't exist.

The truth, of course, is that corridos (ballads), dichos (proverbial sayings), and tallas (jokes) do exist; yet rhetorical studies of these texts remain to be conducted. In *Uncle Remus con chile*, for instance, Américo Paredes presents a talla he collected in the early 1960s and labeled "Juan Huarache:"

> Have you heard about the fellow whose name was Juan Guerra Hinojosa? Y le decían El Huarache. He tried and tried to figure out how he could keep the pelusa from calling him El Huarache. He had read in the papers about so-and-so going to court and changing his name, so he decided he'd become an American and change his name. Then people wouldn't be calling him El Huarache anymore.
>
> So he went down there to change his name. "Vamos a ver," dijo, "vamos a cambiarme el nombre. Juan. Pos es John. Guerra. Pos es War. John War. Y con Hinojosa, ¿pos cómo le hacemos?" No encontró palabra en inglés. "Pos ponle ahi la 'H' [hache] nomás. A ver cómo sale [. . .] John War Hache. ¡Ah, chingados!"
>
> En inglés o en español, como quiera salió huarache. (123)

This talla (and many others like it in Paredes's work) contains the kind of word play rich in inter-cultural and inter-linguistic rhetorical complexity. But again, these and other forms of oral traditions remain to be analyzed. And as Paredes consciously chose not to do, translations of either language would defeat the purpose of this joke entirely. In fact, it seems likely that had texts like this one been introduced systematically in composition classrooms since the sixties, students' abilities to manipulate these two languages by encoding and decoding both would have been enhanced considerably.

In the past, however, teaching writing to first-year college students in the Southwest, as well as everywhere else in the United States, usually involved English-only texts—usually literary texts—to which students were expected to respond, usually in some formulaic manner. These texts, however, continue to be ones that do not contain bilingual or bicultural codes that Southwestern minority students could identify with (encoding) or that could challenge their expanded linguistically-based analytical powers (decoding). Instead, readings in English composition and literature classes, as Sandra Jamieson suggests, have traditionally been used to shape particular kinds of subject formations and reading practices that have neglected the broader, culturally-based experiences of bilingual ethnic minority students.

In a small but important study of bilingual ethnic minority students, Valdés underscores the importance of considering the backgrounds of students:

> Writing researchers must be aware that any research done on writing alone that is not directly grounded in the academic and personal experiences of the minority students in question will contribute little to our understanding of the actual value of writing for these students, of the other factors that influence their academic success, and of the approaches that could be taken to break long-established patterns and expectations. Interesting as the theoretical questions relating to the writing of these students may be, educational researchers must not lose sight of the fact that practical solutions are desperately needed. (119)

As Valdés's work makes clear, the need for studies for and about Southwestern bilingual minority students continues to be one of the most urgently-needed theoretical and practical fields of inquiry facing rhetoric and composition studies. Understanding the backgrounds of bilinguals therefore requires studying the causes historically underlying bilingualism. She states:

> [W]e know that bilingualism is a widespread natural phenomenon that has come about in different places for different reasons and that factors such as movement of peoples, military conquest, and the expansion of religious practices have resulted in the acquisition of a second language (L2) by certain groups of people. We also know that, depending on the particular characteristics of the language contract [contact— sic], individuals who acquire another language in addition to their first and who use both languages in the course of their everyday lives vary in their productive and receptive abilities in both languages. (91)

Each of the factors creating bilingualism in peoples—migration, colonialism, and religion—applies to and historically accounts for the linguistic circumstances creating Southwestern bilinguals. Despite Valdés's warning, composition studies has failed to address the abilities and needs of minority students with bilingual and bicultural backgrounds.

Throughout the Southwest, the factors creating bilingualism have varied considerably. As the Southwest changed colonial hands from the Spanish to the Mexicans and then to Anglo Americans, Southwestern Mexican groups responded differently because of their varied circumstances. As Paredes explains, after the infamous 1848 "Treaty of Guadalupe Hidalgo settled the conflict over territory between Mexico and the United States, officially at least":

> The immediate change in customs demanded of *tejanos, californios,* and *nuevomejicanos* was from regional subcultures of Mexico to occupied territories within the United States.
>
> Such was not the case with the people of the Lower Rio Grande. A very well defined geographic feature—the Rio Grande itself—became the international line. And it was a line that cut right through the middle of what had once been Nuevo Santander. The river, once a focus of regional life, became a symbol of separation. [. . .] More to our point was the general flouting of customs and immigration laws, not so much as a form of social and ethnic protest but as part of the way of life. ("Problem" 25–26)

The exception Paredes makes of the Lower Rio Grande region is important because residents of this region experienced the most violent intercultural conflicts in the entire Southwest. As David Montejano notes, "It was a conflict between two distinct societies; it was, in the portrayal given by Jovita González in 1930, a 'struggle between the New World and the Old' that at the same time was a 'race struggle'" (104). Despite the "race struggle," many residents of the Lower Rio Grande border region before and after the Treaty of Guadalupe Hidalgo, refused to assimilate, unlike many of their counterparts throughout the Southwest. The exceptional situation of Texas Mexican residents from the Lower Rio Grande border region shall be examined later, as their "flouting of customs and immigration laws" represents a tradition of naturalized resistance often overlooked.

In Texas, the negative educational and societal consequences of the "racial struggle" for Texas Mexicans later in the 20th century were widesweeping: "Anglo and Mexican children, for example, understood that separate schooling meant separation of superior and inferior. This meaning was taught to them in countless lessons—the Mexican school was physically inferior, Mexican children were issued textbooks discarded by Anglo children, Mexican teams were not admitted to county athletic leagues, Mexican girls could not enter beauty contests, and so on" (Montejano 230).

The legacy of racial discrimination against Texas Mexicans has been challenged, of course, by efforts at school and curricular reform, aimed at focusing on issues concerning the linguistic and cultural backgrounds of Texas Mexican students from elementary to high school. For instance, Guadalupe San Miguel, Jr. documents how a language arts curriculum for elementary school was developed for Texas Mexicans in 1925 in San Antonio, Texas by Elma A. Neal, a curriculum specialist. She developed a three-unit series wherein "The lessons are developed with the idea of keeping very close to the natural activities and interests of the normal child. [. . .] In all instances, [. . .] natural situations for the teaching of English are created, the encyclopedic selection of facts, for the sake of teaching English, avoided. [. . .] Our immediate purpose is to furnish the non-English speaking child with a vocabulary he may use in expressing his needs in the community in which he lives" (42).

As this series of language lessons suggests, the pedagogical ideas inherent in these lessons all go back to the students' community environment, as well as to the "natural" activities, interests, and situations of Texas Mexicans. By using community-based activities, interests, and situations as part of an English language arts curriculum, this pedagogical scheme clearly aimed to incorporate Texas Mexican cultural contexts for developing English language arts (literacy) skills. The motivation for developing this innovative language arts curriculum was to increase the number of Texas Mexicans matriculating into the secondary grades, something they were failing to do, compared to their Texas Anglo counterparts.

As San Miguel documents, many early Texas Mexican educators echoed Elma Neal's early pedagogical approach and her concern for the education of non-English speaking and writing Texas Mexican children. Such a series of language arts lessons could have arguably gone a long way toward positively developing the literacy skills of Texas Mexicans. But since at least 1925, in fact, these early pedagogical innovations were all but ignored. Because of this neglect, the early part of this century saw many of the innovative curricular changes disappear, as two educational developments ensued that left Texas Mexican students marginalized by exclusionary practices meant to encourage poor school performance:

> In general, state school officials supported and developed an English-only instructional program to rapidly assimilate language minority children into the established cultural norm. This was reflected in the

extension of the existing English-only policy into the nonpublic schools and into the classroom. The purpose of these actions was to Americanize the Mexican student population—that is, to imbue the non-English child with the habits, customs, and ideals for which America stood and particularly to teach her or him the English language.

The assimilationist curricular practices were in contrast to the exclusionary ones promoted by local school administrators. The exclusionist behavior of public school officials can be most readily seen in their establishment of segregated facilities, in their support of inequalities in the provision of public schools, and in their discriminatory and unequal treatment of Texas Mexican school children. (San Miguel 58)

The practices aimed at assimilating Texas Mexican students were intended to have the effect of constructing students' identities in particular modernist ways. As Edward Said has shown, the "political origins of modern English studies" have been "located [. . .] to a significant extent in the system of colonial education imposed on natives of nineteenth-century India" (42). Said shows that "what has conventionally been thought of as a discipline created by and for British youth was first created by early nineteenth-century colonial administrators for the ideological pacification and re-formation of a potentially rebellious Indian population, and then imported into England for a very different but related use there" (*Culture* 42). The English-only instructional programs imposed on Texas Mexican students throughout the 20th century have clearly been intended to have the same effect—the ideological pacification and re-formation of Texas Mexicans. Today, in what should be considered a more enlightened educational time, language arts pedagogies continue to be predominantly English-only. The state of segregation and egregiously under-funded public school districts and universities where Texas Mexicans find themselves also indicates that Texas educational programs have a very short-sighted view of the roles Texas Mexicans will play in that state's future.

Since the sixties, people of Mexican descent have been concentrated in the Southwest, but they especially find themselves in urban areas. The United States has undergone a postmodern shift, where the ethnic integrity of Hispanic minority groups has been dispersed by a host of socioeconomic forces. Contributing to this dispersal has been the nation's transition from a "Fordist" to a "post-Fordist" economy. As Faigley states, "By the 1960s the Fordist model began to be eroded by transnational competition and by more diversified and volatile markets" (11). But prior to the 1990s and before the post-Fordist North American Free Trade Agreement (NAFTA) took effect, the Southwest had already been affected by diversified and volatile market changes which have since swept the U.S. economy. The economies of Mexico and the United States had to undergo tremendous adjustments in the 1980s when Mexican peso devaluations rocked markets on both sides of the border.

As Faigley points out: "Accompanying the transition from Fordism to post-Fordism has been the breakup of mass culture as it was constituted in the United States throughout much of this century into a pluralization of tastes, styles, and practices" (12). In the Southwest, the commercialization of Mexican-origin cultural practices rapidly expanded to include a booming music industry, Mexican food and restaurants, and extensive bilingual advertising campaigns for consumer products. A significant consequence of this postmodern economic and cultural change is the fragmentation of the human subject. In this predominantly urbanized situation, ethnic young people face massive challenges to identity construction. According to Faigley and others, the postmodern condition "rejects the primacy of consciousness and instead has consciousness originating in language, thus arguing that the subject is an effect rather than a cause of discourse. Because the subject is the locus of overlapping and competing discourses, it is a temporary stitching together of a series of often contradictory subject positions" (9).

From a modernist perspective, the primacy of consciousness affords the existence of a stable, coherent self, an essentialist self, as posited by Enlightenment foundational principles. But according to Faigley, such a consciousness is no longer possible because the postmodern subject is constructed by overlapping and competing discourses to form contradictory and often incoherent subject positions. This postmodern principle of identity construction is, and has been, problematic because it cuts in at least two ways. First, the idea that ethnic minorities can be assimilated to be English-only is not possible. But the idea that ethnic minorities can be led to be clearly Other in a postmodern world is also arguably untenable, a notion that obviously undercuts the integrity underlying any ethnic identity.

Moreover, as postmodern changes in identity construction and the economy transform the socioeconomic and cultural lives of ethnic minorities in the Southwest, the role English departments play in teaching critical literacy to ethnic minorities is becoming more complex. Ethnic minority students have not been exposed to readings featuring their cultural backgrounds or histories, but as Jamieson has shown, efforts to introduce multicultural readings into textbooks remain problematic. More problematic still, however, is the question of how alternative readings would be received by students who have been subjected to the forces operating under postmodern and post-Fordist economic conditions. If previous readings "demand that the reader adopt a white, middle-class reading-subject position, which is also still male," alternative readings might force the same kind of demand in identity construction, albeit a different one, on ethnic minority students who may not construct their identities ethnically. The binary set up (either assimilated or Other) thus seems even more problematic when we consider how complex identity construction always is.

Shirley Brice Heath and Milbrey W. McLaughlin inform us that the young people (among them Latinos) in their studies of youth organizations in inner cities did not self-identify with any particular ethnic group, even though many originate from backgrounds where one would have expected such self-identification. As they state: "*Ethnicity* seemed, from the youth perspective, to be more often a label assigned to them by outsiders than an indication of their real sense of self. Many young people told us repeatedly, 'Ethnicity ain't what it's really all about.' To them, ethnic labels could mean something only later on; achieving a sense of belonging and of knowing that they could do something and be someone in the eyes of others had to come first. Ethnicity came to carry import only as it functioned within a host of embedded identities that could get a young person somewhere in the immediate community" ("Introduction" 6). More problematic still, Heath and McLaughlin state that: "[p]olicymakers, educators, and youth workers often think first of strong ethnic identification as something young people need and may even demand. Yet the young people's sense of salience of their own ethnic membership in their daily lives is likely to be either conditional or latent. The voices of urban youth [. . .] contend that their embedded identities, or multilayered self-conceptions, represent far more than simple labels of ethnic or racial membership" (7). Young people such as these are on college campuses nationwide. But according to Heath and McLaughlin, many of these youths originate from families and communities which have suffered "from all or some of the blows of late 20th-century urban life: decaying housing, drug and alcohol abuse, extreme swings of poverty, high rates of crime and violence, and educational neglect" (7). Their circumstances thus place these youths in situations where the construction of identity is at best a precarious and unstable process.

At the other end of the cultural and economic spectrum of ethnic youth, though, Heath and McLaughlin ironically state that:

> In the 1980s, the children of [. . .] advantaged families [of color] found they had to give themselves labels driven by politics and institutional decisions. [. . .] If professional socioeconomic standing had gained them acceptance in predominantly white institutions, they were often likely to have been effectively isolated from having to think of themselves as "minorities." It was not at all uncommon for students whose families of Latino origins had lived for several decades with a mainstream middle-class "American" identity in a midwestern town—speaking English, participating in local social and cultural organizations, and eating hamburgers and roast beef—to be pressured to self-identify as "culturally different" only on college campuses or as "ethnic minorities" for other purposes. ("Ethnicity" 17–18)

Heath and McLaughlin's studies of inner-city youth show how essentialist identity construction has been problematized and is apparently being rejected by some ethnic youth. The dilemma this poses for English departments in terms of how to go about teaching critical literacy to young people such as these, however, is problematized by other developments within English studies.

Wlad Godzich notes that since the sixties American students have shown a decline in the median scores on the verbal part of the standardized tests given for college admission. These scores, he says, represent an "index of the level of academic preparation and achievement of the university entry-level population" (3). University English departments responded to the decline in test scores by arguing that since students do not possess the necessary verbal skills, "they must receive remedial training in the universities if they are to be successful in their field of study, whether it be in the business, engineering, pre-medicine, pre-law, social sciences, or humanities areas of the university curriculum" (3). Many English department faculty, however, blamed low verbal skills on the "vast expansion of higher education to racial and ethnic minorities originating from poor neighborhoods or localities where there was inadequate elementary and secondary schooling, as a result of either insufficient financial means or discrimination" (3).

The decline in test scores led to the establishment and expansion of programs in composition, rhetoric, or writing, and, as a consequence, the regular English (literature) curriculum has stagnated, often with "an outright reduction of the money allocated to it" (4). Godzich adds:

> The professional schools that are part of American universities (schools of engineering, business, medicine, law, forestry, agriculture, hotel management, and so forth), which were the beneficiaries of a major student enrollment shift away from the humanities and the social sciences as a result of the "New Vocationalism" of the seventies and early eighties, have played a determining role in this situation: what they want are students who can write in *their* fields, and thus, not surprisingly, the writing programs have set up different tracks for students on the basis of their future vocational orientation: writing for business, for law, for science, for medicine, for technology, and so on. (4–5)

Significantly, however, "in this process, any pretense of addressing the needs of so-called disadvantaged student populations has quietly evaporated" (5). So what has happened to addressing these needs?

Thoroughly questioned by postmodern theories of identity construction, the modernist process of assimilation the dominant group has imposed on ethnic minorities for decades ironically no longer holds as it was originally intended to under a Fordist economy. But at the same time, the autonomy of marginalized ethnic groups has apparently been dispersed by post-Fordist, transnational economic forces. And a principal agent of identity construction in universities—English departments—has also been subjected to the same post-Fordist economic forces as driven by the "New Vocationalism" to create yet another form of exclusion.

Having appreciated these changes, one thing remains clear: The need to develop critical literacy among bilingual and bicultural ethnic minority students, as Godzich and Valdés note, still remains to be met—and studied. While extensive and persuasive, studies like Heath and McLaughlin's tell us little about how young Latino students are educated to encode and decode discourses. The results of these studies, based on ethnographic research, do not present the perspectives of minority youth; instead, what we see are the views of these youth through the lenses of their researchers.

In "The Fourth Vision: Literate Language at Work," Shirley Brice Heath repeats a Socratic parable: "Of what have you told me—the thing you have seen or the other thing through which you have seen it?" (302). She adds: "Without acknowledging before and during our look through the magnifying glass its larger context and the value system we have adopted that forces much of the community to look at only the smallness of reading, we cannot know what we have seen" (304). Invaluable and revealing as Heath and McLaughlin's studies are about inner-city youth, one nevertheless would like to have seen extended views from the ethnic minority youth's own perspectives confirming their multilayered self-conceptions in contact zones. Had we seen such perspectives, our views of how they interpreted their postmodern situations might have been different. And had we had the perspectives of adults living in comparable contact zones, might their views have been comparable to those of the youth in these studies? But such was not the intention of Heath and McLaughlin's studies, and this is where their efforts fall short. Once again, the perspectives of adults of color are absent.

In "Arts of the Contact Zone," Mary Louise Pratt shows how dominated peoples can respond to discourses that dominant groups produce about them; such "autoethnographic" texts, she says, "involve a selective collaboration with/and appropriation of idioms of the metropolis or the conqueror. These are merged or infiltrated to varying degrees with indigenous idioms to create self-representations intended to intervene in metropolitan modes of understanding. Autoethnographic works are often addressed to both metropolitan audiences and the speaker's own community. Their reception is thus highly indeterminate. Such texts often constitute a marginalized group's point of entry into the dominant circuits of print culture" (183–84). Pratt's example of such a text is a long letter written "in a mixture of Quechua and ungrammatical, expressive Spanish" to King Philip III of Spain by Felipe Guaman Poma de Ayala in 1613 (182). Pratt states that Guaman Poma's letter is an autoethnographic text, by which she means a text "in which people undertake to describe themselves in ways that engage with representations others have made of them. Thus if ethnographic texts are those in which European metropolitan subjects represent to themselves their others (usually their conquered others), autoethnographic texts are representations that the so-defined others construct *in response to* or in dialogue with those texts" (183).

Pratt states that Guaman Poma—a conquered subject—used "the conqueror's language to construct a parodic, oppositional representation of the conqueror's own speech" (185) as a strategy for presenting a revisionist account of the Spanish conquest of the Incas. Poma also "mirrors back to the Spanish (in their language, which is alien to him) an image of themselves that they often suppress and will therefore surely recognize" (185).

Because of the autoethnographic nature of Poma's letter, one could argue it represents a postmodern consciousness: the letter is the locus of over-lapping and competing discourses, "a temporary stitching together of a series of often contradictory subject positions" (Faigley 9).

Texts like Guaman Poma's originate in contact zones where transcul-turation occurs, as Pratt suggests, in "processes whereby members of sub-ordinated or marginal groups select and invent from materials transmitted by a dominant or metropolitan culture" (186). She adds that "while subor-dinate peoples do not usually control what emanates from dominant cul-ture, they do determine to varying extents what gets absorbed into their own and what it gets used for" (186–187). More to the point, though, "auto-ethnography, transculturation, critique, collaboration, bilingualism, medi-ation, parody, denunciations, imaginary dialogue, vernacular expression —these are some of the literate arts of the contact zone. Miscomprehen-sion, incomprehension, dead letters, unread masterpieces, absolute hetero-geneity of meaning—these are some of the perils of writing in the contact zone" (189).

The following epistolary excerpt from Rolando Hinojosa's novel, *Mi querido Rafa*, represents a Texas Mexican autoethnographic text in some ways comparable to Guaman Poma's letter. Hinojosa's novel is set in the Lower Rio Grande Valley, where Texas Mexicans always have "flouted" the dominant group's laws and customs. In this letter, the adult tejano protag-onist, Jehú, describes how he is subjected to a racial comment made by an Anglo woman who apparently didn't appreciate the presence of Texas Mexicans at a political barbecue:

> Una buena señora (bolilla, regordete, y algo miope, diría yo) se sentó a mi lado; yo estaba escuchando un cuento algo largo y raído por no decir caduco (¡uco!) que contaba Mrs. Ben Timmens. Por fin acabó su cuento y casi al instante se lanza la recién llegada: *"Well, just how many Mexicans did Noddy invite?"* Eramos cinco en el group y yo 1) el único raza there; and 2) el más cerca a ella. Trataron de callarla pero ésta seguía dale que dale y los demás no sabían qué hacer con ella hasta que divisó a la Powerhouse y allá se fue. Well now, te puedes imaginar en lo que aquellas mujeres se vieron para disculpar o mejorar o deshacer lo que la amigaza había dicho. (15 emphasis mine)

The situation, while fictional, nevertheless can be read as an allegory for the presence of Texas Mexicans and their artifacts in English studies. Held at the white master's Big House, this social function has allowed Texas Mexicans like Jehú to attend. Their presence, however, does not guarantee respect; they must still experience racial slurs. But as Jehú states in the English rendition of this same letter, "I think it's healthy to see & hear this type of shit once in a while; it's both sobering & reassuring to know that all's not well with the world" (Hinojasa, *Dear Rafe* 21).

Indeed, the white woman's affront does not pass without a response from Jehú, which is revealed later in *Mi querido Rafa* by another Anglo woman sitting at their table:

> Did Jehú ever tell you about something that happened at one of the parties at the Big House? It was silly, but you know the Valley . . . I think it was Travis De Young's wife . . . No. It was Loretta; Wig Birnham's wife. . . . Anyway, she either told a Mexican joke, you know one of those Beto and Lupe jokes, or . . . no, it wasn't that either. Oh, I can't remember just now, but it was something anti-mexicano, don't you know . . . Really! I don't know *what* in the hell Loretta Birnham uses for eyes or for common sense. My God! Well, *we* didn't know what to say or do and then she finally just drifted away.
>
> Jehú didn't say a *word* . . . I remember that . . . Oh, yes: he smiled a bit, and he nodded, to himself, and then the next time he spoke, it was in the most broken English imaginable . . . He's terrible, you know. Anyway, I didn't know what to say.
>
> Oh, wait a minute, now. He *hummed;* yes, I remember that. Know what it was? "Texas Our Texas" . . . I hadn't heard that in years. (88)

Mrs. Timmens's recollection of Birnham's racial innuendo and Jehú's response confirms Hinojosa's text as autoethnographic: Jehú's response collaborates with and appropriates idioms from the dominant group, thus mirroring Pratt's description of how such groups can and do respond to racialized situations. Not only does he speak in "the most broken English imaginable" to parody how Anglos stereotype Texas Mexicans, but he also hums and therefore appropriates for ironic effect the state song of Texas, which not coincidentally, contains the following lyrics in its first stanza: "Texas, our Texas! All hail the mighty State! / Texas, our Texas! So wonderful so great! / Boldest and grandest, Withstanding ev'ry test; / O *Empire* wide and glorious, You stand supremely blest" (Marsh and Wright emphasis mine).

Hinojosa's novel contains all the elements which make up a resilient autoethnographic text, skillfully incorporating the literate arts of the U.S.-Mexico contact zone Valley Texas Mexicans have been using since this zone was "conquered." And as Pratt suggests, these arts "all live among us today in the transnationalized metropolis of the United States and are becoming more widely visible, more pressing, and, like Guaman Poma's text, more decipherable to those who once would have ignored them in defense of a stable, centered sense of knowledge and reality" (189). The importance of studying autoethnographic texts like Hinojosa's in English studies, and particularly in rhetoric and composition studies, is indeed pressing, for therein lie answers for developing critical literacy among bilinguals.

In addition to studying autoethnographic texts like Hinojosa's, compositionists can find that another answer for developing the critical literacy of U.S. bilinguals of Mexican descent lies in having them write about their own families. This writing exercise is autoethnographic and provides opportunities for them to understand and better appreciate the cultural wisdom within their own culture(s). I used this exercise to great effect in a special composition class made up mainly of Texas Mexican—Tejano—students and which I shall discuss shortly in more detail. This kind of assignment reverses the self-doubt bilingual students from borderland cultures often have about their ethnic identity, especially in academic settings.

In "Globalization, Civilization Processes, and the Relocation of Languages and Cultures," Walter D. Mignolo refers to the "cultures of scholarship" in his theoretical investigation of the new ways languages have been affected by globalization. His views resonate well with students who are living the legacy of internal colonialism in which their culture's wisdom is not privileged or legitimized: "Cultures of scholarship were precisely what people outside Europe either lacked (like the Aztecs and the Incas) or, if they happened to possess them (like China, India, and the Islamic world), they became an object of study (e.g., the rise of "Orientalism"). Over the five hundred years of Western expansion and the creation of colleges and universities in colonized areas since the beginning of the sixteenth century, this belief became so strong as to make people doubt their own wisdom, when that wisdom was not articulated in Western educational institutions and languages" (46).

Mignolo's study corroborates how Texas Mexicans in South Texas fall into the quandary of doubting their culture's wisdom unless we, as compositionists in English Studies, intervene to reverse this process of self-doubt. In the composition class I recently taught, my purpose was to exact this type of reversal. The students were community college students from South Texas who were being tracked, through the auspices of a federally-funded grant, into my University's School of Health Professions, where they were highly under-represented. As with all my writing assignments, these students were given readings on which to base their essays. These readings consisted of two chapters (chapters 4 and 5) from Carlos G. Vélez-Ibáñez's *Border Visions: Mexican Cultures of the Southwest United States.*

Vélez-Ibáñez's fourth chapter entitled "Living in *Confianza* and Patriarchy: The Cultural Systems of U.S. Mexican Households" examines in considerable detail the structure of clusters of Mexican American extended families in Tucson, Arizona, where Vélez-Ibáñez conducted his autoethnographic field research. Here, Vélez-Ibáñez maintains that "women's cultural transmission, discussion, and articulation roles, which are part and parcel of both major rituals and their food preparation activities, define them as the interpreters, carriers and creators of Mexican culture in the United States and the borderlands" (177). But the most remarkable finding of Vélez-Ibáñez's study about Mexican American clustered extended families is the great role women play in these kin groups, thereby debunking the common stereotypical notion that Mexican American culture operates under some type of nefarious patriarchy: "If anything, Mexican households are mostly in the control of women; expenditures are made jointly; funds of knowledge are divided by gender but distributed in an even-handed manner; most Mexican children are made responsible very early on for each other regardless of gender; and in fact, it is women, especially in the late stage of development, upon whom the entire structure of the household cluster rests or falls in economic and political terms. As will be seen, single Mexican males especially are emotionally dependent upon mother love and support" (147). More importantly, Vélez-Ibáñez states that women in these households are "the primary agents of change and stability," for "[i]n spite of being part of every change in industrial technology and form of organization, of being unsettled and resettled by need and deportation, and of being pushed into an assimilationist perspective regarding language and cultural identity, Hispano/Mexicano households remain vibrant and creative units because of their ability to mobilize relations in time of need and to reinforce relations through ritual" (181). A writing exercise based on this type of reading cannot but bring to the fore the major source of wisdom that has seldom been recognized through the "cultures of scholarship" for borderlands Mexican American students—women.

In his fifth chapter entitled "The Distribution of Sadness: Poverty, Crime, Drugs, Illness, and War," Vélez-Ibáñez states, "From every reputable demographic source available, there is no doubt that the single most important predictor of the [Hispano/Mexicano] population's mental, physical, economic, social, or cultural well-being is the acquisition of a high-quality educational experience" (186). Two points need to be stressed. First, "even though educational attainment may provide the road to economic well-being, it may also create such cultural conflict that it leads to less than successful emotional adaptation. Individuals who are told to erase themselves culturally in order to be 'good Americans' may very well suffer from extreme internal conflicts that do not portend mental well-being" (186). Second, "[c]oupled with endemic low expectations subtly and unsubtly projected by teachers and administrators, who depend on 'normative' national tests for instruction rather than normative expectations for success, the precious talents, creativity, and intelligence of too many Mexican children are wasted and seldom enhanced in poor schools" (186–187). For middle-class households, "the [Americanized] push for achievement, competitiveness, profit, and mobility [. . .] creates a struggle over cultural reference, a conflict over historical and cultural identity, and a resistance against the loss of children to consumptive and self-absorbed attitudes" (138). Vélez-Ibáñez adds, "The Americanization of educational programs of the past and the monocultural Anglo-dominant schooling of the present create an ethnic situation of cultural conflict, self-doubt, and uncritical acceptance of destructive ethnic stereotypes" (180). But working against this Americanized "push," one finds clustered extended families, with women at the very heart of their control.

Given these important studies of Hispano/Mexicano families, my students, working with computers, produced essays wherein they analyzed their own family backgrounds. Initially, they were stumped both by the Vélez-Ibáñez readings and by having to write about their families, the latter being something none of them had ever been asked to do before. But here again, Vélez-Ibáñez offers some reasons why my students might have first been stumped: "Ideologically [students from] such households may also be hypnotized by national cultural prisms that accentuate patriotism and reduce regional cultural history to self-destructive ethnic reference" (180). That is, these students had no handle on which to begin a discussion of the cultural lives of their own families. In order to break my students' writer's block, I suggested they focus on rituals performed by their families around holidays or family-oriented social functions, like weddings and quinceñeras.

Clustered extended families represent an incredibly complex rhetorical subject to analyze and write about. And because these Tejano students have typically never been asked to think about and write an analysis of a subject they're so much a part of, they predictably had a difficult time knowing where to begin. Luckily, one of the ways Vélez-Ibáñez illustrates and breaks down the complex structure of clustered extended families in his study is by describing yearly rituals these families perform around specific dates like Christmas and Easter. One ritual he describes is the complex task of making tamales for Christmas, something very close to the cultural hearts and appetites of my Tejano students.

Vélez-Ibáñez's description of the tamale making shows how women conduct what he calls an "exchange of funds of knowledge" and direct it towards the children, thereby revealing the otherwise unspoken structure of the family:

> During the tamale-making process, "heads are counted": i.e., who has been reciprocal during the year, the reputation of various household heads, statements of the peccadillos of men, and the "state" of various exchanges; and important for the purposes of this discussion, children are apprised of all these conversations. It is not unusual at this time for eighteen to twenty-four children from various households to be running about licking spoons, sticking their fingers in the corn dough, and using tortillas to make burritos from available fillings. Children are exposed to conversations, value judgments, and commentaries, which set up for them a context for evaluation of others and reinforce whatever expectations are articulated. (172–73)

Casting aside individual variations of how tamales are made, Vélez-Ibáñez moreover adds that "most women will judge the degree of how spicy the chili is associated with how 'Americanized' a recipe will be. Thus the older the recipe, the more Mexican and thus will mark how original and legitimate the tamale maker is as well. Therefore, older women prize their recipes but even more so pride themselves on handing down 'un-Americanized' versions to their children" (174). This brief description of the "dense" relationships involved when tamales are made illustrates the rhetorical dynamics inherent in this ritualistic process. His description also demonstrates how social relations shape the ethnic identities of Southwestern borderland Mexican Americans, with women unquestionably always playing major roles throughout.

With this suggested lead, ritual performances unexpectedly became the central topic of my Texas Mexican students' essays about their family backgrounds. The essays were powerful in many ways and corroborated many of Vélez-Ibáñez's findings. In no uncertain terms, the women in almost all the families of my Texas Mexican students play extraordinary roles in maintaining their family's cohesion as an extended family unit. With only one exception, all the students came from Mexican-origin backgrounds. The one exception, a non-traditional white male, nevertheless corroborates what happens to extended families in the United States, when his family, once an extended family, broke up into nuclear family units, completely disrupting what stability and cohesion existed before this breakup.

Another Texas Mexican student, a female whose surname is non-Hispanic, unwittingly described her rejection of her ethnicity and advanced some of the more pernicious stereotypes about Latinos when she chose to separate herself from her extended family. The stereotypes curiously resulted even after having read Vélez-Ibáñez's studies, and her misreading of the roles women play in Mexican extended families is especially noteworthy. She titled her essay "The Life of a Broken and Dysfunctional Family," and I use her words to confirm points Vélez-Ibáñez's study illustrates and which arguably result from her broken family background:

> Mexicans are stereotyped by many clueless people way too much, especially the women, as they suffer from most of the suppression. This is primarily the issue of inferiority and male domination. That realization upset me very much because I am now forced to deal with the suppression issue. It is one that I'd rather not acknowledge. I want to conduct my life in a way that I suffer from social and racial prejudice as little as possible. Being in school has given me the independence to break out of the many stereotypical statistics that many teenage, single mothers have been classified in. My small family is what I live for and hope to be able to take care of for the rest of my life. (HCOP 28)

This student comes from a broken home, as her parents are divorced, with her father being an Anglo and her mother a Texas Mexican, and she became a single parent at 17. Her younger brother lives a punk lifestyle, creating various problems for his divorced mother. By this time, the student had a three-year old son, but her Mexican grandmother stepped in to babysit, something that signals the student's return to relying on her extended family.

This particular female student never collaborated with fellow students when writing her essay, for had she done so, her classmates undoubtedly would have challenged many of the stereotypes she advanced in her essay. Her views also confirm much of what Vélez-Ibáñez notes about the effects of "national stereotypes and educational values, which accentuate individualism and self-serving vertical mobility" (180). He adds that "These [national stereotypes and educational values] deny the cultural efficacy of the population by framing them within derogatory stereotypes," leaving some Mexican Americans, like this student, to believe self-destructive stereotypes and deny the validity and value of their own ethnic culture, despite important studies like Vélez-Ibáñez's (180). This student's family background stands as a significant counter-example to all the other Texas Mexican students' family backgrounds but nevertheless corroborates what can happen when a family loses the support that most Mexican American clustered extended families create for each other.

The support engendered and cultivated in these extended families operates through "funds of knowledge" critical to the maintenance of the families' cohesion among all the nuclear households clustered to form the extended family. As Vélez-Ibáñez states:

> Such funds [of knowledge] are not only reposited within nuclear settings but are also part of the repertoire of information contained within the clusters of households, in which younger generational cohorts learn the substance of the corpus of information and have the opportunity to experiment with it in a variety of settings. They are, in fact, the currency of exchange not only between generations but also between households, and they therefore form part of the "cultural glue" that maintains exchange relations between kin. Such funds are dynamic in content and are altered according to changes in empirical reality, and they may even mitigate the more pernicious effects of household poverty. (163)

Vélez-Ibáñez adds that "a major characteristic in the transmission of funds of knowledge is that multiple household domains provide an opportunity for the child to be part of a zone of comfort that is familiar yet experimental, where error is not punitively dealt with and where self-esteem is not endangered" (166). Within these clusters of households, then, zones of comfort provide opportunities for the transmission of critical funds of knowledge acting as "cultural glue." The currency of exchange for these funds of knowledge is highly collaborative for U.S. Mexican students originating from such families. In my experience, Mexican American border-lands students with this type of family background more frequently engage in collaborative writing workshops when composing their essays. The students without this type of family background are not as eager to engage in writing their essays collaboratively, as was clearly evidenced in my composition class. Indeed, those students who wrote that they didn't originate from or who were not sustained by clustered extended families not only tended to write alone, but they also tended to refuse any outside help.

The insight gained from assigning this essay topic yielded other significant findings that we, as rhetoricians/compositionists, might want to consider as we contemplate creating future essay assignments for borderlands students. To this end, consider three related points Walter D. Mignolo makes about the effect of globalization on languages:

1. [T]he question is not so much the number of speakers as it is the hegemonic power of colonial languages in the domain of knowledge, intellectual production, and cultures of scholarship. In the domain of literature, for instance, one can write in English and still add to it the density of Spanish/Latin American memories, as Latino/as are doing in this country. (41)

2. [W]hat the current stage of globalization is enacting is (unconsciously) the uncoupling of the "natural" link between languages and nations, languages and national memories, languages and national literature. Thus, it is creating the condition for and enacting the relocation of languages and the fracture of cultures. (42)

3. [I]f English is becoming the universal language of scholarship, English is not carrying with it the conceptual weight and value of Western scholarship. My contention is that something similar to what happens in literature is happening in cultures of scholarship: a border gnoseology is emerging at the intersection of Western epistemology and non-Western knowledge, characterized as "wisdom" by the former. (42–43)

My composition class presented a rare opportunity for me to experiment with a pedagogy that I don't often use. By introducing readings and topics these students can more readily identify with, compositionists can offer students a set of problematics which unquestionably have the potential of empowering them, thereby helping to reverse the process of self-doubt. Readings like Vélez-Ibáñez's autoethnographic anthropological studies present forms of wisdom that are indeed "articulated in Western educational institutions and languages" and which therefore legitimize topics seldom offered to students like Texas Mexicans.

Assigning culturally-based topics that borderlands students of color can identity with and which are based on readings legitimized by Western educational institutions and languages (i.e. legitimized forms of academic discourse) changes the culture of scholarship we might unconsciously be engaged in. Within English studies, we have choices about what kinds of assignments to create and what kind of effect these assignments will have on our students' thinking about the world and the cultures they originate from. Because of the changes caused by transnational forces spawning a stage of globalization which is affecting our language of scholarship, English, as Mignolo insightfully suggests, will increasingly not carry the conceptual "density" of Western scholarship that it once did. Most of my Texas Mexican students' essays are filled with the kind of cultural density which is indeed evidence of the relocation of languages and the fracture of national and academic cultures that Mignolo describes.

In my students' essays, for instance, there are recipes for regional Mexican food, Spanish terms describing rituals based on funds of knowledge, and vivid descriptions of the roles filled by specific genders in their clustered extended families. Together, these essays provide panoramic snapshots of life along the U.S.-Mexico borderlands at the beginning of the 21st century: the effects of crime, inner-city and suburban gang life, illnesses, poverty, as well as of transnational family reunions, religious ceremonies, editing Spanish-language family newsletters, and using e-mail to connect over long distances with family members. Many of the essays, not surprisingly, also include family genealogies extending into Mexico. By laying out these genealogies, the students show not only vestiges of the utter and dire poverty many of them originate from, but also the strength, endurance, and pride with which they've raised themselves up by their bootstraps.

In one essay, a female student writes the following about her family's performance of cultural rituals during Christmas, and as she does, she negotiates a rhetorical dynamic necessary for addressing her topic as well as her intended audience:

My grandmothers along with uncles and cousins talk among themselves while they wait for the food to be served by my aunts. In these rituals performed in Mexican culture, foods are prepared to accompany the celebration. The foods of the Christmas season include tamales, menudo, flour tortillas, sweet bread, and of course buñuelos, which are like flour tortillas, except they are fried and sprinkled with sugar and cinnamon. Other additional foods include caldo de res and caldo de pollo, which are just a combination of vegetables plus beef or chicken, respectively. The main traditional delicacy of the Christmas holidays in my family is a cake called a rosca. The cake contains a little plastic baby within. The person who gets the slice with the baby has to sponsor the next posada, and the same sequence of events continues throughout the next Christmas holidays. (HCOP 26)

Notice at the beginning how the grandmothers appear to be holding court, while the aunts have prepared the food for the occasion. The student then describes in comparable detail the cultural rituals performed by her extended family during Easter.

In "Perez and Company: My Woo Tang Clan," another female student writes,

All of my mother's siblings have a home that is supported more by the working mother rather than the working father. Almost all of the women in my family hold very important and high position jobs. For example, my mother is head inspector of the Food and Drug Administration for Laredo, Texas, and my sister is head secretary to a professor at Texas A&M International University. One of my aunts is chief consultant for a lawyer, while my other aunt has been a teacher for fifteen years and head of the ESL program.

The men within my family, however, are either out of work or looking for any jobs they can find. Jobs that are found are usually low paying and frustrating. The fact that male counterparts are absent from many of the families in my cluster does not support the studies challenged by Vélez-Ibáñez that claim that the U.S. Mexican household is a patriarchal environment. As Vélez-Ibáñez suggests, it is women who support the entire structure of the household itself and are the primary caretakers of economic and political duties. My family is a great example of this observation made by Vélez-Ibáñez. Almost all the women in my family manage a household without a male figure. (HCOP 92)

My teaching experience with these Texas Mexican students leads me to believe that many of them are and will be using e-mail and websites in the future to maintain their extended families' cohesion. The use of this kind of technology is increasing, so while they assimilate within the mainstream, they nonetheless maintain their cultural and ethnic integrity through the dissemination, increasingly through electronic media, of critical funds of knowledge within their families. These extended families, we should remember, are led primarily by women, who protect them from the vagaries of social and political disruptions, vagaries which in turn could cause incredible sadness for them were it not for the cohesion engendered by these clustered extended families. My view of the future is therefore hopeful, and in my opinion, computer technologies will lend themselves to maintaining, rather than disrupting, Southwestern Mexican American cultures among clustered families of this type.

One further point corroborated by my students' essays and highly significant for our understanding of students with backgrounds from these Southwestern Mexican extended family networks should be noted. As the generations of U.S. Mexicans become more acculturated into U.S. mainstream culture, most of them are not breaking up into separate nuclear family units nor moving away from their families. As Vélez-Ibáñez states: "Studies have shown that regardless of class, Mexican extended families in the United States become more extensive and stronger with generational advancement, acculturation, and socioeconomic mobility. Although an assimilationist perspective would indicate that the opposite should be true, this has not been the case" (144). Moreover, while Spanish in some combination with English is the preferred language among families in Vélez-Ibáñez's study (145), he states that: "Even acculturation, as measured by language scales, seems to strengthen extension, and, extended familism is greatest among those who are likely to be English speakers" (144).

The significance of these findings for compositionists confirms Mignolo's point that while English is becoming the universal language of scholarship (even while the numbers of English speakers is declining globally), "English is not carrying with it the conceptual weight and value of Western scholarship" (42–43). Nor is it keeping U.S. Latino/as from adding their cultural density to their writings (41), as is clearly the case with my Texas Mexican students' essays. However, pedagogical approaches creating a high-quality educational experience for composition students originating from zones of comfort engendered in their extended family environments have yet to be systematically developed.

Until such approaches are effectively developed—approaches that incorporate the students' cultural densities and memories—composition classrooms will continue to be potential sites of cultural conflicts. Unless we develop such pedagogical approaches, the educational outcomes will likely be as Vélez-Ibáñez warns: "For the U.S. Mexican adult, who has maneuvered through both culturally constituted zones of comfort and formal educational settings, *self-doubt, negation, and cultural resistance will emerge together*" (167 emphasis mine). From a U.S.-Mexico borderlands perspective, we cannot afford to create sites of cultural conflict where crossover collaborations with students' cultural backgrounds and pedagogies aren't taken advantage of and cultivated. People from all cultural backgrounds, after all, have wisdom they should not doubt and which can help us form what we should all desire—a democracy.

The construction of identity, as many have said, is grounded in language, with consciousness itself originating in language and being an effect and not a cause of discourse (Faigley 9). Today, this postmodern notion about the construction of identity holds that consciousness is the "locus of overlapping and competing discourses," and the resulting consciousness existing as "a temporary stitching together of a series of often contradictory subject positions" (9). In addition to language, however, the "social density" of one's life, or the lack of it, as created by kinships, works to construct one's identity, especially the ethnic identity of groups like Texas Mexicans and Mexican Americans in the Southwest. That is, the social relations that ethnic groups like Tejanos engage in and are a part of, as much as language(s), work to construct identity, especially an ethnic identity. Because I believe this to be so, I can therefore say that among Mexicans in the Greater Southwest borderlands of the United States, the construction of ethnic identity does and can work quite differently, compared to either Mexican immigrants or Anglos. Compositionists seeking to advance the critical literacy of students like these should therefore recognize the family backgrounds of non-mainstream students along the U.S.-Mexico border.

Bilingual and bicultural students learning to encode and decode discourses influencing the construction of their identities must no longer be limited to reading works not marked by the codes characteristic of auto-ethnographic texts like Hinojosa's or those of my students. Nor should collaborative cultural practices engendered in their family backgrounds be overlooked. Such texts and practices have long since quit rattling at the gates of the dominant group; they are already within that domain, transculturally and transnationally overlapping, competing for attention from all of us. In recognition of this fact, the final words here rightfully belong to Rolando Hinojosa, and they go out to scholars and practitioners in postcolonial studies and in rhetoric and composition studies: "'Well, will we then be like the useless servants who did nothing more than that which was commanded of us?'" (*Useless* 184). This quotation is an example of a transcultural appropriation typically found in autoethnographic writings, as it's taken from a biblical source: Luke 17:10.

Louise Rodríguez Connal

HYBRIDITY

A Lens for Understanding Mestizo/a Writers

I am visible—see this Indian face—yet I am invisible.
I both blind them with my beak nose and am their blind spot.
But I exist, we exist. They'd like to think I have melted in the pot.
But I haven't, we haven't.

Gloria Anzaldúa

Edward Said's discussions of orientalism, colonialism, and/or the "Other" apply to the "USAmerican" landscape. Many of the ideas found in his work apply to minority groups within the United States in ways similar to the colonized people about whom he writes. For example, Said claims in his introduction to *Culture and Imperialism* that USAmerican identity is hybridized from its inception: "Before we can agree on what the American identity is made of, we have to concede that as an immigrant settler society superimposed on the ruins of considerable native presence, American identity is too varied to be a unitary and homogeneous thing; indeed the battle within it is between advocates of a unitary identity and those who see the whole as a complex but not reductively unified one. This opposition implies two different perspectives, two historiographies, one linear and subsuming, the other contrapuntal and often nomadic" (xxv). The fact that

USAmerican identity is "too varied to be unitary" suggests a contention between the need to unify and the need for minority voices to assert their points of view.

My understanding from personal reflection and readings is that US-America has colonized others in two ways, through assimilation of immigrants and conquest of territories in war. According to Said, the United States seeks to exert its perceived cultural, military, and political superiority over other countries. All cultures taking part in the enterprise are "involved in one another; none is single and pure, all are hybrid, heterogeneous, extraordinarily differentiated, and unmonolithic" (*Culture* xxv). Said points to the importance of hybridity in postcolonial experience and theory. Hybridity subverts the notion of purity and allows for the means of resistance: "Never was it the case that the imperial encounter pitted an active Western intruder against a supine or inert non-Western native; there was *always* some form of active resistance" (xii).

People resist in various ways, from small transgressions against laws imposed on them to transcultural rhetorics and transculturation. For in the interstices of society, through discussions among themselves, marginalized groups find ways to express themselves. Transcultural rhetorics provide a way of engaging with multiple cultures. They also provide a means of subversion that Anzaldúa and Said call for through the power to narrate one's own story. Transcultural rhetorics allow us to inscribe narratives that people can use to throw off imperial subjugation (Said, *Culture* xiii). Reclaiming our histories becomes an act of inclusion in the national story; such histories and personal narratives become transcultural acts. Keeping silent for too long blurs the histories, and these must then be clarified. Said's assertions are indeed a part of transcultural rhetorics that need to be explored so that the history of events important to us is not forgotten.

The United States remains uncomfortable with its hybridity. Its social, educational, and cultural policies reflect discomfort with perceived and real differences among the various groups of its citizenry. Hybridity occurs when languages and cultures meet. It results from colonization or other human enterprises, such as trade, travel, and migration. Indeed, whenever a society embarks on a colonial venture, or whenever a country opens its doors to people with different cultures and languages, cultural conflicts occur. Since hybridity is part of the process of transculturation, hybrid people become engaged in what I call transcultural rhetorics. Some acts include code switching or rhetorical gestures appropriate to one culture but used in another.

Hyperbole, repetition, excessive politeness, and pronunciation of words that demonstrate the lingering sounds of two languages also contribute to transcultural rhetorics. Transcultural rhetorics demonstrate a fluidity of movement between two languages. The movement may occur in the uses of perspective and problem solving or in other areas where a person draws on the multiple aspects that construct identity and experiences.

Transculturation involves uses of the "reciprocal influences of modes of representation and cultural practices of various kinds of colonies and metropoles" or, as within USAmerican boundaries, the practices of various kinds of cultures (Ashcroft, Griffiths, and Tiffin, *Post-Colonial* 233). Furthermore, transculturation involves the use of hybridity, which "refers to the creation of new *transcultural* forms within the contact zone" (118). I use the term hybridity with a more positive connotation than previous scholars have. I associate it with a creative process of identity construction drawing on the new forms created by hybridity that provide creative engagement with various aspects of life.

As a Puerto Rican and USAmerican, I use transcultural rhetorics. I also understand and present the hybridized viewpoints that Spanish and English, the languages that contribute to my hybridity, can create. Navigation between two cultures and languages allows me to establish a means of communication between them and contributes to the development of transcultural rhetorics. Whether immigrant or second, third, or fourth generation, USAmericans from other cultures learn about the need to address multiple audiences. Like other hybrid USAmericans, I have multiple viewpoints that enrich my understanding of the world. Hybrid USAmericans also understand, especially during interactions with authorities, the need to draw on our understanding of language within the contact zone.

The particular accents, languages, or approaches to writing and other communication are not always valued in our classrooms and society, however, and we feel marginalized within the institutions that we seek to enter. I argue that institutional control over the subject to be taught and over the language in which it is taught repeats the colonization of the lands, customs, and politics of the countries from which our ancestors came. Using a transcultural approach would contribute to the kind of knowledge that enhances all students. *Mestizaje* rarely comes without a struggle. Hence, understanding hybridity leads to a better appreciation of its possible creative uses in various aspects of social life. For example, a study of political processes and issues in Connecticut reveals the creative approaches that those aware of identities of mestizos use. During an election in Connecticut, a campaign manager aware of USAmerican politics appealed to ethnic identity. The understanding of mestizaje provided the successful approach: "Edwin Vargas, whose rhetoric and strategy had a class hue, recognized that ethnicity was a crucial factor in mobilizing Puerto Ricans. In 1985, he tossed aside his socialist ideology to support Nancy Meléndez, the ethnic candidate. Subsequently, whenever he ran a campaign he took advantage of his candidate's position on row B of the ballot by using the slogan Vota por la B de Boricua (Vote for row B, for Boricua), which, instead of reminding voters of issues, appealed to their sense of identity" (Cruz 161).

It is important to understand the concept of hybridity because those of us who teach composition frequently draw on events our students can identify with. One of the more pertinent sources of materials comes from hybrid USAmericans. Using hybrid experiences allows us both to teach transcultural rhetorics and to aid students' development of self-reflective skills. If we understand the conflicts and other aspects of hybridity and transculturation, we can conceive of better ways to interact with "others." We can allow for differences and allow students to understand, acknowledge, and use familiar rhetorical strategies. Students gain knowledge of differences between home and standard rhetorics, history, and point of view. Such awareness leads to critical inquiry and insights useful in other areas of their lives. They may even recognize ways that education contributes to their "standardization."

A growing knowledge of Puerto Rico's history enriched my own understanding of transcultural rhetorics. By learning transcultural rhetorics, students can develop what I call rhetorical intelligence that encourages shifting among rhetorical gestures according to the needs of the situation. In many ways, such a practice allows students to grasp the importance of concepts such as audience and context along with diverse rhetorical gestures. Composition is the perfect context for doing this.

Aristotle, Burke, and the Contact Zone: Expanding Our View of Rhetoric

Rhetoric, though widely understood to relate to politicians' empty promises, has historically meant persuasion. In the same way that scholars view rhetoric as a means of producing meaning within their cultural contexts, hybrids create meanings that reflect the multiplicity that makes up their individual construction and means for producing meaning. From Aristotle we learn that rhetoric is "the means of persuasion available to a public speaker from logical argument, the presentation of the speaker's character, and moving the emotions of the audience. Although this part of rhetoric has come to be known as 'invention,' Aristotle himself offers no general term for it until the transition section at the end of book two, where he refers to it as *dianoia*, 'thought'" (Kennedy 25).

Burke refocuses the definition of rhetoric to mean persuasion through the act of identification. In the introduction to *A Rhetoric of Motives*, Burke seeks to do more than discuss texts as "pure poetry" (xiii); in addition, he studies how identification relates to persuasion. Using the term *identification*, Burke aims "to mark off the areas of rhetoric by showing how a rhetorical motive is often present where it is not usually recognized or thought to belong. In part, we would but rediscover rhetorical elements that had become obscured when rhetoric as a term fell into disuse, and other specialized disciplines [. . .] came to the fore" (xiii). Burke's focus on identification helps those of us in cultural or literary studies understand the relationship between the naturalized rhetorical gestures we use to persuade and the cultural contexts of those acts. Identification with cultural ideas and symbol–making obscures the ideological connections between culture and rhetoric because a relationship between these elements seems "natural." These connections obscure the function of language in creating the identifications we make.

Rhetoric has changed its meaning from Aristotle's definition to Kenneth Burke's model. I use the concept of identity to mean two things. The first involves the ways that we connect to or willingly affiliate ourselves with a particular group, person, or culture; identification, as I understand it, draws from this. The second involves the actions, perceptions, and representations that people use to define themselves. For example, as a Puerto Rican USAmerican woman teacher, I define myself with groups with which I share, mingle, bond, or affiliate. These contexts provide areas of "oneness" or commonality that lead to group cooperation, despite any individual differences between members. Burke's discussion of consubstantiality in *A Rhetoric of Motives* illustrates this aspect of identification (21). Those of us who are bicultural or multicultural identify with more than one cultural ideology. This causes us to select or create new hybrid images in our rhetorics that allow us to negotiate meaning through our identifications.

Hybrids interpret and create a synthesized meaning of cultural texts, laws, rituals, or gender role expectations that they experience. This allows them to combine the diverse aspects of culture with which they engage. Transcultural rhetorics involve more than moving from one context to another. They involve a creative blurring of selection from and synthesis of dual or multiple identities and rhetorics, creating unique learning styles. Transcultural rhetorics benefit others in this diverse society. To understand and engage with people whose home cultures differ, all students can learn about different rhetorics, and transcultural rhetorics can facilitate that understanding. In fact, people do so informally. Yet such a practice in "traditionally populated" classrooms can lead to frustrations. Many students in first-year composition classrooms come from states where issues of diversity are alien concepts. Transcultural rhetorics educate us about the histories, cultures, and issues not discussed in our homes or communities. Since language contributes to our learning, understanding transcultural rhetorics can help us understand that learning styles, like differing rhetorical styles, are positive features of the USAmerican landscape.

Reconstructing Hybrid Identification through Language

Acknowledging and encouraging a linguistic reconstruction of our identities contributes to the creative processes of transcultural rhetorics. Another often-neglected aspect of transculturation involves the reclamation of cultural histories and identities, such as what Anzaldúa writes about in *Borderlands/La Frontera*. If a person has a *mestiza* identity, she should have access to rhetorics that reflect the histories and cultures that contribute to her identity. Transcultural rhetorics in this context become more politicized and can enhance the way we teach language, literature, and identity. Effective teaching allows us to teach rhetorics relevant to a diverse student population.

For example, because I am Latina, I study the ways that Latinas take on the role of subjects, storytellers, or historians of their cultures. In other words, I look at how using transcultural rhetoric works in the enterprise of speaking out, among us and to or with other groups. Anzaldúa's views on breaking the mestiza's silence support my view and reinforce the use of transcultural rhetorics in my classroom.

Anzaldúa addresses the issue of cultural erasure. She advocates an assertive stance, one that allows for chaos, subversion, and control of self-representation. Anzaldúa encourages hybrids to take pride in our heritage and speak out for ourselves: "At the confluence of two or more genetic streams, with chromosomes constantly 'crossing over,' this mixture of races, rather than resulting in an inferior being, provides hybrid progeny, a mutable, more malleable species with a rich gene pool. From this racial, ideological, cultural, and biological cross-pollinization, an 'alien' consciousness is presently in the making—a new mestiza consciousness, *una conciencia de mujer*. It is the consciousness of the Borderlands" (*Borderlands* 77). Anzaldúa asserts that using language in ways that represent who we are helps us to confront assimilation practices that frequently undermine our identity. She teaches us that we must resist and defy cultural losses by using the languages that contribute to and represent our multiplicity: "The new mestiza copes by developing a tolerance for contradictions, a tolerance for ambiguity. She learns to be Indian in Mexican culture, to be Mexican from an Anglo point of view. She learns to juggle cultures. She has a plural personality, she operates in a pluralistic mode—nothing is thrust out [. . .] nothing abandoned. [. . . S]he turns ambivalence into something else" (*Borderlands* 79). The new mestiza reconstructs her identity by taking stock of what she inherits from both cultures and making selections appropriate to her needs for survival and growth. In doing this, she practices transculturation. When she speaks or writes from a position she reconstructs, she practices transcultural rhetoric. This concept is important because it reveals the creative practice that, in fact, is a part of the oral and written composing processes we teach in our composition classrooms. However, what a new mestiza composes are representations of herself, her worldviews, or her history. Instead of composing an essay that meets course requirements, she composes representations that reflect her needs for the survival of those aspects of herself that constitute her identity.

Anzaldúa notes the difficulties of self-representation. She discovers inner resistance to knowing, changing, and letting go of the familiar (*Borderlands* 48). However, she urges herself and other mestizas to continue to cross into the alien territory of conscious knowing. To do otherwise is to stay still. "But if I escape conscious awareness, escape 'knowing,' I won't be moving. [. . .] 'Knowing' is painful because after 'it' happens I can't stay in the same place and be comfortable" (48).

Transculturation means that I select from two or more cultures when acting as subject in my life. It means that I acknowledge my situation as being between two worlds, two languages, and two ways of viewing womanhood. Most importantly, transculturation is a process whereby I, consciously or unconsciously, move between or among two or more languages and cultures. For me, transculturation is a two-way street. I do not believe that the dominant culture remains unaffected by the language and culture it dominates. Moreover, I do not believe that whatever language or culture is dominant remains so or remains so to the same degree. The cultural influences overlap and influence me strongly, particularly in relation to my views of what it means to be a mother, daughter—hybrid.

Definitions of Hybridity Inform Current Theories of Culture and Identity

Fragmentation occurs both when people's homelands are colonized and when people immigrate to other countries. In *Colonial Desire,* Robert J. C. Young notes that the need for "organic metaphors of identity or society implies a countersense of fragmentation and dispersion" (4). Survival dictates the acquisition of "new" or "colonizer's" languages and obedience to laws and customs associated with a colonizer. Likewise, migrating people must acclimate to new contexts. Yet fragmentation between new and old customs and languages remains. Hybridity allows for synthesizing a response to conflicting identities and national narratives discussed in other postcolonial writings. Discussions of hybridity present us with the counterparadigm that grew alongside a sense of fragmentation.

Young's review of hybridity in culture, quite naturally for his purpose, follows the progress of global colonization by Western Europe of countries in the East. Although the global, imperial, and capitalist powers imposed a single unitary economic system, they did so at the expense of local cultures and the dislocation of those cultures and peoples (Young 4).

Young points out that concepts of hybridity were caused by the "mechanics of the intricate processes of cultural contact, intrusion, fusion, and disjunction" (5). These historically receive little attention. He cites findings in other areas of study, such as archeology, where intrusions of cultural contact and conflict are studied in paradigms that diffuse, assimilate, or isolate aspects of culture (5). Some of the areas Young lists include "exchange of commodities, of diseases, of healing systems and of religions" (5). Young finds the area of language and sex or fertility useful in developing a paradigm for studying hybridity. Both language and sex produce hybrid forms (Creole and pidgin languages and miscegenated children) that embody threatening forms of perversion and degeneration and become the basis for endless metaphoric extension in the racial discourse of social commentary (5). Each model, language, or sex shares the same outcome: hybridity. The hybridization of mixed races takes place after all in the womb (Young 19). Hybridity is a metaphor for conflict and synthesis.

Young furthers the argument for hybridity by pointing out the uses and categories Bakhtin finds for it. The issues Young raises coincide with transcultural practices of hybrid people. Since hybrid language practice describes the ability of language to be the same while being different, it explains part of the double-voiced nature found in dialogue, such as Bakhtin discusses in *The Dialogic Imagination*. While double-voice can be found in literature, it also can be found in real people's discourse. Arguments calling for all USAmericans to have one identity ignore the double-voiced realities of people, their ability to identify with two or more cultures and to use double-voiced speech. Bakhtin says, "Unintentional, unconscious hybridization" is one "of the most important modes in the historical life and evolution of all languages" (358). As Young notes, such unconscious hybridization gives birth to "creolization of languages" (21). Hybridity thus occurs without a conscious political purpose, and unconscious hybridity is very valuable in emphasizing the creative aspects of hybridity: "For this kind of unconscious hybridity, whose pregnancy gives birth to new forms of amalgamation rather than contestation, we might employ Brathwaite's term, 'creolization', or the French *métissage,* the imperceptible process a new mode" (21).

New forms indicate the creative consequences of hybridity. Whether we use creolization, métissage, or mestizaje, the concept represented by these words underscores the value of movement between two or more cultures with amalgamated or newly created ideas. However, many of the internal dialogues in which hybrids engage result from the conflicts, social or political, they experience with the dominant culture. As in my case, conflicts of women's roles in the two cultures that influence me create the internal dialogue. Others who experience conflicts, quite naturally, need to organize with others for political redress.

Categories of hybrids allow us to see the synthesis and creativity of transcultural rhetorics at work in the writings of double-voiced, politically charged writers creating points of resistance to counter the dominant discourses. Since language can be seen as living, organic, growing, and changing, the writer can creatively construct her systems of viewing the world. Hence, hybridity as seen by Bakhtin is "an artistically organized system for bringing different languages in contact with one another" (361).

Hybridity and Identification: Bhabha's Approach to Subversion

To develop rhetorics that engage minority students and provide writing role models for them, we look at how hybridity provides ways for people to identify with nondominant writing forms. We can also study how such rhetorics can subvert educational systems that stifle the multiple views of hybrid Americans. Identity, as I understand the term, indicates how a person defines his or her self. I identify with both Puerto Rican and USAmerican cultures; hence, I claim both for my self-definition. Identification, how I identify with specific groups, influences the way I think, speak, and write. Thus, rhetoric that excludes the ability of the audience to identify (to make a connection) with texts or discourse falls short of effectively persuading audiences who cannot see themselves or their ways of viewing the world. Hence, much attention to the creation of identification inhabits discussions about culture and language. Marginalized groups can meet to subvert or challenge an oppressive system. In Homi Bhabha's interrogation of "cultural hybridization," he argues that the interplay among cultures takes place in the in-between places of society: "[The] in-between spaces provide the terrain for elaborating strategies of selfhood—singular or communal —that initiate new signs of identity, and innovative sites of collaboration and contestation, in the act of defining the idea of society itself" (*The Location* 2). Bhabha's image of stairwells in a building creates and contributes to the hierarchical representation of his theory. These stairwells mirror the positions of power in society where those with power are at the top. Bhabha and Pratt claim cultural values are negotiated through the interplay between or among cultures. The interplay among cultures leads to negotiation of cultural values, such as gender roles, child-to-parent roles, and the importance of religion. Anzaldúa's discussion of mestizaje comes to mind again. She and other women of color subvert the system by keeping cultural characteristics that are important to them. They do not create a hierarchical image. Bhabha's concept constructs the movement between cultures; however, the hierarchical nature of his discussion is countered by women of color in their discussions of subject formation or self-representation. While a minority group may be "contesting" the dominant culture for political benefits, it may also be jockeying for cultural authority.

Interestingly, Bhabha uses metaphors that indicate the concept of movement or fluidity in cultural exchanges. He does this in his discussion of theoretical frameworks that focus on the "beyond." For not only do cultural minorities want to move out beyond subjugation, many want to move beyond boundaries set up in previous eras (*The Location* 4). This accounts for generational differences within groups. Bhabha's theories provide the politicization with which people from nondominant groups must engage. One can see the movement of the different groups who seek movement out or beyond what is known, what is expected, or what is revered: "The borderline work of culture demands an encounter with 'newness' that is not part of the continuum of past and present. It creates a sense of the new as an insurgent act of cultural translation" (*The Location* 7).

Hybridity allows for emerging differences among members of society, but difference should not silence people. As we see in Young's discussions of hybridity, the imbrication of race, culture, difference, and language have contributed negative consequences to "different" members of our society. Bhabha, Said, Anzaldúa, and others point to the need to understand and use language in ways that resist political and historical inequities.

Currently, many United States citizens feel a sense of fragmentation and dispersion that leads to the desire for a fixed identity, as exemplified in campaigns for English-only and other measures that provide a sense of unity. Naturally, this feeling prompts public policy debates about educational systems and other social institutions. Yet, as Robert J. C. Young says: "Fixity of identification is only sought in situations of instability and disruption, of conflict and change. Despite these differences, the fundamental model has not altered: fixity implies disparateness; multiplicity must be set against at least a national singularity to have any meaning. In each case identity is self-consciously articulated through setting one term against the other; what has happened is that the hierarchy has now been reversed. Or has it?" (4). The model of fixity that Young writes about plays out in the United States context. Many USAmericans desire and embrace the notion of a "single" culture—a oneness that excludes the changes wrought by the assimilation, acculturation, and multicultural practices in society.

Mestizaje Born of Imperialism and Assimilation

Historically, USAmericans have had to contend with opposing, merging, or collaborative forces—the consequences of colonization—whether military or political. The lack of purity and unity of cultures, races, and languages, or the perceived lack of unity or unifying elements in a diverse society contributes to the discomfort that many USAmericans feel about today's multicultural society. This discomfort in part comes from not understanding hybridity, what it is and how it functions. In *The Predicament of Culture: Twentieth-Century Ethnography, Literature, and Art,* James Clifford attempts to address this discomfort. In doing so, he provides teachers and students alike with a starting point toward understanding the ideas posed by Said and other postcolonial scholars. This leads to the reason that teachers need to study hybridity: in gaining understanding of hybridity, educators can ease the discomfort many people feel with difference.

Clifford points to examples of changes in modern USAmerican cultures. In the introduction to his book he refers to the poem "To Elsie" by William Carlos Williams (a doctor/writer of Puerto Rican descent) that reflects on the poet's discomfort with changes in social mores and traditions. Clifford claims that Williams's discomfort is akin to that of many in current society because Williams finds himself off center among scattered traditions. Modernity, and the condition of "rootlessness" and mobility he confronts, is an increasingly common fate. According to Clifford, "'Elsie' stands simultaneously for a local cultural breakdown and a collective future. [. . .] This feeling of lost authenticity, of 'modernity' ruining some essence or source is not a new one. [. . .] Again and again over the millenia change is configured as disorder, pure products go crazy" (3–4). However, the image of Elsie suggests a new turn. Elsie, the housekeeper for whom Williams writes the poem, becomes symbolic of the ways that hybridization subverts establishment views of order. Hence, the poem also points to the fear among USAmericans of anything that disturbs idealized views of USAmerican life. In the poem, Williams calls the following images to mind:

illegitimate births, poverty and squalor, welfare, and child labor. From the dominant group's point of view, these conditions reflect situations that evolve from changes that occur when new groups enter the USAmerican landscape. Hence, the dominant culture's fear of change and hybridization increases.

The engagement of hybridity with identity relates to the development and interruption of cultural hierarchies. Dual points of identification provide a person with myths of cultural origin that frequently conflict. The hybrid can accept either or neither or create a new myth that represents the hybrid experience. Hybrid identities frequently conflict with either or both cultures that construct the person. Anzaldúa alludes to this in *Borderlands/ La Frontera*. Furthermore, such conflicted identity leads many of us to use our hybrid identities in ways that provide us a means of political action. In *The Post-Colonial Studies Reader,* Ashcroft, Griffiths, and Tiffin agree that national identity is "often based on naturalised myths of racial or cultural origin [. . . and] it was a vital part of the collective political resistance which focused on issues of separate identity and cultural distinctiveness" (183). The fact that hybridity of postcolonial cultures responds to concepts of separate and pure identity demonstrates how hybridity contributes to the creation of resistance. Other aspects of the usefulness of hybridity in discussions of language and cultures are found through the flexibility created by or through the hybridization processes. Ashcroft, Griffiths, and Tiffin note:

> Most postcolonial writing has concerned itself with the hybridised nature of postcolonial culture as strength rather than as weakness. Such writing focuses on the fact that the transaction of the postcolonial world is not a one-way process in which oppression obliterates the oppressed or the coloniser silences the colonised in absolute terms. In practice it rather stresses the mutuality of the process. It lays emphasis on the survival [. . .] of the distinctive aspects of the culture of the oppressed, and shows how these become an integral part of the new formations which arise from the clash of cultures characteristic of imperialism. Finally, it emphasises how hybridity and the power it releases may well be seen to be the characteristic feature and contribution of the postcolonial, allowing a means of evading the replication of the binary categories of the past and developing new anti-monolithic models of cultural exchange and growth. (*Post–Colonial Studies* 183)

Hybridity, therefore, can be seen as a means of resistance to duplicating colonial models by the colonized who blend colonial models with their own cultural performance, language, or values.

Although USAmerican–Puerto Rican students may not have the benefit of knowing the history of Puerto Rico, many literacy workers do. Conflicts among USAmerican *Borinqueño/as* arise from the erasure of our history and the imposition of an English-only language policy on us. Understanding the effects of history on the lives of students, sociolinguist Ana Celia Zentella includes an overview of the history of Puerto Rican migrations to the United States. In "The Language Situation of Puerto Ricans," Zentella seeks to explain the distinctiveness of their experiences and the consequences on not only economic factors but also on literacy education and practices. Her historical overview links the changes of Puerto Rican economy after its conquest by the United States to that which the United States and Puerto Rican workers (especially during the 1945–55 era following World War II) became involved in: "[T]his push-pull, between hardship conditions that push Puerto Ricans out of either the United States or Puerto Rico on the one hand and the promise of better opportunities, which pull them toward the other shore, is shaped by the economic forces set in motion in Washington D.C., which create favorable or unfavorable working and living conditions in the metropolis and the colony" (140).

Zentella's findings highlight the transcultural rhetorics among Puerto Ricans. She says, "They soon feel attacked because they speak Puerto Rican Spanish, because they speak black English vernacular or Puerto Rican English, because they want to speak Spanish and English too, and because they speak both languages together" (158). Teachers, whether in monolingual or bilingual classroom settings, unaware of the features of the particular Spanish and English spoken by Puerto Ricans, stigmatize them (158). Hence we as teachers are obligated to "become aware of the factors that determine language choice . . . in the community and of the discourse strategies accomplished by code-switching" (Zentella 158). Transcultural rhetorics require that we become aware of our language patterns. The study of the linguistic patterns and codes used by our students becomes essential in composition classrooms. Teaching transcultural rhetorics in ways that require self-reflection and critique contributes to extending our linguistic, cultural, and cognitive experiences or practices in our lives and in the endeavor to communicate with others—across cultures.

In the United States, the desire to integrate immigrants into the social and cultural landscape influences the impetus for a standardized, unifying language. This desire leads to problems concerning how to educate minority or poor students, for Zentella's studies indicate that many students from blue-collar families do not speak or write in USAmerican standard English dialect. Thus, even in a situation that does not involve military takeovers, issues of language dominance occur. The justifications posed by dominant groups do not, however, take into account the realities of those not in power. One example of interest comes from discussions of mestizas.

The New Mestiza: Reclaiming Subject Positions

There are women historically and in today's society for whom writing, or the concept of writing, politically or otherwise, still does not occur as easily as our needs indicate it should. We hybridized USAmericans encounter conflicts with acceptance of our transcultural ways of thinking, perceiving, and writing. Many of us are not aware of writers whose backgrounds are similar to our own, for such writers are unknown or untaught in our schools and homes.

The conflicts in these women's subject positions, both within US-American culture and their immigrant or ethnic cultures, highlight rhetorics of indirection and survival or, as is found among earlier writers, a rhetoric of submissive subversion. Jan Swearingen, using what she calls an "archeology of ideologies concerning educated and rhetorical women," calls such rhetorical gestures "tropes of self-abnegation" and "ironic self-deprecation" ("Methinks" 4–5). Although Swearingen and others look upon these as sincere expressions of the writers of past eras, I see them as submissive gestures that women used for their purposes in the past. These can work in today's world. Swearingen claims submissive strategies are born of frustrated intellectual and creative minds finding ways to express themselves and engage with the worlds they lived in. While Swearingen's archeology of cultural ideology dips into the past, I note that present-day students from Latina backgrounds share in rhetorical self-deprecation or self-abnegation.

The strategies of submissive subversion and indirection that Latinas use, though not always valued in our culture's direct, to-the-point writing style, can teach us much about students who use indirect writing strategies.

Although these strategies are sometimes used because women must engage with cultural authorities, at other times the rhetorical gestures allow them to engage with their hybrid cultures by addressing two or more audiences. Mothers pass down cultural and linguistic "styles" to daughters before formal education insists on a different academic rhetorical style. Additionally, such women's understanding of racial and gendered issues in their lives makes them reticent to speak out; therefore, their writings require closer readings. In addition to the cultural crossings many of us engage in, we also, as bell hooks points out, deal with patriarchal structures across two cultural systems. For example, because mothers are responsible for teaching cultural values and roles to their daughters, we frequently see a generational conflict. For women of color, whose mothers espouse patriarchal ideals, the problem is magnified, as seen in the Taylor, Gilligan, and Sullivan study *Between Voice and Silence*. Olivia, one of the participants in the study, provides us with an example: "In Olivia's interviews there is a clear tension between her mother's cultural values and her own thinking. [. . .] With passion and a well-developed contempt for 'falseness' in relationships, Olivia describes how her mother suffers because of her 'niceness' and 'goodness'" (83). The context of the study demonstrates the values that the mother learned. She wishes to pass these along to her daughter. These values include being of service and smiling even when she does not desire to do what people in authority ask of her. However, the study also demonstrates that Olivia's Americanization creates conflicts for her. She sees her mother as a doormat whose "niceness," "goodness," and service-oriented actions are "false." Therefore, Olivia does not speak of these concepts or qualities in the same terms and meaning as does her mother. The problem for Olivia and other girls like her lies in the need to fulfill her own potential in an environment alien to her mother while being a compliant daughter (85).

Although they may seem less willing to share their experiences, these women possess rhetorical strategies that serve their entry into public discussions. This is where the multiplicity begins. For example, the subjects of Taylor, Gilligan, and Sullivan's study articulate their hesitancy for engaging in public discourse: "Being Spanish, [. . .] you've got to watch yourself, you've got to, because a lot of people misinterpret Spanish people. A lot of people are different, they have these ways of thinking about these people, they think they know about these Puerto Rican people and stuff like that, and Salvadoran people too" (83). Please note the need for Puerto Rican girls to identify themselves as Spanish. All of my life, I have understood this to mean that in the eyes of many Puerto Ricans the term "Spanish" connotes a higher social status, one encumbered with less racial stigma. Within Puerto Rican culture, to be Spanish is to identify with the former ruling class on the Island. Hence, to be Spanish is to identify with a nonracialized group, one perceived as superior and one with social standing. The young women in the study are as aware of their place in USAmerican society as were women of previous eras.

In our efforts to understand the reasons for women's reluctance to speak out politically in current composition classes, many who teach composition have studied the work of Belenky, Clinchy, Goldberger, and Tarule. We may find facile comparisons between the women depicted in *Women's Ways of Knowing: The Development of Self, Voice, and Mind* and Latinas in composition classrooms. However, other factors, such as race and culture, add to Latinas' hesitation to write or speak out. For some teachers, it may seem as if Latinas' writing demonstrates rhetorical gestures that correspond to the categories found in the Belenky et al. work. However, women of color have complex reasons for nonlinear rhetorical approaches. Many Latinas feel that they do not fit in to the dominant cultural landscape. Experience of cultural colonization may also create resistance or hesitancy to write. The conflicts of living in two cultures and addressing two or more power systems complicate the lives of women of color. Yet, the complication challenges us to find ways to write or speak out, to break silence in ways that use our cultural identities.

Transcultural Rhetorics, Hybridity, and Writing

In her address to the 1997 Conference on Communication and Composition, Patricia Bizzell rightly notes the seeming ease with which hybrid USAmericans move from one language to another. This observation leads her to claim that one hybrid language should be taught. I believe this approach negates the language diversity found in the contact zone. This diversity, formed from the diverse language communities, needs diverse expression. That is, diversity in language use more naturally mirrors the communities, experiences, and political status of citizens in the contact zone. Transcultural rhetorics allow the writer or student to develop the ability to decide what to do in particular contexts. More importantly, transcultural rhetorics allow speakers or writers to create new uses of language and rhetorical gestures within old contexts, as well as in new ones. It would underscore the importance of changing rhetorical gestures according to one's audience. Transcultural rhetorics allow us to create and use gestures that meet the needs of multiple audiences. It would do more than teaching one hybridized language would do. Most importantly, transcultural rhetorics would not antagonize those making public policy as much as teaching a hybrid language would because standard language would still be taught. Too many people still look at hybridity as mongrelization. Failure to address both the purpose and use of hybridity in order to claim that we should teach a hybrid language minimizes the complexities of hybridity and its function within the USAmerican landscape. Furthermore, Bizzell's idea for teaching hybrid discourse ignores transcultural rhetorics that give a writer or speaker more choices. The choices in part provide hybrid USAmericans ways with which to subvert linguistic codes, sites, or contexts not useful in the process of reclaiming stories or histories and systems that oppress women and minorities.

Women of color demonstrate the importance of maintaining their identities and of crossing into other cultures and mediums of communication for expressing their identities and experiences. As Gloria Anzaldúa points out, "until I can accept as legitimate Chicano Texas Spanish, Tex-Mex, and all the other languages I speak, I cannot accept the legitimacy of myself" (*Borderlands* 39). Members of society must use language education that relates to people's realities. Additionally, writing is important for those who must negotiate cultural and linguistic differences. Writing and differences in "englishes," as pointed out by Bhabha, are important elements in the construction of a means with which to engage others' points of view and methods of representing diverse experiences. Writing provides a method for accomplishing a transcultural experience. Trinh T. Minh-ha states: "Writing, in a way, is listening to the others' language and reading with the others' eyes. The more ears I'm able to hear with, the farther I see the plurality of meaning and the less I lend myself to the illusion of a single message" (*Woman* 30). In *Reclaiming Medusa: Short Stories by Contemporary Puerto Rican Women*, Diana L. Velez describes the artistic production of the anthology and explains the multiple approaches and languages of the anthology's contributors: "Writing is a complex working out of wishes, and since daydreaming and artistic production both stem from the same source, all art may best be described as serious play. Thus, as the writer inscribes her desire through the symbolic order of language, she weaves narratives, which, in their imaginative relation to her life, undercut its suffocating reality" (ii). Thus, Minh-ha and Anzaldúa, among other women of color, demand we use our hybridity to explore our mestiza imaginations. We should not develop a hybrid language as Bizzell suggests. However, when dealing with political issues in our lives, we should select from the dialects and ways of knowing available to us. We should write in ways that confront and challenge issues that oppress us, as the authors of *Reclaiming Medusa* and others have done.

Pamela Gay

THE POLITICS OF LOCATION

Using Flare-Ups to Spark "Reflexive Dialogue"

in the Ever-Changing Classroom Text

One fall in upstate New York when the leaves were beginning to turn and it was time to give the course I agreed to teach in the spring a title, a theme, to make plans, I wondered how far I could open up a classroom through various forms of face-to-face and computer-mediated dialogue. In an effort to promote student agency, I decided to make "voice" a pedagogical site in a 1995 graduate course I had entitled "Teaching Writing from a Postcolonial Perspective."

Classroom Story

Like computer-networked discussion, a listserv opens up a subtext of voices seldom heard in our classrooms. The discussion list in this class of twenty-four students enrolled in a Master's program in English was wide open—we could use this space however we wanted. When we were reading Bakhtin's "Discourse in the Novel" (*Dialogic* 259–422), we used the listserv to continue our face-to-face discussion. More often, however, we didn't decide as a group a specific topic for electronic discussion. Participants would simply try to get some conversation going about whatever they wanted to talk about related to the course work.

Prior to this class, most students didn't have e-mail accounts, although a few were regular Internet users and subscribed to electronic discussion lists. The newcomers groped to locate themselves in this new environment they were also creating. They stumbled, argued, lurked, pouted, and screamed. Overwhelmed by the sheer volume of messages and annoyed by voices they didn't want to hear, some skimmed through the messages and rapidly deleted them. Two women wrote a collaborative message complaining that when their voices went out there, no one picked them up, so to speak, but the guys always got responses. Many complained about the exclusionary voice of the resident theorist who spoke "grad-speak." He was upset because "inclusion" was part of his political stance and to be accused of sounding exclusive was shocking. Furthermore, he was puzzled: he didn't understand why they didn't understand. He thought he was being perfectly clear. I quietly inserted my voice: "Ask him what he means." Instead of simply reacting in a huff and going away, I wanted students to engage these voices. How could I move them from monologue to dialogue? How could I move them from waiting in line for their turn and not listening (D.C. politician-style) to turning around and listening?

A number of students finishing their Master's degree at the end of this term expressed anxiety about finding jobs. A few white males were vocal about their belief that they would be discriminated against on two counts: gender and race. One angry male denied white-skin privilege and started (it seemed) yelling at bell hooks, whose book *Teaching to Transgress* (1994) we had started to read. Liz, wearing a "Radical Teacher" t-shirt, looked at me from across the seminar table as if to say, "Are you going to let him get away with this?" The tension was high. I dramatized this moment by standing up and asking, "Shall I throw this book out the window?" One student quickly responded, "If you do, I'll run around and catch the book." The tension was momentarily broken, and, fortunately, it was time for spring break.

A Flare-Up

Around this time there was a nationwide debate on Western civilization versus multiculturalism, and "American Culture" curriculum debates at Stanford were well publicized. Did multiculturalism mean teaching people about different cultures and offering different viewpoints? Did multiculturalism mean diversity? Some feared diversity would translate into "oppression studies." Indeed, one proposal for a diversity requirement at Binghamton University included this statement: "In the sense of 'diversity' here intended, such courses consider as central issues: the inequalities of power, the nature of oppression, and relations of dominance among various groups of people, as well as resistances to these structures." This proposal did not pass. Discussions, nationally and locally, were heated. Nobody seemed to be listening.

At the end of spring break, Tom, who had been reading bell hooks furiously in both senses, clicked on the class listserv and asserted his voice:

Sun, 26 Mar 1995

I know that I'm walking into a spider's pit, but before I start, let me post a disclaimer. Those of you who don't read it and then flame me will receive no mercy from me when I slam you. I am Hispanic from my mother's side, and Native American on my father's side. I don't consider myself white.

I don't think that studying cultures other than Western civilization —whatever that means—is totally pointless, but it's pretty close. Face it, when will African languages or Japanese history come in handy to us? We descend from a primary cultural inheritance—Homer on down. What I mean by 'we' is the political entity known as US. But you may say, what about immigrants? Shouldn't they study their own voices, and shouldn't we? Try emigrating to China and see if they listen to your voice.

Second, I think it's getting pretty late in the day for this poppycock over Western Civ. There is no one Western civ. There are many. Those of you who don't believe it, try reconciling Greek culture with Irish, and Lithuanian with Danish. Doesn't work. Western civ is a myth. Those who say that they've been bludgeoned with too much Western civ and want to hear something different are truly the epitome of ignorance and need to study a little more Western civ to get it.

As for our resisting students, let them. Multiculturalism is a joke. It is just another excuse for bigotry and hate. If you don't believe me, try counting how many "whites" there are in African Studies classes, or for that matter, how many African-Americans take Whitman or Shakespeare. Also, see what happens to "white" students when they do speak up in their Africana class. They get shouted down.

I think that we've been brainwashed a little too long, and it's time to derail the train. Get on with something a little more noteworthy and that matters more. If you think multiculturalism is a good thing, take a trip to Bosnia sometime.

As I've said, I'm Hispanic and Native American. I accept 'western civ' as my own, and study it for its beauty, depth of expression, and high currency. This does not mean that we shouldn't read non-Western literature. I just say we stop forcing people to read outside their cultural tradition. It doesn't do anyone any good, unless you plan on living in Nigeria or Japan. Nazis read Tibetan authors too!

Tom sent this post on Sunday, 26 March 1995. Immediately afterward, Tom replied to a request by Mike, the class's computer-mediated communication specialist, for a meeting in the computer classroom to help with any technological problems.[1] Here's Tom's reply:

I'm feeling better. [Tom had been ill with a flu.] So better that I just posted an inflammatory message onto the list. Hopefully it will cause some controversy. More likely just hate mail.
The only day I have free is . . .
See ya.
Tom

Tom's "inflammatory message" got an immediate reaction from Mike, who did not want to throw bell hooks out of the class.

Here's the opening of Mike's response sent to the class listserv, followed by excerpts from two single-spaced, typed pages:

first thing that strikes me about tom's post is how angry it makes me.
monologic/monolithic culture (western/european) as it is taught in schools denies . . . my experience as a working-class/catholic/left/ EASTERN european/mediterranean—but not as a white male, although my sicilian-ness would have landed me non-white status in the 40s—duh—how could race be biological if irish and italians could suddenly 'become' white?
. . . you say that there are many different 'western' cultures. Bravo. There are also many non-western cultures. Together these two helped to bring about many layers of what we understand as american culture.
. . . I really don't see where you are arguing from. . . . If stonewall jackson is a hero and not a murderer . . . it changes the relationship in my mind between the 'indians' and 'cowboys.' . . . Doesn't saying that you are descended from 'indians' but associating yourself with the 'victor,' that is, white jackson, erase yourself? Isn't it a contradiction to say 'i am indian' *and* 'my culture is stonewall jackson's culture?'

The opening line of Tom's reply was: "An :-P to you too." [(:-P is an emoticon for a smiley face sticking its tongue out.] And Tom went on for one page:

> . . . I don't erase myself by saying I am an indian/hispanic but yet read 'western literature' and value it more than anything. I just don't see what the big deal is. I'm supposedly oppressed. . . . If I were, I wouldn't have posted in the first place. I resent being called 'oppressed.' . . . Check one. Hispanic, Black, Native American, White. Why is it so important? . . . I'm just saying that, along with Richard Rodriguez, that I am personally sick and tired of getting goodies by marking off "Hispanic" on my apps. My performance is not linked to my racial identity. Binghamton is the first place I've ever been called white. I didn't learn English until I was 9. I've been called a Pancho in Texas. I thought it would be great to come to 'civilized' NY and not be marginalized for my Hispanic origins. I have found an even greater insult—being accepted into 'whiteness.'
>
> I'd rather be called a spic. Thank you very much. But this spic reads Shakespeare.

Tom ended his post and clicked "send" apparently too quickly, immediately sending another post (excerpted as follows):

> Date: Sun, 26 Mar 1995
> From: Tom
> To: Multiple recipients of list . . .
> Subject: tom's post
>   More drivel. No, I don't expect that my membership in the 'oppressed' would shelter me from attack. I was reacting to this idea that some people have of my 'whiteness' just because I study 'white' culture. . . . I think that multiculturalism has been dreamed up by guilty white people. . . . Take it from a Hispanic/Native American. . . . Tom

✍

Tom and Mike sparred on the list for several days.

Tom: I don't expect that my membership in the 'oppressed' would shelter me from attack.

Mike: i don't accept this

Tom: And I don't accept your unacceptance of my stance. Oppression is a myth dreamed up by intellectuals. In Panama, where I am from, people were tortured in prison, families were killed by death squads, etc. That's oppression.

Tom: Stop feeling guilty about your 'cultural superiority.' It's okay. You can sleep at night.

Mike: but that's just it. I don't feel 'superior.' I don't care about what you call white culture. I find it boring.

Tom: (I am conscious of my own inflammatory rhetoric): Whites turn their beady colonial eyes on nonwestern culture. They see that it is different from their own. They lump it all together and legitimize it as 'multicultural.' Boom, the postcolonial is objectified as Other. . . . Whites have won. You thus write history. Which means that we read it. (Those of you who have been following my argument are now smiling, I see.)

Date: Tue, 28 Mar 1995
From: Tom
To: Multiple recipients of list

In no way am I saying that reading about other cultures is 'bad.' When I study medieval romance, I necessarily read Arabic love poetry, Sufi mysticism, the Chinese poetry that influenced the sufis, etc. What I don't like is the forcing. Multiculturalism also lumps different cultures into one giant Other. I find this utterly revolting. . . . So what if you read Toni Morrison and Scott Momaday. Read Dante and The [Epic of] Gilgamesh, then come talk to me.

Yours in elitism, Tom

Date: Tue, 28 Mar 1995
From: Mike
To: Multiple recipients of list

tom, I'm not sure i want to react on the personal level you've chosen to respond from . . . your elitism is disturbing. . . . why do students turn to the simpsons and beavis and butthead? It is relevant and it is fun and part of the students' context.

Tom replied a few hours later:

Mike, I find your last posting intriguing. . . . I may be old-fashioned, but I thought the idea of teaching was supposed to be to lift students out of their context and into a new light.

This exchange took place over three days (Sunday, Monday, and Tuesday) prior to the first meeting in a conventional classroom after spring break. I don't know if any students were smiling, as Tom imagined. In fact, several students who returned from the break and casually tuned into the list were upset. Many were offended by Tom's tone. Someone posted a message for the boys to take it outside.

Upon realizing that a number of students had not visited the list after the break, I decided not to bring up what had happened there until everyone had a chance to read the posts. Instead, I divided the class into three discussion groups to talk about the week's reading. Tom and Mike were in different groups. I pulled up a chair and found myself sitting next to Tom. Part way through class, Mike got up and wrote on the corner of the blackboard: *Let's talk about multiculturalism.* (In this class, we often wrote messages on the board. I'd write something. Someone would go to the board at some point and reply. I think this was a carryover from our e-mail and networked discussions. We were used to letting all our voices out.)

Tom turned to see what Mike had written and then snarled, "I'll kill'im —No, I don't want to talk about IT. Don't even get me started." I took him seriously. He was very angry and sat agitated in his chair. There was no way I was going to open the class up then and there, especially since many had not tuned into the list and hadn't a clue about what was going on.

Tom asked to see me after this three-hour class, and we talked for two hours. He asked me if he could debate Mike in front of the whole class about whether or not multiculturalism should be forced on students. "I'll kill him," he told me. "And I'll win," he exclaimed, adding that he was trained in debate. As an American, he had also been exposed to a public model of confrontation between competing discourses. Was there another alternative to a win-lose resolution? How can we as teachers allow an eruption to occur between two students without their monopolizing the classroom? I told Tom I would think about what had happened and meet with him the next day.

Meanwhile everyone read Tom's post and the heated exchange. Amy asserted her view calmly on the class listserv: "We cannot just write off multiculturalism. Multiculturalism is not just replacing one thing with another but using this idea of 'critical thinking' to examine why certain things have and haven't been included in the traditions of a certain discipline." These excerpts from Tom's response (28 March) provide some context for the remark *Multiculturalism is a joke* that went up like a flare in this class in this particular historical moment. Tom wrote:

> Multiculturalism would be a good thing if it indeed did encourage critical thinking and was used to look at different cultures. However, I have found it does not. . . . . A multicultural class I took at UT [University of Texas, Austin] was an excuse to blame the white man for Mexicans' and Indians' problems. As a hispanic and native american, I felt angry and embarrassed that the two or three white colleagues in the class were being pilloried. That's not the vision I had. It breeded hate and contempt. I think the energy could have been used a lot better had we examined the beautiful in all of our cultures. . . . Let's get over it. . . . Divisiveness is not our goal; that was the old way. Let's get together and agree on things instead of fighting.

Amy countered another of Tom's arguments:

> i don't buy the argument that we are 'forcing' marginalized writers down people's throats because whether we pick canonized texts or non-canonized texts, we are still imposing our beliefs on our students, in a sense. Whatever we choose, we should think about the implications of our choices.

> Tom: We are forcing it because students under D2 [Proposal 2 for a diversity requirement under debate at Binghamton at the time] would have to take 2 classes in 'oppression' studies. Do we ask students to take Rush Limbaugh 101? No. Just because we've set up multiculturalism as the radical left (and therefore good) does not mean that the 'old' western canon is reactionary right (and therefore bad).

Not everyone responded like Amy. Some deleted the messages; others lurked around; and still others fired more words. "One person's outburst," as Dixon and Archibald explain, "may create the conditions for another person's silence" (xi). One student reported that he stopped checking the list: "The discussion depressed me so much that I didn't participate. Deliberately stayed silent."

Tom [and now readers may imagine him smiling] fired this post directly to Mike:

> Date: Tues, 28 Mar 1995
> Subject: hee hee

Miguel,

I think we have you on the run, meng.

:-) Tom

P.S. I'll quote what a member of the San Antonio Barrio told me once when my car broke down in a BAD part of town. 'Hey, meng, chu got life insurance?'

Please take that in the spirit it is offered.

ঞ

One student, a self-proclaimed anarchist sent this message to "multiple re-cipients" of the list (30 Mar 1995):

people, can we please be careful with each other? passionate disagree-ments, yes; vicious verbal warfare and personal attacks, no. . . . please *chill*

On my way to class, I saw some of the students sitting on a bench outdoors by the fountain talking about—what else?—and I shouted, "I don't want to let in all the voices. I don't want to hear any more voices!"—and we all had a good laugh. The laughter felt good—the class was consuming us. We talked about it in the hallways and byways of academe. And those who did-n't post their views posted them to me in person.

The angry discussion string about multiculturalism, however, did pre-sent me with an opportunity to move beyond inclusion and to begin to ex-plore engagement. There were time constraints. We had only four or five meetings left before our end-course conference, and we had more reading planned. Most of the students wanted to move on and let Tom and Mike settle their differences—or not.

There was also another undercurrent in this classroom text. Mike was sitting in on this class. He had already taken a different version of this class with me earlier and did not need the credit. But he was interested in post-colonialism and writing instruction and the reading we were doing and my pedagogical project: using technology to open up the classroom. Further-more, this class was unusually large for a graduate course, and I welcomed Mike's help. I was able to hold a face-to-face seminar with twelve students, for example, while the other twelve went to a computer classroom for an electronic synchronous discussion with Mike's help. He also planned to go into the field of composition studies (with a concentration in computers and writing). In other words, Mike, who had begun reading in the field and had explored uses of technology in the writing classroom, was in quite a different location than these M.A. students with concentrations in literature or creative writing and who were new to composition studies as well as the ways we were using technology. Some students felt intimidated, annoyed, or bullied, depending on their own locations. After some class discussion and with the end-course presentations in mind, I suggested that Tom and Mike work on some way of exploring their different perspectives and present their findings.

Working Toward a Methodology for Engaging Voices

> The point is not simply that one should have a voice; the more crucial question concerns the sort of voice one comes to have as a result of one's location.
>
> Chandra Talpade Mohanty, "On Race" 208

After small-group class discussions, I used "quickwriting" in a variety of ways to help students explore their locations as listeners and/or speakers. I also asked students to write about whether or not they felt silenced in the discussion, about who got to speak and how and why. We tried to examine the power relations in various groups. For some, this self-study was an eye-opener. One male, for example, had not realized that he had been dominating his small-group discussion. He was excited about what he had to say and anxious to speak but assumed others would join in if they wanted and was surprised to learn that they felt silenced. He was horrified. This group worked on changing the group dynamics. Would this kind of work carry over to electronic discussions? Transcripts of electronic discussions could be printed and studied—but we didn't take time to do so in this class. It was late in the course. We did at least get started as a class working toward some kind of methodology. What I want to focus on is the pedagogy I began to explore in my work with Tom and Mike.

I began this "researchable moment" with these questions: What prompted Tom to write what was bound in this classroom context to be perceived as an inflammatory post?[2] How did Tom come to speak those words that sent so many people running for cover or counterattacking?

What intersections formed his current location or nexus of identities? Was Tom one of the students who passed for white and was shouted down in an Africana studies class when he spoke up? What's the story behind Tom's remarks? And why was Mike *so* upset?

I sent Tom and Mike e-mail messages suggesting that they go offstage and e-mail each other privately. But I didn't just want the boys to "take it outside." I wanted to see if they could back up and learn to listen, *really* listen, that is, to see the world through another set of eyes. I found two essays that I thought could be helpful for thinking about a methodology to engage voices (that represent difference): "Working Together Across Difference" by Uma Narayan and "Collaboration as 'Reflexive Dialogue'" by Donna Qualley and Elizabeth Chiseri-Strater.

Uma Narayan describes two necessary stances the listener must assume to move toward greater understanding: methodological humility and methodological caution. Methodological humility requires that the listener "sincerely conduct herself under the assumption that, as an outsider, she may be missing something, and that what appears to be a mistake on the part of the insider may make sense if she had a fuller understanding of the context" (38). Methodological caution requires that the listener "carry out her attempted criticism of the insider's perceptions in such a way that it does not attempt to, or even seem to amount to an attempt to disparage or dismiss entirely the validity of the insider's point of view" (38). What in their life stories led Tom and Mike to different stances? I hoped they would assume that they had missed something and would fill in the gaps so that they would better understand their differences, a necessary first step in moving toward engagement.

Donna Qualley and Elizabeth Chiseri-Strater, drawing on the work of Kurt Spellmeyer, ask how can we develop a dialogic pedagogy that "values difference as a common resource for the enlargement of life-worlds" (111)? They contend: "If collaboration is to provide a way for students to negotiate multiple (and often contradictory) positions, it must involve two recursive moves: a dialectical encounter with an 'other' (a person or idea) and a reflexive engagement with the self" (111). Difference, they continue, can become "the basis for further dialogue and reflexivity" (113). They argue that "reflexive dialogue—dialogue that may lead to the construction and examination of one's own position—should be the aim of a pedagogy intent on enlarging, complicating, or challenging students' experiences and belief systems" (113). This looking back-and-ahead movement, this process of (re)construction in which a later self engages in dialogue with an earlier self, Bakhtin calls one's "ideological becoming." Ultimately, I wanted Tom and Mike not just to understand each other better but to engage in dialogue with their earlier selves and to see themselves from another perspective. This kind of dialogue leads us to question an earlier perspective and to see the world from a larger perspective. Ironically, it seems Tom would agree. Recall the statement Tom made about teaching in a post to Mike: "I thought the idea of teaching was supposed to be to lift students out of their context and into a new light."

Given the time constraints, I encouraged Tom and Mike to let the reading frame their e-mail conversation and to try to move toward understanding. This was my only intervention besides asking them to "cc" their exchanges to me. Although I wanted a record of their dialogue as a teacher-researcher and certainly was not monitoring their discussion, the teacher is always the teacher and carries with her the larger narrative of the teacher's gaze (and sometimes glare). Regarding my proposal, Tom replied:

> sounds good to me. I'm game. I too think that a classroom "debate" will dissolve into meaningless noise and shouting, and some incredibly ugly things will be said, because like I told you, I've been trained as an attack dog (unfortunately) and will react thus. Mike, I fear, has the same background.

No, I didn't want a face-to-face repeat of the flare-up that followed Tom's inflammatory post, though I doubted participants would shout and say "incredibly ugly things" offscreen. Notice that Tom immediately began searching for ways he and Mike were compatible.

Mike e-mailed this message to Tom:

> tom, i agree that we need to continue this discussion, and i want to allow a cool down. but i think we are *not* understanding each other's positions. that's the rub. we've been screaming *past* each other.

Exactly, I thought to myself. And exactly the problem in most heated classroom discussions.

Tom replied: "Would it be possible to imagine the two of us team-teaching a course." Imagining Mike :-)ing, Tom quickly answered his own question: "The guffaws resound through the halls." He then went on to mention their differences from his point of view.

> For instance, you love computers in your class; I don't trust them be-yond the "wow-gee" stage. . . . You're a writing person and I'm a liter-ature person. . . . You want a dangerous classroom (in bell hooks's def.) while I suspect them; I'm much more comfortable in a "safe" class-room (whatever that means). I'm sure we could think of more major differences . . . In fact, why don't we? . . . our argument is not *just* about (multi)culturalism, its about a lot of stuff. Tomas

Leith and Myerson in *The Power of Address* present a different view of argument from the commonly held one that views argument as negative or destructive; they offer what they call a rhetorical view of argument cen-tered on address (82). Understanding is achieved through the concept of address. They argue that "when another view is encountered, a response is made not only *to* that view, but also *at* the source of that view" (87). They maintain that "the two characters seem to be talking to each other so in-tensely because what they say (in words) is saturated by the views of the person to whom they are addressed and also by the presence of that per-son" (87). As Tom wrote, "[o]ur argument is not *just* about (multi)cul-turalism, its about a lot of stuff." How can we move from argument as opposition (opposing views) to engagement? As Leith and Myerson would put it, how can we *address* each other?

While Tom and Mike didn't plan a course together, they discussed their different cultural backgrounds (Hispanic/Native American and Sicilian/Lithuanian). Tom surprised Mike with his historical knowledge of Lithuan-ian culture. Prompted by Tom's definition of Mike as "white," Mike re-flected on his upbringing. Instead of sparring with Tom, Mike uses Tom's label as an opportunity to look back and wrestle with his own identification:

> My grandparents . . . were fiercely proud of their home cultures and determined to maintain them. My mother and father both were raised with that classic tension between being proud of themselves and their heritage and their american-ness in the dominant mcdonalds and french fry sense. . . . My mother knew french, lithuanian, and english. my dad knew a little sicilian, but took german in high school (in rebellion, I think). so i grew up english first and only. . . . my point is that i am monocultural in my upbringing. . . . my parents raised me to be 'white.'

Mike was no longer just "another white guy," and Tom and Mike were no longer "screaming *past* each other." In this same post, Mike turned the talk back to multiculturalism and reflected on his earlier stance. While trying to fill Tom in on why he used the label and found his line "Multiculturalism is a joke" offensive, Mike arrives at his own understanding:

> perhaps i was wrong in insisting that texts can be labelled 'multicultural,' . . . however, the layers of definitions of 'american' that exist come together, in my mind, to create 'multiculturalism' sometimes for better, sometimes for worse. the label is effective for me because it counters suburban deadness.

For Mike, the term "multiculturalism" is no joke. Mike closed this post to Tom with "this feels good, let's continue" and suggested a direction for further dialogue:

> i am curious about your father's story. . . . are there connections between his (and your!) stories that fit some idea of the immigrant story?

Notice the change of tone from "Let's talk about multiculturalism" scribbled on the blackboard following Tom's inflammatory post. Seeing through another set of eyes now, Tom replied:

> I can see how your upbringing was 'monocultural.' In ways, my dad did a lot toward discouraging my discovery (is that a good word) of my Cayuga and Hispanic heritages. Even though we were a bilingual household, english did have some kind of hegemony. . . . He had taken a lot of heat for being a 'redskin' and didn't want me to feel that kind of pain.

Tom exclaimed, "This is FUN!" which I read differently than a post he had sent me earlier: "Electronic brawls are fun(?) but pretty useless, especially when we all start insulting (primary instigator talking here!)."

At the end of their e-mail correspondence, Tom and Mike sat next to each other in class. They had found some common ground, which turned out to be *Star Wars*. Tom to Mike: "Did you ever experience a strange sense of loss when Han Solo was frozen in carbonite, and a thrill when 50 trillion years later they finally finished a *Return of the Jedi* and the trailers showed a Han Solo alive and well?"

Everyone was e-mailing titles and abstracts to the class listserv so the class would have some idea of the presentations for our end-course Developing Teachers' conference. Here's Tom's post:

Subject: Tom and Mike's presentation

"Pendejos y Ungie-mingie: Error and Collaboration in (Trans)Cultural Dialogics"

Tom's an ungie-mingie.

Mike's a pendejo.

And then we worked it out.

A collaborative explication of problematic discourse through dialogics.

Be there.

Tom and Mike decided to show the class that they had made peace and perhaps wanted to make peace with the class.

Toward a New Pedagogy of Voice

"Coming to voice" for Bakhtin refers to the struggle against authority. Bakhtin argues that there is always a power struggle—dialogic tension—between what he calls "authoritative" and "internally persuasive" discourse. Authoritative discourse is removed in what Bakhtin describes as a "distanced zone" where it does not come into contact or interact with other voices. There is no competition. Authoritative discourse is not called into question; it is transmitted, received, and frequently (in educational settings) parroted back. The internally persuasive word, on the other hand, is "half-ours, half-someone else's," writes Bakhtin. It "does not remain in an isolated and static condition. It is not so much interpreted by us as it is further, that is, freely, developed, applied to new material, new conditions; it enters into interanimating relationships with new contexts" (345–46).

Incidents from other classrooms reveal some problems when words are "freely developed" in new contexts. A white college student wore a t-shirt to her exercise class with these words run together (like an e-mail or Internet address) on the front: nappybluedenim. One African American woman looked at the words and gave her "hate looks" throughout the class. Afterward, the wearer of the tee-message posed this question to another African American woman whom she felt she knew well enough to ask, "Is this [pointing to her tee] offensive?" The woman shrugged and replied, "It's just a brand name."

"Nappy" may be "just a name" to the woman who shrugged, but in another classroom story that made the national news, an African American parent organized a protest when a white elementary school teacher in Brooklyn brought "nappy" into the classroom. The protesters claimed that the teacher who read the book *Nappy Hair* to her students was feeding into a negative stereotype, and they demanded the teacher be fired. While both teacher and author hoped to build self-esteem among African American children, it took just one parent seeing the word "nappy" and an illustration of nappy hair in a book in her daughter's backpack to call up her own memories and a whole social history of this word (Holloway B3). Sadly, there was no attempt to engage these voices. The teacher felt threatened and was moved to another school—and the book was removed.

At the University of Wisconsin at Madison a black student who was also president of the Black Student Union at the time, objected to a professor's use of the word "niggardly" in the classroom. The professor had described one of the main characters in the prologue of *The Canterbury Tales* as niggardly. When the student told the professor that she was offended, he told her that "niggardly" had no association with the racial slur and opened up his next lecture with a discussion of the meaning of the word, using the word a number of times. The *Oxford English Dictionary (OED)* defines niggardly as "stingy or miserly." Although niggardly sounds similar to "nigger," the two words share no etymological link; niggardly, according to *Webster's Third New International Dictionary of the English Language*, is of Scandinavian origin. (The two words do appear in large bold print opposite each other at the top of the same page in the *OED*.) The distressed student, while listening to the professor's "authoritative discourse," glanced at the notes of a student sitting next to her—the student had mistakenly written "niggerly" (Maguer A11).

To return to Bakhtin, the "internally persuasive word [multicultural, nappy, niggardly] does not remain in an isolated and static condition. [. . . It] enters into interanimating relationships with new contexts" (345–46) and gets drawn into the "contact zone" where a struggle (for voice, for authority) is constantly being waged. Recall Tom's remark: "[O]ur argument is not * just * about (multi)culturalism, its about a lot of stuff." And "'nappy' isn't about nappy at all," according to one vocal reader of the news ("Nappy").

Albert Memmi in *The Colonizer and the Colonized* views the inequality between the colonizer and colonized imposed by imperialism as a form of discrimination or racism. *What's wrong with them?* "The colonialist," Memmi points out, "stresses those things which keep him separate rather than emphasizing that which might contribute to the foundation of a joint community" (71). Let's return to the flare-up between the professor and student concerning the word "niggardly."

The professor accepts the *OED* as authority and asserts his institutional authority over the student. The student struggles for authority, but the professor does not engage in the struggle. He does not invite dialogue with the student-other (one of *them*). He chooses not to travel to her world and identify with her. Nor does he, at least in this news report, call his perspective into question. Imagine this student arguing that the professor does not own the word "niggardly," which he obviously views differently from his privileged position. This scenario, as unimaginable as this professor being removed, raises an interesting question. Does opening up classroom culture as a "dialogized space" include teachers (us) as well as students (them)? Both parties are guilty for refusing to see that persons have different points of view, but the professor has a way of externalizing his authority while the student is only a minority of one. Are we teachers open to posing fundamental questions to our own viewpoints? Or will our differences in status (and authority) prevent us from decolonizing our pedagogical practices? We may find that what we really want as teachers is for the others (students) to engage our difference in relation to their lesser status difference.

I have assumed that trying to engage voices that represent difference is a worthy goal. It helps to create a larger sense of fairness and justice so we don't kill each other (no more L.A. riots) and it enlarges our perspective. Life is richer when we know more points of view than our own. But there are some knotty problems to be addressed.

After hearing my classroom story at a Bakhtin seminar at Penn State (1995), Bakhtin scholar Caryl Emerson said to me: "So what you are saying is that while dialogue is endless, human energy is not." Yes, that's part of the story. What about our human limitations? How much can we—each of us *and* together as a classroom community—take in? And, as I have written elsewhere, can we—any of us—"bear the discomfort truly letting all the voices out or in may bring to our lives in the classroom community"? ("Improving" 157). I am referring to the risk of being forced to face the error of our "constructs," in a George Kelly sense, which can be terrifying, depending on how deep the construct. Further, should anyone be forced to engage in dialogue with a Detested Other? Are there some voices we may not want to "address"? Do we want to travel to the world of Albert Speer or neo-Nazi Buford Furrow who hates difference (Jews, blacks, and homosexuals)? What do we have to lose? While we may not have these extremes in *our* classrooms, we may have students who write from racist, sexist, or homophobic perspectives (Rothgery). How can we help students (and teachers) engage in what Beverly Guy-Sheftall calls "difficult dialogues"? How can we learn to talk productively through the differences we encounter in each other?

Uma Narayan, writing in the 1980s, put outsider-insider in binary opposition, but understanding is more complicated than crossing over and coming to some Benneton-style "living in harmony" understanding. Maybe other/other (with the slash indicating dialogic tension) is more appropriate. However, just letting students see and hear different voices, like simply adding multi-ethnic texts to a curriculum, is not enough to enlarge understanding. Engagement goes beyond even understanding "the sort of voice one comes to have as a result of one's location" (Mohanty, "On Race" 208). Engagement requires "world-traveling": seeing "ourselves in their eyes" (Lugones 401)—and calling our earlier selves or perspectives into question. "Travelling to someone's 'world' is a way of identifying with them," Lugones explains (398). "[T]ravelling to their 'world' we can understand what it is like to be them and what it is like to be ourselves in their eyes" (401).

"Voicing" exists at levels of both particularity and generality. When the general level is solely in operation, we can disconnect from the person behind the voice and deal in stereotypes, but when we go down the abstraction ladder, we inevitably connect with the person behind the voice and a different dynamic ensues. The issue is not voicing but persons *behind* the voices. We can use our voices to connect with other persons or to hide or deny self or other. "In Bakhtin's system, we are all *cuzoj* [other] to one another by definition: each of us has his or her own language, point of view, conceptual system that to all others is *cuzoj*," explains Michael Holquist, editor and co-translator of *The Dialogic Imagination* (Bakhtin 423). It does not imply estrangement (like "alien" in English) or exoticism (like the contemporary use of "other"). But we connect to an *other* only when personhood is offered.

Initially, the word multiculturalism sent Tom and Mike in different directions because of their different contexts. However, when Tom listened to

Mike (when he traveled to his world), he began to realize that Mike wasn't "just another white guy." And Mike began to see Tom's outburst as part of a larger story. Tom and Mike were able to work their way out of their grand opposition only when they started seeing each other as located in an ongoing narrative. Their antagonism was negotiated because they received enough support to *stay* in conversation and through that staying they came to entertain the idea that there was an-other point of view. Tom and Mike made peace; they connected with each other as opposed to declaring a truce, which is passively refusing to connect with a person. Through "voice" pedagogy, they found a strategy for getting to the other side of dichotomous opposition.

Cecilia Milanés tells a story about an unexpected (and uninvited) voice in a classroom where she was trying to enact dialogic pedagogy. She asked her students to divide into small discussion groups in two rooms and audio-taped one group to see if they followed directed questions. When she returned to the main classroom at the end of class, she saw a young Latino talking into the tape recorder surrounded by a group of young men chuckling. When she listened to the tape that night, she was shocked to hear this voice that "hides or denies self or other:" "This teacher is a feminist and her views are fucked up" (117).

Milanés was still angry when she approached him after the next class. He apologized before she said anything, and as he talked, the context for his hostile remark became clear. He said he had had his "share of feminist teachers," and he felt she was pushing her ideas on him. He told her of the various injustices he suffered, including guilt by association (male and therefore oppressor). He complained that four of the first five stories they read were by women and that the stories were politically loaded. And he told her he was speaking for the "other guys" in the class (117–18). His talk eventually revealed another of his voices, that of the person behind the Latino who made the derogatory remark.

The classroom as a dialogized space includes contexts as well as texts: Who speaks? Who listens? Why? Like Milanés's tape recorder, computer-mediated communication gives us a record of class discussion, making it possible for us to look and look again, allowing for a reframing not possible with ongoing spoken texts. Dialogic pedagogy is sometimes simply counterposed to transmission pedagogy or trivialized to multivocality. But "dialogic" is not just about giving students "voice" or exchanging views and reaching some kind of consensus ("and then we worked it out"). Critical, dialogic *engaged* pedagogy views coming to voice as a struggle for power/ authority.

To confront colonial inequality and work toward a more critical, dialogic pedagogy, difference has to be more than acknowledged, tolerated, or celebrated—difference needs to be engaged. "If we want our students to seriously engage with other perspectives," writes Qualley, "we need to provide them with a method of inquiry and the time and opportunity to use it" (*Turns* 135). Without dissent, the classroom would be monologic (tidy). To engage difference, a struggle is necessary. Can we, as educators rather than politicians, develop another model besides a win-lose resolution, such as one that sparks the possibility for reflexive dialogue?

To engage in reflexive dialogue requires critical listening—to imagine yourself as the Other, to look, *really* look, at an Other's point of view, which requires suspending your "I" for a little while. Only through the temporary suspension of "I" can the possibility for dialogue occur. Resolution may not happen because of time constraints and the limitations of human energy. The classroom, however, can be a space for the beginning of dialogue. Reflexive dialogue enabled Tom and Mike to listen to each other's voice and move from a win-lose situation. A two-tiered pedagogy of voice can encourage all of us to re-see and re-accent, not just re-produce, the word and the world. Through telling and interrogating more stories from our classrooms, perhaps we can relocate "voice" as a site of struggle—and then choose our struggles as teachers, students, and classroom communities.

C. Jan Swearingen

THE NEW LITERACY/ORALITY DEBATES

Ebonics and the Redefinition of Literacy in Multicultural Settings

On interstate 30 between Fort Worth and Dallas a large billboard invites enrollments in a private Christian Academy. Large bold text surrounded by golden trumpets and white lilies announces: "no guns, no condoms, no sex education, no tolerance, no diversity." A conversation overheard in a Pennzoil waiting room amplified the force and illuminated the appeal of these refusals. Two suburban soccer dads, fresh from a golf game, began to talk about the new language arts curriculum at their respective neighborhood schools, curriculum that used rewards, stickers, and candies for good performance, and featured new readings by "some Spanish and Black writers." One dad said to the other, "You know we've been having meetings at our church about this new curriculum and how to get rid of it; it's from California. Some are saying that it's Satanist. We've put together a kit that explains what words to look for: tolerance, diversity, multicultural, ethnic. When I was in school they knew how to teach: we had *one* American literature course, not five, your choice of color and language. And if we got out of line the coach would take a two-by-four to our backsides. That's what we've got to get back to, not all this bean sprout liberal, feel good, self-esteem candy and sticker stuff."

As I listened, I was both fascinated and horrified. Fascinated that the reaction against multiculturalism had become so codified and so unapologetically associated with reading literature by minorities; horrified that it was equated with Satanism. Although California has not yet been granted the status of official home of Satan in the United States, it has, along with Texas, engaged in some troubling Satanizing activities directed at illegal immigrants and affirmative action. Texas has currently suspended all use of minority categories in hiring, school admissions, promotions, and scholarships, effectively ending civil rights–based affirmative action as we have known it. California's recent anti–affirmative action legislation is being challenged, but still holds. Numerous English-only bills have been advanced in state legislatures and congress; if passed, many of them could end Headstart and bilingual programs. As if the climate were not yet quite bad enough, media responses to the Oakland School Board's Ebonics proposal rocketed into the national consciousness like evil stars sent by Satan, wherever his home is these days. Whoopi Goldberg and Bill Cosby were among the first to weigh in. They were joined by a chorus of shockingly hateful, mocking, frightened, and ignorant responses.

Why the increasingly hardened refusal to accept multicultural curricula, diversity, and even the concept of tolerance? Why the race to rally behind English-only legislation at both the state and national levels? Why the wave of repeals in affirmative action and other legacies of the Civil Rights Acts of the sixties? Most dramatically, why the hysterical reaction against the Oakland School Board's plan to adopt a program for inner-city youth that had been used in numerous inner-city schools for over fifteen years with varying degrees of success—and some failures? I attempt to unravel some of these waves of resistance and misunderstanding. Debates about Ebonics, dissent about the proper scholarly conduct of studies in orality and literacy, and reactions against multiculturalism are three sides of one issue: different names for very much the same set of literary, cultural, and linguistic issues and revealing indicators of how far we have come and of how much farther we have to go.

Ebonics

Linguistics, the study of ancient and modern languages to observe change and evolution across time and cultures, is hardly "professional crackpotism," as one editorial charged in denouncing the linguists who testified in support of the Oakland School Board's Ebonics proposal. How quickly we forget that American English was regarded as defective British English well into the twentieth century; many Brits still consider it so. American literature was not deemed culturally worthy of study in university English courses until the 1940s; no modern vernacular literature was studied at the university level until the 1890s. A longer view might help diffuse some of the wild paranoia directed at African American Vernacular, or Ebonics.

What it means to "teach Ebonics" has been perhaps the most distorted element in reports of Oakland's School Board proposal. Several critics of the Oakland plan cited a parallel court-mandated program in Ann Arbor, Michigan. In *Martin Luther King, Jr. Elementary School Children et al. v. Ann Arbor School District,* the "Black English trial" of 1979, Judge John Joiner of the federal district court mandated special teacher-training programs to improve teachers' understanding of African American Vernacular speakers and their culture. Alarmed pundits announced that the Oakland School Board proposed to invoke Judge Joiner's federal court order affirming the students' right to be "educated in Ebonics." This was neither the claim nor the request of the plaintiffs in the Ann Arbor case in which parents of twelve elementary schoolchildren alleged the students had been denied equal opportunity to an education by being placed in remedial or learning deficit tracks because they are Black English speakers. In his decision, Judge Joiner did not "institute special language programs for black students," as one Ebonics editorial claimed. The initial *problem* in the Ann Arbor case was that there were already special segregated programs for Black English speakers: remedial tracks into which students were placed early on in elementary school, often without formal evaluation, and from which they rarely escaped. In some cases Blacks who were not Black English speakers had been placed in such tracks before they had opened their mouths, without being tested. Similar incidents have continued in schools across the United States. It is in this system, and not in one that will be created by teaching Ebonics, that weak students will continue to be passed on without learning standard English. What the judge in the *King Elementary School* decision *did* require was a teacher-training program in which teachers would be taught the basics of African American Vernacular so that they could more readily teach standard English to Black English speakers. Unfortunately, within a year of the Ann Arbor decision the teachers had come to resent the program, and the Ann Arbor school district chose to lose its federal funding rather than comply.

The shameful editorial rhetoric at work in the Ebonics discussion repeated the error by reducing several complex issues to red flags: the claim that Oakland's plan was to teach Ebonics to students, the report that proponents of Ebonics believe it is a genetic language, and the indictment of the Oakland board for wanting only to get its hands on federal bilingual funding. Linguists working on African American Vernacular phonology have noted that many of the sound patterns of spoken Black English can be traced to the pronunciation of African languages. Sound patterns travel within and across dialects and languages. Studies in historical linguistics have found that the origin—the genesis—of many Black English pronunciations can be found in African languages. Misquoting this assertion to depict Oakland School Board members as believers in "genetic," inheritable linguistic behaviors constitutes a slur with double racial overtones, for it implicated the School Board members in an erroneous, foolish, and racist claim, and served to mock any tracing of literary and linguistic origins to African roots.

On the charge of misusing federal funds, many editorials denounced this stimulus as a money-grabbing ploy, and linked it to the alleged poor track record of Ebonics and bilingual programs. The development of bilingual and now Ebonics programs was indeed fueled by the availability of federal funding for specialized language instruction. Are any and all such programs now under indictment? One blanket claim was that "there is no evidence that Ebonics has improved the English of Black students." School by school and case by case the facts are very different. It depends on how the teacher's understandings of Ebonics are used in class day by day in teaching standard English, and in adopting a nonpunitive attitude toward Black English speakers. The attitudes of teachers and parents toward the students' language, whether it is Spanish or African American, are key contexts for language learning and for the achievement of bidialectalism.

In one of the first Head Start programs near Corpus Christi, Texas, I served as a recreation supervisor during the summers of 1966 and 1967. At that time, it was common to "teach" Spanish-speaking students English by locking them in closets, rapping their knuckles, and denying them the bathroom. Since most of the first-generation Head Start teachers were public school teachers seeking summer employment, and not specialists in second language instruction, traditional punitive methods for teaching English were carried over into the first Head Start classes. The objections raised to teacher attitudes toward Ebonics—the speech of many Black inner-city students—are reminders of a similar history for the case of African American Vernacular. A traditional and very effective vehicle for enforcing the learning of Standard English within as well as outside African American communities—practiced by Black and White teachers and parents—has been the depiction of Black English as "broken." It is clear that an older system of teaching that would punish by demeaning Black English or Spanish is being called for in many editorials that react to the therapeutic, feel good, affirmative goals of more recent bilingual programs. Let's go back to the basics of the good old days and that coach with the two-by-four ready at the bat.

Two points in the Ebonics resolution passed at the January 1997 meetings of the Linguistic Society of America state the alternative pedagogical goal succinctly: "Characterizations of Ebonics as 'slang', 'mutant', 'lazy', 'defective', or 'broken English' are incorrect and demeaning; [. . .] and [. . .] the Oakland School Board's decision to recognize the vernacular of African American students in teaching them Standard English is linguistically and pedagogically sound" ("Resolution"). Of course this resolution brought gales of laughter and gross misrepresentations from the bloodthirsty editorialists. The meetings of the Linguistic Society were enthusiastically mocked and selectively quoted to create that familiar caricature of the professor as a multicultural crazy and bleeding heart liberal—the "professional crackpot."

The Ebonics incident led a surprising number of journalists and educators to take strong anti-Ebonics positions, in some cases with inaccurate information about what the Oakland School Board had proposed. The degree of misunderstanding and fear of Ebonics suggests that there has been virtually no widespread understanding of the curriculum, purposes, failures, and successes not only of Ebonics as proposed in Oakland but, much more widely, of virtually all federally mandated desegregation and bilingual education programs going back over thirty years. The speech of inner-city youth—Ebonics—is more divergent from mainstream English than it was twenty years ago. This should function as an argument in favor of Ebonics bidialectical curriculum, but instead has drawn out attitudes of retrenchment, paranoia, and refusal of federal and state monies to needy inner-city schools.

While the tone of resistance and discord concerning Ebonics is still in the air, it seems particularly important to develop improved definitions of the purposes for which African American Vernacular English (AAVE) has been codified and adapted in classroom uses. Not only language educators, but also historians and teachers of American literature have become increasingly knowledgeable about the development and cultural legacies of AAVE. The Ebonics incident underscores a tragic lack of connection between what academicians know and do and what the public understands. For more than twenty-five years Black English has been a major object of study by linguists, curriculum developers in English at all levels, and literary scholars. An OpEd by James Baldwin in response to the Ann Arbor trial asked in its title: "If Black English Isn't a Language, What Is It?" He was in the United States to participate in an international conference at Wayne State University following the *King Elementary School* decision. The collected conference papers, Geneva Smitherman's *Black English and the Education of Black Children and Youth*, are unfortunately out of print, but subsequent studies have continued the work and were drawn on by the Oakland educators.

One cannot read Zora Neale Hurston without reveling in her joy in the vernacular, and in her ability to let it tell marvelous brilliant tales. Toni Morrison's Nobel Prize acceptance speech affirms the importance of living spoken vernaculars alongside the dead languages we all must learn in a common culture. We read Hurston remembering, thanks to Alice Walker's recovery of her work, that many key figures in the Harlem Renaissance found her work repugnant because it employed—and enjoyed—the vernacular. Understanding this and other moments in the history of AAVE is a vitally important body of knowledge for students, teachers, and scholars, because otherwise, quite obviously, we will in ignorance repeat the past.

Taken as a whole, the flood of Ebonics editorials manifests an astonishing degree of resistance, misunderstanding, distortions, dismissal and thinly veiled racism. Is Black English defective standard English or not? Should it be "taught?" Like English as a Second Language and bilingual programs, programs that recognize Black English as the lingua franca of many Black students are directed at speeding the entrance of Black English speakers into mainstream Standard English classrooms. This purpose was clear, alongside other purposes in the Oakland School Board proposal, but got very little play in the initial round of editorials. The media, who ought to know better or, at the very least, be capable of more than cursory research, shamelessly waved the red flags calculated to draw public enmity. "Texonics," retorted one Texas newspaper columnist. An initial editorial by Black columnist William Raspberry took a New York cab driver's patois as an example of what the Oakland School Board proposed "teaching."[1] Bill Cosby and Whoopi Goldberg made sneering remarks on various television shows about slang and gutter talk, illustrating that the heated controversy about Ebonics goes on within as well as outside of the African American community. Like Jesse Jackson, Raspberry later relented, a bit, with the explanation that he now understood the proposal as similar to longstanding ESL and bilingual pedagogies. The Oakland School Board clarified some of the unfortunate wording they had chosen, wording that was too easily misinterpreted as a claim that Black English has genetic roots, and that it should therefore be "taught" *instead of* Standard English. Perhaps, in the end, the Ebonics incident will serve to promote improved education for inner-city youth rather than fueling anti–affirmative action legislation and the dismantling of bilingual education programs.

In a somewhat bizarre coincidence, during the initial weeks of the Ebonics brouhaha, Oakland's neighbor, Berkeley, heard the University of California explaining the merit of a new course of study in Afrikaans. One defense was offered by a visiting professor from South Africa, a linguist who studies the evolution of Afrikaans among Black and White South Africans. The language, culture, and literature of South Africa, including its schooling and religious traditions, has been indelibly, irrevocably shaped by Afrikaans. Imposed upon Blacks in township schools, it was deeply resented, and prompted widespread riots in the 1970s. The revolt against the language of the oppressive Apartheid regime formed a crucial turning point in the anti-Apartheid movement. South African Blacks in the resistance movement had long admired and drawn on U.S. scholarship on Black English, and found it especially supportive during the anti-Afrikaans movement. Several academic disciplines trace the heritage that Black English has contributed to the language, art, music, literature, and religious traditions of the United States. Robert MacNeil's acclaimed public television series, *The Story of English,* included an entire segment on Black English that spanned all these subjects and went on to emphasize the often ignored point that the speech of White and Black southerners shares identical roots in the 300-plus year history of linguistic and social interaction between Whites and Blacks in the south. Many southerners, in short, speak Black English. One Ebonics editorial pointed out that Elvis sang Black English. The author of the editorial defending Texonics illustrated this in his title: "we mizewell admit what language is." We can and we do, but why is the wealth of information, scholarship, and pedagogical wisdom disappearing down a black hole?

Alongside the Ebonics discussions in the media, in that parallel universe known as academia, e-mail lists and editorials in the *Chronicle of Higher Education*[2] manifested much anguish over the failure of academicians to communicate with the public. There is division among teachers, scholars, and students about how Black English and African American culture, history, and literature should be studied at the college level. There is much dispute among African Americans concerning Black English study and pedagogies, a difference of opinions that was helpfully summarized in Robert MacNeil's Black English segment almost a decade ago. Nonetheless, high school, college, and university courses in linguistics, English, and history cover ample materials in African American language and culture, often within Black Studies programs, but just as often within traditional disciplinary majors; high school teachers flock to summer institutes to study African American literature and history in order to supplement existing classroom materials. Many designers of writing courses at universities are conversant with African American Vernacular English alongside other dialects and languages so that they can more effectively bridge the gap between the students' home culture, language, and learning styles and those required by university study.

Why, then, the flood of diatribes scorning Ebonics as the teaching of slang, lambasting the divisiveness of the liberal politically correct agenda, and claiming that twenty years of bilingual education and ESL, the counterparts to the Oakland curriculum, simply don't work? I fear the thinly veiled racism that weaves its way through these hysterical, willfully distorted innuendoes. Some of those who adopt the back-to-the-basics tone assumed by propounders of "traditional" curriculum are reminiscent of one Bureau of Indian Affairs administrator setting up Indian Schools at the end of the nineteenth century. Defending the forced exportation of Indian children from their homes to boarding schools, he asserted that if English was good enough for the white man and good enough for Jesus Christ it was sure good enough for the red man. Today the same tone is struck by those who say get to work and quit whining; we have no problem that can't be solved by good teaching and disciplined students. The implication: we no longer have race problems. Or, we no longer want to define any of our problems in terms of race. Many opponents of affirmative action, multicultural curriculum, and Ebonics—variously defined—seem to have concluded that the entire civil rights agenda, the attempt to define and solve problems in terms of race and language has been divisive and ineffective. The verdict is in: the civil rights movement has failed.

In trying to sift through the deluge of editorial tones and topics spawned by the Ebonics discussion, I came up with several very tentative conclusions. Racism is alive and well, as evidenced by the easy sneer adopted in two-thirds of the Ebonics editorials. Little Rascals' Buckwheat and not Zora Neale Hurston was cited as emblematic of the African American Vernacular whose diversity is as great as the diversity of Spanish variants spoken within the United States, or of the dialects that distinguish White speakers from Minneapolis and those from Baton Rouge. Racism is manifest in most of the quick dismissals of Ebonics as slang, as broken English, as something you would not want your child to learn or your daughter to marry. The easy reduction of Black English to the status of gutter talk, and the assumption that this designation is somehow amusing, is fear-driven, a racist denigration of a language and culture that has contributed to our language and culture a wealth of terms and concepts, including denigration. Sure, Black English is "slang," in part and in some settings, but so is the colloquial English that all of us use in different settings as we engage in what linguists call "code switching."

As the Ebonics discussion progressed in the editorial columns, happily, some more thoughtful voices began to get into the discussions. The growing divergence of the speech of Black inner-city youth is a concern of parents, educators, and linguistic demographers. If bridges between their language and culture and that of schools cannot be reinforced, we continue to march toward the ominous situation that already exists in many states—more per capita spent on prisoners than students; more funds allocated to prisons than to schools. Creating the necessary bridges will take good will on both sides and, yes, some of that tolerance for diversity that everyone seems to be so tired of hearing about. Ultimately, however, this is not simply a linguistic issue. The larger forces that lead inner-city youth to deliberately avoid using Standard English, and even to deliberately avoid making good grades because doing so is "white," need solutions created by the village: families and school boards and teachers and state funding agencies working together in agreement that there is a problem (Gates, *Loose Canons* 32; Gilyard, *Voices of the Self* 46). The problem *is* racism, in concert with the compound economic issues evolving in the global economy's effects on our local economies. The solutions are not easy to define. The Oakland School Board's steps in the right direction should not be so quickly mocked. Instead, let us turn to the wealth of knowledge and mutual cultural heritage that can be shared, that already has been shared within the village that we create together. The alternative is not hard to define; we see it every day because it is reported to us every day: chaos, race wars, and very dead dreams.

Literacy/Orality Studies: Linking Language and Literature

Watching the second installment of George Lucas's reissued trilogy *Star Wars*, I was reminded of Eric Havelock's presentation to the Conference on College Composition and Communication entitled "Literacy, Orality, and *Star Wars*." The lecture emphasized the universality of oral-epic narrative plot and the typical aggregative, epithet-laden, paratactic syntax of oral language practice across many cultures and languages. In a memorable discussion in which Havelock equated the zero-copula speech of the pre-Socratic philosophers with Black English, and linked this characteristic of orality with the logic of narrative syntax, a sharp contrast with predicative copular syntax and logic emerged. The Ebonics furor underscores the need to return to these understandings of oral language and narrative that only ten years ago were readily available in casual discussion. As we await the *Return of the Jedi* perhaps we can review what *Star Wars* preserves of our oral-epic roots.

In composing *Star Wars*, George Lucas very deliberately drew upon several key elements in oral tradition and myth, the array of elements that have been so ably and amply defined in the work of Walter Ong, Eric Havelock, and Albert Lord, among other exponents of oral tradition and oral composition. These are heavy characters: you know who is wearing the white hat; there could be no clearer example of this than Darth Vader's menacing black Samurai helmet and the deep African American cadences of James Earl Jones's voice. Memorable lines appear in the form of aphorisms and epithets: "It is your destiny." The story is one of quest, struggle, identity, and redemption. It is a tale of mistaken romance—found, and lost, and recovered. The purity of youth's hope, idealism, and sacrifice redeems an almost dead and decadent culture; the hero's faith restores a father to an eternal life. The power of such stories is universal, inspiring, and that day in the theater, I yearned for it in a way that brought tears to my eyes as I watched the teenagers file into the rows ahead. The unruly group of high school classmates made their way into the seats in front of us; they were decked out in the usual array of pierced noses, ears, eyebrows, navels, and no doubt other locations we don't want to know about. They wore ragged blue jeans, sported dyed black and orange hair, and noisily spouted ritual verbal rebukes and abuse. They fell silent as the opening narrative rolled across the screen, and hardly moved for the next two and a half hours. As Luke was stalked and maimed by Darth Vader in battle after battle, and was told, "you *will* turn to the dark side of the force," they crouched and cowered and winced—as did we all, for such is the power of myth and of orality. Nothing can match the identification and total immersion it brings with it, and nothing should be regarded as more dangerous when it is in the hands of the dark side of the force.

These young people, still children in so many ways, were not even born when the first *Star Wars* film appeared in 1978; like my sixteen-year-old son, they were only three or four when the second episode appeared in 1983. The Darth Vader character scared them to death. They have known this film primarily through video viewings; its story has nonetheless become part of their mythology, and they are flocking to see it for the first time on the big screen. It is moving and also encouraging to see the response of the jaded junior sophisticates to *Star Wars*. Lucas had hoped that its message would reach this audience and find a home there.

And what is the value of that force, the force of believing that good will triumph over evil, that the young can redeem—and be redeemed by—the old, that true love can be distinguished from fleeting infatuation? What is the value of the resounding epithets that myth and religion transmit through the acoustics of orality: "it is your destiny," "may the force be with you," "Thy will be done," "I will fear no evil." My constant companions, recited like a mantra throughout the year I was up for tenure, were the first lines of Psalm 1: "Blessed is the man who walketh not in the counsel of the ungodly nor standeth in the way of sinners nor sitteth in the seat of the scornful." What can the continuing presence of such words and their power tell us about the state of our understandings of literacy and orality today? And what does our current selection of canonical epithets tell us, diagnostically, about our culture? On these points the methods used by scholars in studies of literacy and orality have begun to differ, sometimes heatedly.

After more than two decades of debate, the directions of studies in literacy and orality are more diverse than they were in the sixties and seventies when an entire group of scholars' work converged: Buckminster Fuller's and Marshall McLuhan's celebrations of the Global Village were the first in a series of waves of global consciousness and interest in new telecommunications media, now extending to explorations of not just orality, not just literacy, but "electracy"—the internet medium. In the decade of Fuller and McLuhan, Jack Goody's *The Consequences of Literacy* appeared, along with Havelock's *Preface to Plato*, and Walter Ong's many works on technology, consciousness, orality, vernacular literacies, and the presence of the Word. The work of Lord and Parry was revived and adapted by many scholars— Walter Ong, Roger Abrahams, and Henry Louis Gates, among others—and directed at the study of African American vernacular forms such as rapping, flyting, and playing the dozens, as well as at the powerful poetic and rhetorical traditions of African American preaching. Subsequent scholars and writers have adapted this line of study even further for the study of literature and oral tradition in African American and other American ethnic cultures.[3]

Alice Walker's novels, alongside her works as an essayist, have contributed much to an understanding of the *range* of Black vernaculars among African Americans. Walker is single-handedly responsible for marking the grave and recovering the work of Zora Neale Hurston who, in the thirties and forties, wrote novels preserving the vernaculars of southern rural blacks. Henry Louis Gates and others have extended these earlier studies of African American orality into the study of African American rhetorical traditions. His work on Frederick Douglass emphasizes that rhetorical tropes are produced spontaneously in powerful oral poetry and oratory; our names for chiasmus, antiphrasis, synechdoche, and the host of rhetorical schemes and figures known to historians of rhetoric—these are the tools of the taxonomist, not the "genetic" origin of rhetoric. In emphasizing this point, Gates joins Ong and Havelock in propounding the universality of rhetoric and of orality as powerful vehicles—encyclopedias and repositories of human cultures everywhere, regardless of whether they have "studied" rhetoric.

Considering the richness of the ongoing study of orality and literacy and of their relationship to one another, it has been troubling to witness the emergence of the Empire striking back at our happy Ewok global village. Why and to what end? Oral traditions, as these are customarily studied, are within each culture conservative and conserving, uniform and cohesive repositories of cultural lore; individual performances may change, but the core story remains the same. You know what you can recall, and what you can recall is preserved in song and poem and narrative by memorable epic encyclopedias: the *Iliad* and *Odyssey*, the Hebrew Scriptures, the New Testament gospels, the Yiddish stories collected by Gershom Sholem, the Talkin' and Testifyin' of the Black church in America. The study of literacy has become increasingly differential, with emphasis on different kinds and uses of literacy. The work of Shirley Brice Heath, Beth Daniell, Beverly Moss, and a number of other scholars has challenged the global claims made for the effects of literacy on consciousness in early literacy/orality studies.[4]

Beth Daniell writes, "In the sixties and seventies scholars theorized that literacy per se causes structural changes in human cognition, changes that bring about radical alterations in cultures. This theory portrays literacy and orality as binary opposites and posits a great cognitive leap between literate persons and cultures on the one hand and oral persons and cultures on the other. The autonomous, great leap model of literacy has now been challenged by work in psychology, history, sociolinguistics, anthropology, and ethnographies of speaking. Because the great leap view presents literacy and orality as cognitive states and as binary opposites, it fails to consider both the economic, political, social, and cultural conditions that influence and constrain literacy, and the complex interrelationships between the spoken and the written word. Literacy should be approached as multiple, local, particular, rhetorical, and contextual" (private correspondence). In this example from Daniell, and in many others, several grounds and purposes are advanced in refutations of global or universalist models of literacy and orality. First, it is charged that any notion of a universal human consciousness is unscientific, unprovable, Eurocentric, elitist, and a remnant of Enlightenment humanism that we would do well to dispense with. Second, it is argued that if literacy is always local and specific, shaped by individual family, school, and village uses and contexts, then orality must be as well. Third, and most recently, many models of orality, particularly those that have been applied to the study of African American language, literature, and culture, have been charged with racism. According to this view, to say that African American language or culture is fundamentally or essentially oral is a racist romanticizing of a certain variant of African American*ism* and should be disbanded in favor of a carefully qualified plural definition of African American language, literature, and culture. The politics of identity have met literacy/orality studies in the multicultural academic village. In *Loose Canons,*

Gates illustrates this problem, by providing the following excerpt from the college admission essay he wrote for Yale in 1969: "My grandfather was colored, my father was a Negro, and I am Black" (134).

I have not the space to respond at length to each of the criticisms advanced against global or universalist literacy / orality studies. I can, however, define the following starting points for answers. First, on the charge of pseudoscientism leveled at claims of innate or universal characteristics of the human mind and consciousness that are altered by literacy: most scholars who study the universal or common features of literacy and orality do not present themselves exclusively as scientists. Rather, the literacy-orality contrast has been pursued as an heuristic, as an interpretive method for generalizing about significant differences between literate and oral literatures and cultures, and significant similarities across literate and literary traditions, on the one hand, and oral traditions on the other. Similarly, Enlightenment —and earlier—humanists advanced universal claims about human consciousness, the human mind, political and moral social contracts, not as empirical scientists but as philosophers. The claims were moral, ethical, and theological, especially when measured by today's canons of scientific proof and evidence. Statements regarding human cultures and consciousness are affirmations of value and descriptions of beliefs as often as they are assertions of facts. When Ong classifies the characteristics of the literate mind in contrast to the oral mind by generalizing about textual features, he is asserting very general hypotheses based on the observations of prominent textual features, not defining neurological wiring. When Havelock observes that words and metaphors changed as Greek culture moved into the "eye" world of literacy rather than the "ear" world of acoustic orality, he is very clearly presenting a conjecture about what might have been happening in self-understandings of mind and consciousness.[5]

Second, to the recommendation that we pursue local and not global practices and definitions of literacy, I would issue a warning that parallels the warnings leveled against Ebonics curricula. To pursue only local, and not global, practices, habits, customs, considerations, and definitions of humanity, human value, political, social, and moral value is to foster a sense of difference without its necessary coordinate: sameness, or commonality. That is exactly what many critics of Ebonics and, more broadly, of multiculturalism fear. Further, to combine a local-only rule for literacy studies with a politically based objection to ethnic cultural designations such as

Black oral culture would seem to impede the goal of local studies by erasing the terms needed for defining local identities. There would be no one
and nothing to talk about. It is noteworthy that in anti-affirmative action
legislation as well there is a movement away from any references to Black,
White, Hispanic, and other designating categories. If these, along with oral,
literate, Western, Eastern, and other names for identifying and understanding self-designated as well as Other-designated human communities are to
be struck from the record on the grounds that they are essentialist, or racist,
what strange new label-less world will we live in?

Literacy, Orality, and Culture Wars

It may be that an inability to coordinate the politics—the culture wars—
behind the study of multicultural literatures and languages is bringing multiculturalism, like bidialectalism, to a screeching halt. In theory, that is, but
certainly not in practice, or we would have no Ebonics debate. Charlayne
Hunter–Gault's autobiography *In My Place* provides a reminder, and a gentle
rejoinder. The reminder: it was not until 1961, seven years after Brown
vs. Board of Education, that Hunter–Gault and her classmate Hamilton
Holmes integrated the University of Georgia, escorted in the sadly familiar
scene by Federal marshals to protect them from a jeering crowd of White
onlookers and students. In her account, Hunter–Gault credits a long line of
forebears from village and city, civilian and army life, secular and church
worlds. They are thanked for the calm resolve and even sense of humor
that she and "Ham" sustained in the face of spitting, jeering, and dormi-
tory bomb threats. Her account reminds us not only of how recently we
have begun to try to adapt to integrated schooling and schools. Hunter–
Gault has become an acclaimed journalist. Her television presence conveys
an audible refusal to adopt the sanitized accents of speech-coached television journalism, and a visible eclecticism in dress and hairstyle. Early on in
her college career as a journalism major, and then during her first years in
newspaper and television work, she was repeatedly told that her "slow slurry
speech" would take care of itself—with practice and a voice coach. In a
gentle rejoinder, she remarks that it just never did. No one needs to give
Hunter–Gault lessons in identity politics. Her self-presentation in speech and
dress proclaim that she will not be typecast; the variety of self-presentations

she uses provides a refreshing vision of pluralism at its best: one identity, one unique individual expressing herself through many voices, all of them authentic (Royster).

The presence of Hunter–Gault's words and story provides a refreshing example of the aims of cultural pluralism, multiculturalism, and increased tolerance for diversity in language and literature. What she has become, an integrated human person in several senses, would have been impossible, she emphasizes, without her understanding of the different, painfully divided, cultures that contributed to her upbringing, education, voices, and identity. Like Frederick Douglass's *Narrative of the Life of Frederick Douglass*, Richard Wright's *Black Boy*, Mike Rose's *Lives on the Boundary*, Richard Rodriguez's *Hunger of Memory*, Victor Villanueva's *Bootstraps*, and Keith Gilyard's *Voices of the Self*, Hunter–Gault's story is in part a literacy narrative, an account of how she moved into education, standard language, and the cultures of schools. These stories remind us that pronunciation has yet to overcome pigmentation, to dissolve the barriers or resolve the discord that divides Black, Brown, and White in the United States. We need to read these stories of what it is that divides us to better understand what it is that may unite us—our common grounds, common values, and common places.

In *Loose Canons,* Henry Louis Gates provides a succinct definition of why and how multiculturalism has begun to draw fire—not only from soccer dads, but from many academicians as well. He notes that John Henry Newman defended as the university's primary task "the power of viewing many things at once as one whole, referring them severally to their true place in the universal system, and of understanding their respective values, and determining their mutual dependence" (qtd. in Gates xv). Gates continues:

> If multiculturalism represents an age-old ideal—the dream known, in the seventeenth century, as *mathesis universalis* —why has it been the target of such ferocious attacks? Pluralism sees culture as porous, dynamic, and interactive, rather than as the fixed property of particular ethnic groups. Thus, the idea of a monolithic, homogeneous 'West' itself comes into question. Historians have pointed out that the concept of 'Western culture' may date back only to the eighteenth century. But rather than mourning—or celebrating—the loss of some putative ancestral purity, we can recognize what is valuable, resilient, resonant, cohesive, or even coherent. Some of the most formally complex

and compelling Black writers—such as Jean Toomer, Sterling Brown, Langston Hughes, Ralph Ellison, James Baldwin, Toni Morrison, and Gwendolyn Brooks—have always blended forms of Western literature with African American vernacular and written traditions. Even a vernacular form like the spiritual took as its texts the King James version of the Old and New Testaments. Toni Morrison's master's thesis was on Virginia Woolf and Faulkner. African American culture has been a model of multiculturalism and plurality, and represents the very best hope for us, collectively, to forge a new and vital common American culture in the twenty-first century" (Gates xvi–xvii).

What Gates says of African American culture, or cultures, has already been extended to history and to literary studies. The ongoing furor over Ebonics illustrates that we have yet to extend the best principles of tolerance and respect for diversity to spoken and written language variety outside of literature proper. Clearly many Whites and Blacks resent and fear the idea that we should encourage appreciation and respect for Ebonics, even though it is already present in literary and artistic representations: Douglass, Twain, Faulkner; Zora Neale Hurston; rap, blues, jazz, and Jumpin' Jack Flash.

Alongside Julia Kristeva—with reference to Eastern European genocide and rape—and Edward Said—with reference to Middle Eastern conflict—Gates is calling for very precise methods for affirming diversity without sacrificing concepts of unity, shared value, and universals of human culture. Yet, Gates notes, multiculturalism clearly represents—"either refreshingly or frighteningly—a radical departure. Like most claims of cultural novelty or revolution, this one is more than a little exaggerated. For both the challenge of cultural pluralism and the varied forms of political resistance to it go back to the founding of our republic" (*Loose Canons* xiv). The only way to transcend those divisions—to forge, for once, a civic culture that respects both differences and commonalities—is through education that seeks to comprehend the diversity of human culture. As Gates argues, "There is no tolerance without respect, and no respect without knowledge" (xv). The mindless celebration of difference for its own sake is not more tenable than the nostalgic return to some monochrome homogeneity. We all must search for a middle way and commit ourselves to its construction.

Composition and Postcolonial Studies

1. Doing so was always problematic, given the institutionalization of composition and the overwhelming tendency to commodify students and their work, tendencies with which composition has too often been complicit.

2. In a foreword to Greenbaum's text, Gary Olson sets up a dichotomy between expressivism and theory in composition calling those who espouse some form of expressivist pedagogy "boss compositionists" (a term deployed by Jim Sledd for very different purposes) and charging that they seek to "set back our disciplinary clock" in opposition to those offering important theoretical challenges (xii). This dichotomy seems particularly unfortunate as well as overdrawn. While many in composition have offered critiques of expressivism, it would be misguided to fail to recognize that expressivism, especially in its romantic incarnations, has a deep theoretical base.

3. Aniel Rallin points out that the borderlands metaphor informed both the 2003 National Association of Ethnic Studies meeting (whose theme was "Borderlands and Beyond: Examining Intersections of Race, Ethnicity, Class, Gender, Sexuality, and Nation") and the 2003 International Communication Association meeting (theme: "Communication in Borderlands").

4. See the collection *Alt.Dis: Alternative Discourses and the Academy*, ed. Christopher Schroeder, Helen Fox, and Patricia Bizzell.

Toward a Mestiza Rhetoric: Gloria Anzaldúa on Composition and Postcoloniality

1. Lahoucine Ouzgane contributed half of the questions for this interview.

Terms of Engagement: Postcolonialism, Transnationalism, and Composition Studies

1. Academic acknowledgment of the importance of multiculturalism is signaled in Ronald Takaki's 1989 essay "An Educated and Culturally Literate Person Must Study America's Multicultural Reality" in *The Chronicle of Higher Education*. On a more cynical note, Spivak suggests "the stage at which transnational trade is now, world trade

one should say, it is necessary for people in the United States to 'know other cultures'" ("Transnationality and Multiculturalist Ideology" 82–83).

2. See, for instance, Gauri Viswanathan's *Masks of Conquest*; Ngugi wa Thiong'o's *Decolonising the Mind*; Albert Wendt's "Education." Postcolonial works that treat this theme include Simi Bedford's *Yoruba Girl Dancing*; Jill Ker Conway's *The Road from Coorain: Recollections of a Harsh and Beautiful Journey into Adulthood*; Tsitsi Dangarembga's *Nervous Conditions*; Merle Hodge's *Crick, Crack, Monkey*; and George Lamming's *In the Castle of My Skin*.

3. See, for example, Jarratt, Poulakos, Vitanza's "Taking," Welch's "Interpreting."

4. Spivak's ironic self-description in her interview "Postmarked Calcutta, India."

5. See Chow's *Writing in the Diaspora* (especially "Where Have All the Natives Gone?"); Shohat's "The Struggle over Representation;" and Spivak's "Can the Subaltern Speak?"

6. See Bahri's "Once More with Feeling: What is Postcolonialism?"; Dirlik's "The Postcolonial Aura: Third World Criticism in the Age of Global Capitalism;" McClintock's "The Angel of Progress: Pitfalls of the Term 'Post-Colonialism;'" Shohat's "Notes on the Postcolonial" for critiques of the term "postcolonial."

7. For a robust critique of the essay, see Schwarz and Ray's "Postcolonial Discourse: The Raw and the Cooked."

8. See the double issues of *Social Text* 31/32 (1992) on "Third World and Postcolonial Issues," and of *ARIEL: A Review of International English Literature* 26.1/2 (1995) on the special topic "Postcolonialism and its Discontents." See also the spring 1994 issue of the *Yale Journal of Criticism* 7.1.

9. For the record, the second edition of the *American Heritage Dictionary* defines it as "of, relating to, or being the time following the establishment of independence in a colony" (968).

10. This admittedly cynical and paranoid factoid on multiculturalism is at least devoid of confusion about the conceptual meaning of the term: "Multiculturalism is a malleable buzzword which serves to legitimize several different racially and culturally oriented cosmologies that are primarily exclusive (as opposed to inclusive). The term multiculturalism is also often used as a validation for the creation of a new cultural identity as well as the reinterpretation of alleged history for sects of *minority racial and religious groups* that want (and desperately need) to constantly reaffirm their status as victims. Multiculturalism tends to be advocated by second, third, or fourth generation Americans as opposed to new immigrants. Multiculturalism equals monocentrism" (emphasis mine; "A Primer on the Subject of Multiculturalism").

11. A July 1994 issue of the journal *Counseling Psychologist* carried an article titled "Disability as Cultural Diversity." As I pondered the title, it occurred to me that it would not, perhaps, be unfair to suggest that our culture, in an ironic reversal, perceives diversity, particularly racial and sexual, as disability.

12. Visit the following site for a sampling of conservative responses to multiculturalism: <<http://www.olywa.net/alan/essay/cultural.html>>.

Encountering the Other: Postcolonial Theory and Composition Scholarship

1. I am not advocating a form of ethical relativism or a return to a neoromantic individualism that is incognizant of the power of culture, ideology, and social context. I am referring to the notion that within the social contexts of our interactions we constantly make choices, and *what* choices we make, despite the absence of external strictures, situates us firmly in the ethical domain. Also, this notion of ethics is distinct from existential ethics, the former being based on abstract reasoning and an assertion of self, the latter on mutual benefit.

2. This position is associated particularly with the work of Emmanuel Levinas and is elaborated in the work of Luce Irigaray (see Hirsh and Olson).

3. One of the finest works I know on the subject is Evelyn Ashton-Jones's "Collaboration, Conversation, and the Politics of Gender."

4. This is not to deny the power of ideology in forming the choices we make. At the same time that postmodern theory illustrates the need to participate actively in our ethical decision making, it also reveals the extent to which our ideological frameworks can work to limit the very choices we make or are able to make.

5. Of course, direct discussion of ethics is becoming more common, as indicated by this book and by the work of James Porter. Also see Moore and Kleine.

6. Interestingly, Patricia Bizzell has even argued that the contact zone can be used as a way to reorganize literary study: "This concept can aid us both because it emphasizes the conditions of difficulty and struggle under which literatures from different cultures come together (thus forestalling the disrespectful glossing over of differences), and because it gives us a conceptual base for bringing these literatures together, namely, when they occur in or are brought to the same site of struggle or 'contact zone'" ("Contact" 166).

7. A revised version of Pratt's "Arts of the Contact Zone" serves as the introduction of her book *Imperial Eyes: Studies in Travel Writing and Transculturation*.

8. Giroux makes a similar point about how compositionists and literacy scholars have appropriated the work of Freire: "What has been increasingly lost in the North American and Western appropriation of Freire's work is the profound and radical nature of its theory and practice as an anti-colonial and postcolonial discourse" ("Paulo" 193).

9. A telling indication of the deradicalizing of a potent concept like contact zone is that textbooks are beginning to emerge that attempt to "apply" contact zone theory in their overall pedagogy. If, as Kathleen Welch argues, textbooks are the most conservative repositories of our knowledge at any given moment, then one wonders what the implications are of contact zone theory being packaged in textbooks. I'm reminded, too, of C.H. Knoblauch's observation about social construction: "One can be quite sure, however, that when roving, and normally warring, bands of cognitive psychologists, text linguists, philosophers of composition, historians of rhetoric, Marxist critics, poststructuralists, and reader response theorists all wax equally enthusiastic about 'the social construction of reality,' there is a good chance that the expression has long since lost its capacity to name anything important or even very interesting" (54).

10. There are, of course, notable exceptions, but few if any draw on the kind of postcolonial theory I will be discussing shortly.

11. In *Pedagogy of the Oppressed*, Freire discusses the dynamic in which the oppressed desire to become like the oppressor, and he warns literacy workers to be prepared for such desire as the oppressed gain critical consciousness (chapter 1 *passim*, especially 29).

12. The story that Pratt tells of Guaman Poma's *New Chronicle* illustrates this very point, in that Poma provides a revisionist history, "written in a mixture of Quechua and ungrammatical, expressive Spanish," that imitates and parodies the official discourse: "Guaman Poma constructs his text by appropriating and adapting pieces of the representational repertoire of the invaders" ("Arts," 34, 36).

13. In a recent interview, Freire addresses misreadings of his position on teacher authority and the ethical obligation of teachers to exercise their authority (Olson).

14. A notable recent work on the subject is Xin Liu Gale's *Teacher Authority in the Postmodern Classroom*, a winner of the W. Ross Winterowd Award for the most outstanding book on composition theory.

15. One encouraging development is *JAC*'s special issue (18.1) on postcolonial theory and composition.

Pratt and Pratfalls: Revisioning Contact Zones

1. Pratt says she borrows this term from linguistics. See *Imperial Eyes* (7).

2. We did not find any reviews of Pratt's book in composition or rhetoric journals.

3. The three reviewers in the literature journals define Pratt's contact zones by quoting from Pratt, but they do not choose the same quotations. The review in *World Literature Written in English* defines Pratt's contact zones as "the space in which peoples geographically and historically separated come into contact with each other and establish ongoing relations" (6 qtd. in Pratt 125). *Research in African Literatures* offers an extended definition: "The contact zone is 'the space of colonial encounters, the space in which peoples geographically and historically separated come into contact with each other and establish ongoing relations, usually involving conditions of coercion, radical inequality, and intractable conflict' (6). Although often synonymous with 'colonial frontier,' the term 'contact zone' represents an attempt to step outside a European expansionist perspective and to recognize that both colonizers and colonized, or travelers and 'travelees,' are 'constituted in and by their relations to each other' (7) as well as that an imbalance of power governs those relations. It extends the question of how European travel writing has produced 'the rest of the world' to that of how 'Europe's constructions of subordinated others' (6) have been both shaped and appropriated by those others." (155)

The review in *Novel* notes that Pratt employs several idiosyncratic terms, such as "contact zone," which are sure to become (if they are not already) common parlance in discussions of imperialism. "Contact zones" are "social spaces where disparate cultures meet, clash, and grapple with each other, often in highly asymmetrical relations of domination and subordination" (4). As Pratt points out, "contact zone" is often syn-onymous with "colonial frontier;" her use of the former term illustrates her effort to avoid the "European expansionist perspective" (7) associated not only with the latter term but with studies of the travel genre as well (364).

Beside Ourselves: Rhetoric and Representation in Postcolonial Feminist Writing

1. In the Roof and Wiegman collection, see especially essays by Leslie Bow, Dympna Callaghan, and Sabina Sawhney.

2. See Mailloux for a related definition of rhetoric incorporating political effectiv-ity and trope.

3. Chandra Talpade Mohanty's "Introduction: Cartographies of Struggle" offers a revealing critique of the ways some Western feminists have performed a similar opera-tion on "Third-World women" by beginning their analyses with the descriptive category of "woman" (59). In the research she cites, universal groupings such as "women of Africa" become "homogeneous sociological grouping[s] characterized by common de-pendencies or powerlessness" (59). Mohanty explains the ways resistance activities of Third World women—i.e., efforts toward representing themselves politically—are ob-scured by the assumption that they are "legal minors (read 'they-are-still-not-conscious-of-their-rights')" (72).

4. For similar treatments of metaphor as the "trope of privilege" (DeMan 158), see Jakobson, Johnson, Laclau and Mouffe, Ryan, and Sommer.

5. Originally titled *Me llamo Rigoberta Menchú y así me nació la conciencia*, the book was published in English in 1984 as *I, Rigoberta Menchú. An Indian Woman in Guatemala*, before Menchú Tum married and changed her name.

6. My choice of three women as representative of postcolonial feminism per-forms the kind of metaphorical substitution I analyze in the essay. I choose Spivak and Trinh because they revel in the act of writing, working over and through the problem of representation with a painful sensitivity I find appealing; Menchú, because of the urgency of her situation. I choose them because I love to read them, each for different reasons. One of my purposes for writing this essay was to direct my responses away from a "conventional ethics of altruism" (Gunn 165) or an "uncritical hero-worship" (Sommer 69), and toward a "respect [that] is the condition of possibility for the kind of love that takes care not to simply appropriate its object" (Sommer 69).

7. Robert Con Davis and David S. Gross analyze Spivak's rhetoric in terms of ethos, raising some of the issues discussed below toward the end of pointing a direc-tion for an ethical practice of cultural studies. They characterize Spivak's style in terms of "theatricality" (69) and imagine the voice of the subaltern as produced by a kind of "ventriloquism" (76).

8. In the analysis of Davis and Gross, the subaltern ethos does not refer to a par-ticular group but rather to the impossibility of any discourse of the "other" available to the colonizer that has not been "defined by and related to the master discourse" (77).

9. Spivak differentiates her work from the "information retrieval" taking place in

anthropology, political science, history, and sociology. She applies her critique of subaltern representation across these disciplinary boundaries, warning of potential for violence when historians and others assume a consciousness of the subject under examination ("Subaltern" 295). Benita Perry takes issue with Spivak and others on this point, arguing that an overscrupulous concern for such "violence" can have the effect of quelling efforts toward uncovering knowledge of colonized peoples and their resistant practices For Spivak's most recent revision of the "Subaltern" essay, see her *A Critique of Colonial Reason.*

10. See Hennessy (14–31) for a discussion of a related theory: Pecheux's concept of "dis-identification." Hennessy defines it as the practice of *"working on* the subject-form"; "a critical discourse that is distinguished by its intervention in the pre-constructed categories on which the interdiscourse depends."

11. In a survey of work at the borders of feminism and rhetoric, Lisa Ede, Cheryl Glenn, and Andrea Lunsford discuss women's alternative styles and the challenge by feminists of color to white feminists on issues of representation (420–28).

12. See Ede, Glenn, and Lunsford for a discussion of feminist alternatives to classical rhetorical arrangement (414–20).

13. See Jarratt and Reynolds for a related revision of classical ethos through postmodern feminist theory.

14. Although this discussion of Spivak and Trinh is focused more on theorizing than pedagogy, I have assigned portions of Trinh's book to upper-division undergraduates in classes crosslisted with Women's Studies and English. I know at least one colleague who has used her chapter "Grandma's Story" with first-year composition students, and another who has taught Spivak in undergraduate feminist theory courses.

15. I use the past tense to indicate that Menchú's literacy has changed in the twenty years since she provided the oral account that led to the publication of her testimonio. In 1982, she had been studying spoken Spanish for three years. She has since published two books in Spanish: *Clamor de la Tierra. Trenzando el Futuro : Luchas Campensinas en la Historia Reciente de Guatemala,* con Comité de Unidad Campesina (Donostia, Gipúzkoa [Spain]: Tercera Prensa, 1992) and *Rigoberta, la Nieta de los Mayas,* con la colaboración de Gianni Minà y Dante Liano (Madrid: El País-Aguilar, 1998).

16. The postcoloniality of Guatemala is multilayered. As Menchú Tum explains in her book, the Spanish conquest of Central America left as part of its legacy a three-layered society, with the indigenous Indian groups at the bottom; *ladinos,* Spanish-speaking, assimilated *mestizos,* in the middle; and upper-class descendants of the Spanish conquerors at the top.

17. Susan Morgan makes this point eloquently in her recent book on Victorian women writers in southeast Asia, arguing (through the title) that *Place Matters.* She points out major differences among Singapore, Thailand, and India in their histories of contact with the West, economies, and social structures, and shows how those differences matter in our interpretations of colonial and postcolonial literatures.

18. Other examples of testimonio include Domitilia Barrios, *Let Me Speak;* Eugenia Claribel Alegría, *They Won't Take Me Alive;* and Elvia Alvarado, *Don't Be Afraid, Gringo.*

The Politics of Location: Using Flare-Ups to Spark "Reflexive Dialogue" in the Ever-Changing Classroom Text

1. Tom and Mike gave me permission to use their names and e-mail exchange.

2. In her introduction to an edited collection entitled *Outbursts in Academe: Multiculturalism and Other Sources of Conflict,* Kathleen Dixon views outbursts as "researchable moments in the lives of teachers and students."

The New Literacy/Orality Debates: Ebonics and the Redefinition of Literacy in Multicultural Settings

1. Geneva Smitherman has compiled the editorial and media responses to the King Elementary School decision and Ebonics debate in "Ebonics, King, and Oakland: Some Folk Don't Believe Fat Meat is Greasy."

2. Fuller references to the work of Lord, Parry, Ong, and others may be found in a special issue of *Pre/Text* 7 (1986) entitled "The Literacy/Orality Wars."

3. See also Beth Daniell's "Against the Great Leap of Literacy," Shirley Brice Heath's "Protean Shapes in Literacy Events: Ever-Shifting Oral and Literate Traditions," and J. Beverly Moss's *A Community Text Arises: A Literate Text and a Literacy Tradition in African American Churches.*

4. Further assessments of Havelock and Ong may be found in *Pre/Text* 7 (1986).

Bibliography

Ahmad, Aijaz. *In Theory: Classes, Nations, Literatures*. London: Verso, 1992.

Alcoff, Linda. "The Problem of Speaking for Others." *Cultural Critique* 20 (1991–92): 5–32.

Alegría, Eugenia Claribel. *They Won't Take Me Alive*. Trans. Amanda Hopkinson. London: Women's, 1987.

Allen, Julia M., and Lester Faigley. "Discursive Strategies for Social Change: An Alternative Rhetoric of Argument." *Rhetoric Review* 14 (1995): 142–72.

Alvarado, Elvia. *Don't Be Afraid, Gringo*. Trans and Ed. Medea Benjamin. San Francisco: Institute for Food and Development Policy, 1987.

Anderson, Benedict. *Imagined Communities: Reflections on the Origins and Spread of Nationalism*. London: Verso, 1983.

Anzaldúa, Gloria. *Borderlands/La Frontera: The New Mestiza*. San Francisco: Aunt Lute, 1987.

———. Introduction. *Making Face, Making Soul: Haciendo Caras, Creative and Critical Perspectives by Women of Color*. Ed. Gloria Anzaldúa. San Francisco: Aunt Lute, 1990.

———. "La Prieta." *This Bridge Called My Back: Writings by Radical Women of Color*. Ed. Cherríe L. Moraga and Gloria Anzaldúa. 198–209.

Appiah, Kwame Anthony. *In My Father's House: Africa in the Philosophy of Culture*. New York: Oxford UP, 1992.

Ashcroft, Bill. "Modernity's First Born: Latin America and Postcolonial Transformation." *ARIEL* 29 (1998): 7–29.

Ashcroft, Bill, Gareth Griffiths, and Helen Tiffin. *The Empire Writes Back: Theory and Practice in Post-Colonial Literatures*. New York: Routledge, 1989.

———. *Post-Colonial Studies: The Key Concepts*. London: Routledge, 1998.

———. *The Post-Colonial Studies Reader*. London: Routledge, 1995.

Ashton-Jones, Evelyn. "Collaboration, Conversation, and the Politics of Gender." *Feminine Principles and Women's Experience in American Composition and Rhetoric*. Ed. Louise Wetherbee Phelps and Janet Emig. Pittsburgh: U of Pittsburgh P, 1995. 5–26.

"Attention: Potential Contributors." *Novel* 28 (1995): 2.

Bahri, Deepika. "Marginally Off-Center: Postcolonialism in the Teaching Machine." *College English* 59 (1997): 277–98.

———. "Once More with Feeling: What is Postcolonialism?" *ARIEL: A Review of International English Literature* 26 (1995): 51–82.

———. "Terms of Engagement: Postcolonialism, Transnationalism, and Composition Studies." *Exploring Borderlands* 29–44.

Bahri, Deepika, and Mary Vasudeva. *Between the Lines: South Asians and Postcoloniality*. Philadelphia: Temple UP, 1996.

————. Introduction. Ed. Bahri and Basudeva. 1–34.

Bakhtin, M. M. *The Dialogic Imagination: Four Essays*. Ed. Michael Holquist and trans. Caryl Emerson and Michael Holquist. Austin: U of Texas P, 1981.

Baldwin, James. "If Black English Isn't a Language, Then Tell Me, What is It?" 1979. *The Black Scholar* 27 (1997): 5–6.

Barrios de Chungara, Domatila. *Let Me Speak!: Testimony of Domitila, a Woman of the Bolivian Mines*. Trans. Victoria Ortiz. New York: Monthly Review, 1978.

Bartholomae, David. *Facts, Artifacts, and Counterfacts: Theory and Method for a Reading and Writing Course*. Portsmouth, N.H.: Boynton / Cook, 1986.

Bartholomae, David and Anthony Petrosky, eds. *Ways of Reading: An Anthology for Writers*. 5th ed. Boston: Bedford, 1999.

Bauman, Zygmunt. *Postmodern Ethics*. Cambridge: Blackwell, 1993.

Belenky, Mary Field, Blythe McVicker Clinchy, Nancy Rule Goldberger, and Jill Mattuck Tarule. *Women's Ways of Knowing: The Development of Self, Voice, and Mind*. New York: Basic, 1986.

Bell, Steven M. "A Prolegomenon." *Critical Theory, Cultural Politics, and Latin American Narratives*. Ed. Steven M. Bell, Albert H. LeMay, and Leonard Orr. Notre Dame, IN: U of Notre Dame P, 1993. 1–32.

Berlin, James. "Poststructuralism, Cultural Studies, and the Composition Classroom: Postmodern Theory in Practice." *Professing the New Rhetorics: A Sourcebook*. Ed. Theresa Enos and Stuart Brown. Englewood Cliffs, NJ: Prentice Hall, 1994.

————. *Rhetoric and Reality: Writing Instruction in American Colleges, 1900–1985*. Carbondale, IL: Southern Illinois UP, 1987.

————. *Rhetorics, Poetics, and Culture: Refiguring College English Studies*. Urbana, IL: NCTE, 1996.

Beverley, John. *Against Literature*. Minneapolis: U of Minnesota P, 1993.

————. "The Margin at the Center: On *Testimonio* (Testimonial Narrative)." *Modern Fiction Studies* 35 (1989): 11–28. Rpt. in *De / Colonizing the Subject: The Politics of Gender in Women's Autobiography*. Ed. Sidonie Smith and Julia Watson. Minneapolis: U of Minnesota P, 1992. 91–114.

Bhabha, Homi. *The Location of Culture*. London: Routledge, 1994.

————. "Signs Taken for Wonders: Questions of Ambivalence and Authority Under a Tree Outside Delhi." *Critical Inquiry* 12 (1985): 144–65.

Bickford, Susan. "In the Presence of Others: Arendt and Anzaldúa on the Paradox of Public Appearance." *Feminist Interpretations of Hannah Arendt*. Ed. Bonnie Honig. State College, PA: Pennsylvania State UP, 1995. 313–35.

Bitzer, Lloyd. "The Rhetorical Situation." *Philosophy and Rhetoric* 1 (1968): 1–14.

Bizzell, Patricia. *Academic Discourse and Critical Consciousness*. Pittsburgh: U of Pittsburgh P, 1992.

————. "'Contact Zones' and English Studies." *College English* 56 (1994): 163–69.

————. "Rhetoric and Social Change." Address. Conference of College Composition and Communication. Phoenix, 1997.

————. "Why, What, How: Hybridity." *Corporate Studies* 27 (1999): 7–22.

Blake, Susan. L. Rev. of *Imperial Eyes*, by Mary Louise Pratt. *Research in African Literatures* 24 (1993): 155–56.

Brady, Laura. "The Reproduction of Othering." *Feminism and Composition Studies*. Ed. Susan C. Jarratt and Lynn Worsham. New York: MCA, 21–44.

Brinton, Alan. "Situation in the Theory of Rhetoric." *Philosophy and Rhetoric* 14 (1981): 234–48.

Brodkey, Linda. *Writing Permitted in Designated Areas Only*. Minneapolis: U of Minnesota P, 1996.

Brown, Stephen Gilbert. *Words in the Wilderness: Critical Literacy in the Borderlands*. Albany, NY: State U of New York P, 2000.

Bullock, Richard and John Trimbur, eds. *The Politics of Writing Instruction*. Portsmouth, N.H.: Boynton/Cook, 1991.

Burke, Kenneth. *A Rhetoric of Motives*. Berkeley: U of California P, 1969.

———. *The Philosophy of Literary Form: Studies in Symbolic Action*. Berkeley: U of California P, 1969.

Campbell, Mary. Rev. of *Imperial Eyes*, by Mary Louise Pratt. *American Ethnologist* 21 (1994): 931–33.

Canagarajah, A. Suresh. "'Nondiscursive' Requirements in Academic Publishing, Material Resources of Periphery Scholars, and the Politics of Knowledge Production." *Written Communication* 13 (1996.): 435–72.

Carpenter, Edmond S. "Witch-fear among the Aivilik Eskimos." *Eskimo of the Canadian Arctic*. Ed. Victor F. Valentine and Frank G. Vallee. Toronto: McClelland, 1968. 53–66.

Carroll, David. Rev. of *Imperial Eyes*, by Mary Louise Pratt. *The Journal of Imperial and Commonwealth History* 21 (1993): 157–58.

Castillo, Ana. "Universally Speaking." *Austin American-Statesman* 24 May 1998, H1.

Chow, Rey. *Writing in the Diaspora: Tactics of Intervention in Contemporary Cultural Studies*. Bloomington: Indiana UP, 1993.

Cixous, Hélène and Catherine Clément. *The Newly Born Woman*. Trans. Betsy Wing. Minneapolis: U of Minnesota P, 1986.

Cliff, Michelle. "A Journey Into Speech." *The Graywolf Annual Five: Multicultural Literacy*. Ed. Rick Simonson and Scott Walker. Saint Paul, MN: Graywolf P, 1988. 57–62.

Clifford, James. *The Predicament of Culture: Twentieth-Century Ethnography, Literature, and Art*. Cambridge, MA: Harvard UP, 1988.

Clifford, John, and John Schlib, eds. *Writing Theory and Critical Theory*. New York: MLA, 1994.

Code, Lorraine. *Rhetorical Spaces: Essays on Gendered Locations*. New York: Routledge, 1995.

Coe, Richard M. "An Apology for Form; or, Who took the Form out of the Process?" *College English* 49 (1987): 13–28.

———. "Genre Theory: Australian and North American Approaches." *Theorizing Composition: A Critical Sourcebook in Contemporary Composition Studies*. Westport, CT: Greenwood, 1998. 3–19.

Connors, Robert, and Cheryl Glenn. *The St. Martin's Guide to Teaching Writing*. New York: St. Martin's, 1995.

Conway, Jill Ker. *The Road from Coorain: Recollections of a Harsh and Beautiful Journey into Adulthood*. New York: Knopf, 1989.

Coombs, Kate. "Technical Problems Derail English Only Case in Supreme Court." *The NCTE Council Chronicle* (1997): 3.

Couling, Scott. "Traveling Reviews." *World Literature Written in English* 32 (1993): 123–25.

Cruz, José E. *Identity and Power: Puerto Rican Politics and the Challenge of Ethnicity*. Philadelphia: Temple UP, 1998.

Cummins, James. "The Role of Primary Language Development in Promoting Educational Success for Language Minority Students." *Schooling and Language Minority Students: A Theoretical Framework*. Los Angeles: Evaluation, Dissemination and Assessment Center, California State University, 1981: 4–49.

Dangarembga, Tsitsi. *Nervous Conditions*. Aberystwyth, Wales: Women's, 1988.

Daniell, Beth. "Against the Great Leap Theory of Literacy." *Pre/Text* 7 (1986): 181-94.

Davies, Carole B. "Collaboration and the Ordering Imperative in Life Story Production." *De/Colonizing the Subject: The Politics of Gender in Women's Autobiography*. Ed. Sidonie Smith and Julia Watson. Minneapolis: U of Minnesota P, 1992. 3–19.

Davis, Deborah. "Censorship in America." *The American Voice* 17 (1989): 66–80.

Davis, Robert Con, and David S. Gross. "Gayatri Chakravorty Spivak and the *Ethos* of the Subaltern." *Ethos: New Essays in Rhetorical and Critical Theory*. Ed. James S. Baumlin and Tita French Baumlin. Dallas: Southern Methodist, 1994. 65–89.

Dirlik, Arif. "The Postcolonial Aura: Third World Criticism in the Age of Global Capitalism." *Critical Inquiry* 20 (1994): 328–56.

Dixon, Kathleen, ed. *Outbursts in Academe: Multiculturalism and Other Sources of Conflict*. Portsmouth, N.H.: Boynton/Cook, 1998.

Dixon, Kathleen, and William Archibald. Introduction. Ed. Dixon. ?–?.

Douglass, Frederick. *Narrative of the Life of Frederick Douglass, An American Slave*. Cambridge, MA: Harvard UP, 1960.

D'Souza, Dinesh. *Illiberal Education: The Politics of Race and Sex on Campus*. New York: Vintage, 1991.

Ede, Lisa, Cheryl Glenn, and Andrea Lunsford. "Border Crossings: Intersections of Rhetoric and Feminism." *Rhetorica* 13 (1995): 401–41.

Elbow, Peter. *Writing with Power: Techniques for Mastering the Writing Process*. New York: Oxford UP, 1981.

Faigley, Lester. *Fragments of Rationality: Postmodernity and the Subject of Composition*. Pittsburgh: U of Pittsburgh P, 1992.

Fanon, Frantz. *The Wretched of the Earth*. Trans. C. Farrington. New York: Grove, 1968.

Ferguson, Moira. Rev. of *Imperial Eyes*, by Mary Louise Pratt. *Eighteenth-Century Studies* 26 (1993): 481–84.

Fitts, Karen, and Alan W. France. *Left Margins: Cultural Studies and Composition Pedagogy*. New York: State U of New York P, 1995.

Flower, Linda, Elenore Long, and Lorraine D. Higgins. *Learning to Rival: A Literate Practice for Intercultural Inquiry*. Mahwah, NJ: Lawrence Erlbaum Associates, 2000.

Flynn, Elizabeth A. *Feminism Beyond Modernism*. Carbondale, IL: Southern Illinois UP, 2002.

Fox, Helen. *Listening to the World: Cultural Issues in Academic Writing*. Urbana, IL: NCTE, 1994.

Fox, Tom. *Defending Access: A Critique of Standards in Higher Education*. Portsmouth, N.H.: Boynton/Cook-Heinemann, 1999.

Franklin, Phyllis. "From the Editor." *Profession* 91 (1991): 1–2.

Freire, Paulo. *Education: The Practice of Freedom*. New York: Writers & Readers, 1976.

———. *Pedagogy of the Oppressed*. Trans. Myra Bergman Ramos. New York: Continuum, 1989.

Gale, Xin Liu. *Teachers, Discourses, and Authority in the Postmodern Composition Classroom*. Albany, NY: State U of New York P, 1996.

Gates, Henry Louis. *Loose Canons*. New York: Oxford UP, 1992.

Gay, Pamela. "Improving Classroom Culture: Using Electronic Dialogue to Face Difference." *The Online Writing Classroom*. Ed. Michael Day, Susanmarie Harrington, and Rebecca Rickly. Cresskill, NJ: Hampton, 2000. 147–58.

Gelles, Paul H. "Testimonio, Ethnography and Processes of Authorship." *Anthropology Newsletter* (1998): 16–17.

Gere, Anne Ruggles, Ed. *Into the Field: Sites of Composition Studies*. New York: MLA, 1993.

Gilyard, Keith. *Race, Rhetoric, and Composition*. Portsmouth, N.H.: Boynton/Cook, 1999.

———. *Voices of the Self: A Study of Language Competence*. Detroit: Wayne State UP, 1991.

Giroux, Henry. *Living Dangerously: Multiculturalism and the Politics of Difference, Vol 1*. Ed. J. L Kincheloe and S. R. Steinberg. New York: Lang, 1993.

———. "Paulo Freire and the Politics of Postcolonialism." *Composition Theory in the Postmodern Classroom*. Ed. Gary A. Olson and Sidney I. Dobrin. Albany, NY: State U of New York P, 1994. 193–204.

Giroux, Henry and Peter McLaren. *Between Borders: Pedagogy and the Politics of Cultural Studies*. New York: Routledge, 1994.

Godfrey, Brian J. Rev. of *Imperial Eyes*, by Mary Louise Pratt. *The Annals of the Association of American Geographers* 83 (1993): 542–44.

Godzich, Wlad. *The Culture of Literacy*. Cambridge: Harvard UP, 1994.

Goody, Jack and Ian Watt. *The Consequences of Literacy*. Indianapolis, Bobbs-Merrill, 1963.

Greenbaum, Andrea. *Insurrections: Approaches to Resistance in Composition Studies*. Albany, NY: State U of New York P, 2001.

Guamán Poma de Ayala, Felipe. *New Cronicle [sic] and Good Government: An Indian Account of the Pre-Incas and Incas of Peru*. Trans. G.R. Coulthard. Kingston, Jamaica: University of the West Indies, 1968.

Guerra, Juan. *Close to Home: Oral and Literate Practices in a Transnational Mexican Community*. New York: Teachers College, 1998.

Guha, Ranajit. "Preface." *Selected Subaltern Studies*. Ed. Ranajit Guha and Gayatri Chakravorty Spivak. New York: Oxford UP, 1988. 35–36.

Gupta, Sunil, ed. *Disrupted Borders: An Intervention in Definitions of Boundaries*. London: Rivers Oram P, 1993.

Guy-Sheftall, Beverly. Address. Conference on Gender Issues in Higher Education. October 1994. Burlington, Vermont.

Hall, Catherine. Rev. of *Women's Orients: English Women and the Middle East, 1718–1918*, by Billie Melman, *Discourses of Difference: An Analysis of Women's Travel Writing and Colonialism*, by Sara Mills, and *Imperial Eyes: Travel Writing and Transculturation*, by Mary Louise Pratt. *Feminist Review* 45 (1993): 132–35.

Hall, Stuart. "Cultural Identity and Diaspora." *Contemporary Postcolonial Theory: A Reader.* Ed. Padmini Mongia. New York: Arnold, 1996.

Harkin, Patricia, and John Schilb, eds. *Contending with Words: Composition and Rhetoric in a Postmodern Age.* New York: MLA, 1991.

Hammersley, Martyn. *What's Wrong With Ethnography?* London: Routledge, 1992.

Harlow, Barbara. *Resistance Literature.* New York: Methuen, 1987.

Harris, Joseph. *A Teaching Subject: Composition Since 1966.* Upper Saddle River, NJ: Prentice Hall, 1997.

——. "Negotiating the Contact Zone." *Journal of Basic Writing* 14 (1995): 27–42.

Havelock, Eric. "After Words: A Post Script." *Pre/Text* 7 (1986): 201–8.

——. "Orality, Literacy, and *Star Wars*, Discussion." *Pre/Text* 7 (1986): 123–44.

——. *Preface to Plato.* Cambridge, MA: Harvard UP, 1963.

HCOP 1998 Essays. Health Career Opportunity Program. Collection of unpublished student essays. Southwest Texas State University, San Marcos, Texas.

"Headcount of Employees by Campus." Available at <www.calstate.edu/HR/Fall2000CSUProfiles.pdf> 25 Jan. 2001.

Heath, Shirley Brice. "Protean Shapes in Literacy Events: Ever-Shifting Oral and Literate Traditions." *Spoken and Written Language: Exploring Orality and Literacy.* Ed. Deborah Tannen. Norwood, NJ: Ablex, 1982. 91-117.

——. "The Fourth Vision: Literate Language at Work." *The Right to Literacy.* Ed. Andrea A. Lunsford, Helene Moglen, and James Slevin. New York: MLA, 1990. 289–306.

Heath, Shirley Brice and Milbrey W. McLaughlin, eds. *Identity and Inner-City Youth: Beyond Ethnicity and Gender.* New York: Teachers College, 1993.

——. "Ethnicity and Gender in Theory and Practice: The Youth Perspective." Heath and Milbrey 13–35.

——. Introduction. Heath and Milbrey 1–12.

Helmers, Marguerite H. *Writing Students: Composition Testimonials and Representations of Students.* Albany, NY: State U of New York P, 1994.

Hennessy, R. "Women's Lives / Feminist Knowledge: Feminist Standpoint as Ideology Critique." *Hypatia* 8 (Winter 1993): 14–31.

Henwood, Patricia G. "Disability as Cultural Diversity: Counseling the Hearing Impaired." *Counseling Psychologist* 22 (1994): 489–503.

Hinojosa, Rolando. *Mi querido Rafa.* Houston: Arte Público, 1981.

——. *Dear Rafe.* Houston: Arte Público Press, 1985.

——. *The Useless Servants.* Houston: Arte Público Press, 1993.

Hirsh, Elizabeth and Gary A. Olson. "'Je—Luce Irigaray': A Meeting with Luce Irigaray."

Women Writing Culture. Ed. Gary A. Olson and Elizabeth Hirsh. Albany, NY: State U of New York P, 1995. 141–66.

Hoang, Haivan. "Flexible Rhetorics: Viet-Americans Discursively Effect Community." Diss. Ohio State University.

Hodge, Merle. *Crick, Crack, Monkey.* Portsmouth, N.H.: Heinemann, 2001.

Holloway, Lynette. "Unswayed by Debate on Children's Book." *New York Times* 10 Dec. 1998: B3.

Holquist, Michael. Introduction. *The Dialogic Imagination: Four Essays.* Trans. Caryl Emerson and Michael Holquist. Austin: U of Texas P, 1981. xv–xxxiv.

hooks, bell. *Teaching to Transgress: Education as the Practice of Freedom.* New York: Routledge, 1994.

———. "Third World Diva Girls: Politics of Feminist Solidarity." *The Woman-Centered Economy: Ideals, Reality, and the Space In Between.* Ed. Loraine Edwards and Midge Stocker. Chicago: Third Side, 1995. 265–80.

Horner, Bruce. "Mapping Errors and Expectations for Basic Writing: From the 'Frontier Field' to 'Border Country.'" *English Education* 26 (1994): 29–51.

———. *Terms of Work for Composition: A Materialist Critique.* Albany, NY: State U of New York P, 2000.

Horno-Delgado, Asuncion, Eliana Ortega, Nina M. Scott, and Nancy Spaporta Sternbach, eds. *Breaking Boundaries: Latina Writing and Critical Readings.* Amherst: U of Massachusetts P, 1989.

Hull, Glynda and Mike Rose. "Rethinking Remediation: Toward a Social-Cognitive Understanding of Problematic Reading and Writing." *Written Communication* 6 (1989): 139–54.

Hull, Glynda, Mike Rose, Kay Losey Fraser, and Marisa Castellano. "Remediation as Social Construct: Perspectives from an Analysis of Classroom Discourse." *College Composition and Communication* 42 (1991): 299–329.

Hunter-Gault, Charlayne. *In My Place.* New York: Random, 1995.

Hutcheon, Linda. "Circling the Downspout of Empire: Post-Colonialism and Postmodernism." *Past the Last Post: Theorizing Post-Colonialism and Post-Modernism.* Ed. Ian Adam and Helen Tiffin. Calgary: U of Calgary P, 1990. 167–89.

Hymes, Dell. "Notes Toward (An Understanding Of) Supreme Fictions." *Studies in Historical Change.* Ed. Ralph Cohen. Charlottesville: U of Virginia P, 1992. 128–78.

Ireland, Jeannette. "Ideology, Myth and Maintenance of Cultural Identity." *English Language Research Journal* 3 (1989): 95–136.

Irigaray, Luce. *This Sex Which Is Not One.* Trans. Catherine Porter. Ithaca: Cornell UP, 1985.

Jakobson, Roman. "Two Aspects of Language and Two Types of Linguistic Disturbances." *Fundamentals of Language.* Ed. Roman Jakobson and Morris Halle. The Hague: Mouton, 1956.

Jamieson, Kathleen Hall. "Antecedent Genre as Rhetorical Constraint." *Quarterly Journal of Speech* 61 (1975): 406–15.

———. "Generic Constraints and the Rhetorical Situation." *Philosophy and Rhetoric* 6 (1973): 162–70.

Jamieson, Kathleen Hall and Karlyn Kohrs Campbell. "Form and Genre in Rhetorical Criticism: An Introduction." *Form and Genre: Shaping Rhetorical Action* Ed. K. Jamieson and K. Campbell. Falls Church, VA: Speech Communication Association, 1978. 9–32.

———. "Rhetorical Hybrids: Fusions of Generic Elements." *Quarterly Journal of Speech* 68 (1982): 146–57.

Jamieson, Sandra. "The United Colors of Multiculturalism: Rereading Composition Textbooks in the 90's." Unpublished manuscript. 1993.

JanMohamed, Abdul J. "The Economy of Manichean Allegory: The Function of Racial Difference in Colonialist Literature." *Critical Inquiry* 12 (1985): 59–87.

Jarratt, Susan C. "In Excess: Radical Extensions of Neopragmatism." *Rhetoric, Sophistry, Pragmatism.* Ed. Steven Mailloux. Cambridge: Cambridge UP, 1995. 206–27.

Jarratt, Susan, and Lynn Worsham, eds. *Feminism and Composition Studies.* New York: MLA 1998.

Jay, Gregory S. "Knowledge, Power, and the Struggle for Representation." *College English* 56 (1994): 9–29.

Keating, AnaLouise. *Women Reading/Women Writing: Self-Invention in Paula Gunn Allen, Gloria Anzaldúa, and Audre Lorde.* Philadelphia: Temple UP, 1996.

Kelly, George. *A Theory of Personality: The Psychology of Personal Constructs.* New York: Norton, 1963.

Kennedy, George A., ed. *On Rhetoric: A Theory of Civic Discourse.* New York: Oxford UP, 1991.

King, Richard C. *Postcolonial America.* Urbana, IL: U of Illinois P, 2000.

Knoblauch, C. H. "Some Observations on Freire's *Pedagogy of the Oppressed.*" *Journal of Advanced Composition* 8 (1988): 50–54.

Krashen, Stephen D. "Bilingual Education and Second Language Acquisition Theory." *Schooling and Language Minority Students: A Theoretical Framework.* Los Angeles: Evaluation, Dissemination and Assessment Center, California State University, 1981: 51–79.

Krauss, Clifford. "Guatemala's War: Ideology Is the Latest Excuse." *The New York Times.* 9 Apr. 1995. E5.

Kreisberg, Seth. *Transforming Power: Domination, Empowerment, and Education.* Albany, NY: State Un of New York P, 1992.

Kristeva, Julia. *Strangers to Ourselves.* Trans. Leon S. Roudiez. Hemel. Hempstead, UK: Harvester Wheatsheaf, 1991.

Krupat, Arnold. *For Those Who Came After: A Study of American Indian Autobiography.* Berkeley: U of California P, 1985.

Lakoff, George and Mark Johnson. *Metaphors We Live By.* Chicago: U of Chicago P, 1980.

Lamb, Catherine E. "Beyond Argument in Feminist Composition." *The Writing Teacher's Sourcebook,* 3d ed. Ed. Gary Tate, Edward P. J. Corbett, and Nancy Myers. New York: Oxford UP, 1994. 195–206.

————. "Less Distance, More Space: A Feminist Theory of Power and Writer/Audience Relationships." *Rhetoric and Ideology: Compositions and Criticisms of Power.* Ed. Charles W. Kneupper. Arlington: Rhetoric Society of America, 1989. 99–104.

Lamming, George. *In the Castle of My Skin.* Ann Arbor: U of Michigan P, 1991.

Landry, Donna and Gerald MacLean, eds. *The Spivak Reader.* New York: Routledge, 1996.

Latour, Bruno. *Science in Action: How to Follow Scientists and Engineers through Society.* Cambridge: Harvard UP, 1987.

Legarreta-Marcaida, Dorothy. "Effective Use of the Primary Language in the Classroom." *Schooling and Language Minority Students: A Theoretical Framework.* Los Angeles: Evaluation, Dissemination and Assessment Center, California State University, 1981. 83–116.

Leitch, Vincent B. *Cultural Criticism, Literary Theory, Poststructuralism.* New York: Columbia UP, 1992.

Leith, Dick and George Myerson. *The Power of Address: Explorations in Rhetoric.* London: Routledge, 1989.

Lejeune, Philippe. *On Autobiography.* Trans. Katherine Leary. Minneapolis: U of Minnesota P, 1989.

Linguistic Society of America. "Resolution on the Oakland Ebonics Issue." 1997. <http://www.lsadc.org/ebonics.htm>

Logan, Shirley Wilson. *"We Are Coming."* Carbondale, IL: Southern Illinois UP, 1999.

Lorimer, Douglas A. Rev. of *Imperial Eyes*, by Mary Louise Pratt. *Journal of Modern History* 68 (1996): 429–31.

Lu, Min-Zhan. "Conflict and Struggle: The Enemies or Preconditions of Basic Writing?" *College English* 54 (1992): 887–913.

————. "Defining the Literate Self: The Politics of Cultural Affirmation." *CCC* 51 (1999): 172–94.

————. "Professing Multiculturalism: The Politics of Style in the Contact Zone." *College English* 45 (1994): 442–58.

————. "Reading and Writing Difference: The Problematic of 'Experience.'" *Feminism and Composition Studies: In Other Words.* Ed. Susan C. Jarratt and Lynn Worsham. New York: MLA, 1998.

Lugones, Maria. "Playfulness, 'World'-Travelling, and Loving Perception." *Making Face, Making Soul.* Ed. Gloria Anzaldúa. San Francisco: Aunt Lute, 1990. 390–402.

Lunsford, Andrea A., ed. *Reclaiming Rhetorica: Women in the Rhetorical Tradition.* Pittsburgh: U of Pittsburgh P, 1995.

Lunsford, Andrea and Lahoucine Ouzgane. *Exploring Borderlands: Postcolonial and Composition Studies.* Spec. issue of *JAC: A Journal of Composition Theory* 18 (1998).

Lunsford, Andrea and Lisa Ede. "Representing Audience: 'Successful' Discourse and Disciplinary Critique." *CCC* 47 (1996): 167–79.

Magner, Denise K. "Wisconsin Student Complains about Professor's Use of the Word 'Niggardly.'" *The Chronicle of Higher Education* 12 Feb. 1999: A11.

Maher, Jane. *Mina P. Shaughnessy: Her Life Work.* Urbana, IL: NCTE, 1997.

Mailloux, Steven, ed. *Rhetoric, Sophistry, Pragmatism.* Cambridge: Cambridge UP, 1995.

Malinowski, Bronislaw. *Myth in Primitive Psychology*. New York: Norton, 1926.

Mani, Lata. "Multiple Mediations: Feminist Scholarship in the Age of Multinational Reception." *Feminist Review* 35 (1990): 24–41.

Marcus, George E. and Dick Cushman. "Ethnographies as Texts." *Annual Review of Anthropology* 11 (1982): 25–69.

Marín, Lynda. "Speaking Out Together: Testimonials of Latin American Women." *Latin American Perspectives* 18 (1991): 51–68.

Marsh, William J. and Gladys Yoakum Wright. "Texas, Our Texas." San Antonio: Southern Music Company, 1929.

Marx, Karl. "The Eighteenth Brumaire of Louis Bonaparte." *The Marx Reader*. 2nd ed. Ed. Robert C. Tucker. New York: Norton, 1978. 594–617.

Mason, Peter. "Review Essay: Figures of America." *Eighteenth-Century Life* 20 (1996): 107–116.

McClintock, Anne. "The Angel of Progress: Pitfalls of the Term 'Post-Colonialism,'" *Social Text* 31/32 (1992): 84–98.

McComiskey, Bruce. *Gorgias and the New Sophistic Rhetoric*. Carbondale, IL: Southern Illinois UP, 2002.

McCrum, Robert, Robert McNeil, and William Cram. *The Story of English*. New York: Penguin, 2003.

McGrath, Robin. *Canadian Inuit Literature: The Development of a Tradition*. Ottawa: National Museums of Canada, 1984.

———. "Oral Influence in Contemporary Inuit Literature." *The Native in Literature*. Ed. Thomas King, Cheryl Calver, and Helen Hoy. Oakville: ECW, 1987. 159–73.

McWilliam, Henry O. A. *The Development of Education in Ghana*. New York: International Association of Schools of Social Work, 1977.

Memmi, Albert. *The Colonizer and the Colonized*. Trans. Howard Greenfeld. Boston: Beacon, 1992.

Menchú, Rigoberta. *I, Rigoberta Menchu: An Indian Woman in Guatemala*. Ed. Elisabeth Burgos-Debray. Trans. Ann Wright. London: Verso, 1984.

Mignolo, Walter D. "Globalization, Civilization Processes, and the Relocation of Languages and Cultures." *The Cultures of Globalization*. Eds. Fredric Jameson and Masao Miyoshi. Durham: Duke UP, 1998. 32–53.

Milanés, Cecilia Rodríguez. "Journey toward Voice; or, Constructing One Latina's Poetics." *Other Sisterhoods: Literary Theory and Women of Color*. Ed. Sandra Kumamoto Stanley. Urbana, IL: U of Illinois P, 1998.

———. "Risks, Resistance, and Rewards: One Teacher's Story." *Composition and Resistance*. Ed. C. Mark Hurlbert and Michael Blitz. Portsmouth, N.H.: Boynton/Cook, 1994. 115–24.

Miller, Carolyn R. "Genre as Social Action." *Quarterly Journal of Speech* 70 (1984): 161–67.

Miller, Richard E. "Composing English Studies: Towards a Social History of the Discipline." *College Composition and Communication* 45 (1994): 164–79.

———. "Fault Lines in the Contact Zone." *College English* 56 (1994): 389–408.

Miller, Susan. *Textual Carnivals: The Politics of Composition*. Carbondale, IL: Southern Illinois UP, 1991.

Mills, Sara. Rev. of *Imperial Eyes*, by Mary Louise Pratt. *Journal of Historical Geography* 20 (1994): 497–98.

Minh-ha, Trinh T. "Cotton and Iron." *Out There: Marginalization and Contemporary Cultures.* Ed. Russell Ferguson, Martha Gever, Trinh T. Minh-ha, and Cornel West. Cambridge, MA: MIT Press, 1990. 327–36.

———. "Outside *When the Moon Waxes Red.*" New York: Routledge, 1991.

———. *Woman, Native, Other: Writing, Postcoloniality and Feminism.* Bloomington: Indiana UP, 1989.

Mohanty, Chandra Talpade. "Defining Genealogies: Feminist Reflections on Being South Asian in North America." *Our Feet Walk the Sky: Writers of the South Asian Diaspora.* Eds. The Women of South Asian Descent Collective. San Francisco: Aunt Lute, 1993. 351–58.

———. "Introduction: Cartographies of Struggle, Third World Women and the Politics of Feminism." *Third World Women and the Politics of Feminism.* Ed. Chandra Talpade Mohanty, Ann Russo, and Lourdes Torres. Bloomington: Indiana UP, 1991. 1–47.

———. "On Race and Voice: Challenges for Liberal Education in the 1990s." Giroux and McLaren 145–66.

———. "On Race and Voice: Challenges for Liberal Education in the 1990s." *Cultural Critique* 14 (1989–1990): 179–208.

Mohanty, S. P. "'Us and Them': On the Philosophical Bases of Political Criticism." *New Formations* 8 (1989): 55–80.

Mohr, Nicholasa. "Puerto Rican Writers in the U.S., Puerto Rican Writers in Puerto Rico: A Separation Beyond Language (testimonio)." Horno-Delgado et. al. 111–16.

———. *Rituals of Survival: A Woman's Portfolio.* Houston: Arte Publico, 1986.

Moi, Toril. "Feminism, Postmodernism, and Style: Recent Feminist Criticism in the United States." *Cultural Critique* 9 (1988): 3–24.

Mongia, Padmini, ed. *Contemporary Postcolonial Theory: A Reader.* New York: Arnold, 1996.

Montejano, David. *Anglos and Mexicans in the Making of Texas, 1836–1986.* Austin: U of Texas P, 1987.

Moore, Sandy and Michael Kleine. "Toward an Ethics of Teaching Writing in a Hazardous Context—The University." *Composition Theory for the Postmodern Classroom.* Ed. Gary A. Olson and Sidney I. Dobrin. Albany, NY: State U of New York P, 1994. 93–104.

Moraga, Cherríe and Gloria Anzaldúa. *This Bridge Called My Back: Writings by Radical Women of Color.* New York: Women of Color, 1983.

Moss, Beverly J. *A Community Text Arises: A Literate Text and a Literacy Tradition in African American Churches.* Creskill, NJ: Hampton P, 2003.

"'Nappy' Isn't About 'Nappy' At All," letter, *Chicago Sun-Times* 13 Dec. 1998.

Narayan, Uma. "Working Together across Difference: Some Considerations on Emotions and Political Practice." *Hypatia* 3 (1988): 31–47.

Nuligak. *I, Nuligak: The Autobiography of a Canadian Eskimo.* Ed. Maurice Metayer. Richmond Hill, ON: Pocket, 1966.

Olson, Gary A. "History, *Praxis*, and Change: Paulo Freire and the Politics of Literacy."

(Inter)views: Cross-Disciplinary Perspectives on Rhetoric and Literacy. Ed. Gary A. Olson and Irene Gale. Carbondale, IL: Southern Illinois UP, 1991: 155–68.

Ortega, Eliana. "Poetic Discourse of the Puerto Rican Woman in the U. S.: New Voices of Anacaonian Liberation." Horno-Delgado et. al. 122–35.

Oxford English Dictionary. 1993 ed.

Paredes, Américo. "The Problem of Identity in a Changing Culture: Popular Expressions of Culture Conflict along the Lower Rio Grande Border." *Folklore and Culture on the Texas-Mexican Border.* Ed. Richard Bauman. Austin: CMAS Books, 1993. 19–47.

———. *Uncle Remus con chile.* Houston: Arte Público, 1993.

Parry, Benita. "Problems in Current Theories of Colonial Discourse." *Oxford Literary Review* 9 (1987): 27–58.

Pecheux, Michel. *Language, Semantics and Ideology.* New York: St. Martin's Press, 1975.

Pennycook, A. "Borrowing Others' Words: Text, Ownership, Memory, and Plagiarism." *TESOL Quarterly* 30 (1996): 201–30.

Perry, Donna. *Backtalk: Women Writers Speak Out.* New Brunswick, NJ: Rutgers UP, 1993.

Phelps, Louise Wetherbee, and Janet Emig, eds. *Feminine Principles and Women's Experience in American Composition and Rhetoric.* Pittsburgh: U of Pittsburgh P, 1995.

Porter, James E. "Developing a Postmodern Ethics of Rhetoric and Composition." *Defining the New Rhetorics.* Ed. Theresa Enos and Stuart C. Brown. Newbury Park, CA: Sage, 1993. 207–26.

Pratt, Mary Louise. "Arts of the Contact Zone." *Profession* 91 (1991): 33–40. Rpt. "Arts of the Contact Zone." *Reading the Lives of Others: A Sequence for Writers.* Ed. David Bartholomae and Anthony Petrosky. Boston: St. Martin's, 1995. 180–95.

———. "Criticism in the Contact Zone: Decentering Community and Nation." *Critical Theory, Cultural Politics, and Latin American Narratives.* Ed. Steven M. Bell, Albert H. LeMay, and Leonard Orr. Notre Dame, IN: U of Notre Dame P, 1993. 83–102.

———. *Imperial Eyes: Travel Writing and Transculturation.* London: Routledge, 1992.

"A Primer on the Subject of Multiculturalism, Xenophobia, Racism, Dubious Crookedness and Honest Moneymaking in the Real World and Cyberspace." <http://www.phantom.com/~blam1/lie.html>.

Poulakos, Takis. "Human Agency in the History of Rhetoric: Gorgias's *Encomium of Helen.*" Ed. Victor J. Vitanza. 59–80.

Probyn, Elspeth. "Locating the Local." *Sight Works Volume One: Several Inquiries.* Ed. Marysia Lewandowska. London: Chance, 1988. N. pag.

Qualley, Donna. *Turns of Thought: Teaching Composition as Reflexive Inquiry.* Portsmouth, N.H.: Boynton/Cook, 1997.

Qualley, Donna and Elizabeth Chiseri-Strater. "Collaboration as 'Reflexive Dialogue': A Knowing 'Deeper than Reason.'" *Journal of Composition Theory* (1994): 111–30.

Raspberry, William. "Diversity Changing Twin Cities' Schools." *St. Louis Post Dispatch* 21 Nov. 1988: 2B.

Reder, Stephen. "Practice-Engagement Theory: A Sociocultural Approach to Literacy Across Languages and Cultures." *Literacy Across Languages and Cultures.* Ed. Bernardo M. Ferdman, Rose-Marie Weber, Arnulfo G. Ramirez. Albany, NY: State U of New York P, 1994. 33–74.

Reitz, Caroline. "Narratives of/as Travel." Rev. of *Imperial Eyes*, by Mary Louise Pratt and *Penelope Voyages*, by Karen R. Lawrence. *Novel* 28 (1995): 363–66.

Rich, Adrienne. *On Lies, Secrets, and Silence*. New York: Norton, 1979.

Rimstead, Roxanne. "Mediated Lives: Oral Histories and Cultural Memory." *Essays on Canadian Writing* 60 (1996): 139–65.

Ritvo, Harriet. "Rev. of *Imperial Eyes*, by Mary Louise Pratt." *Victorian Studies* 36 (1993): 498–500.

Rodríguez, Abraham, Jr. "The Boy Without a Flag." *Boricuas: Influential Puerto Rican Writings—An Anthology*. Ed. Roberto Santiago. New York: Ballantine, 1995. 30–46.

Rodriguez, Richard. *Hunger of Memory: The Education of Richard Rodriguez*. New York: Bantam, 1983.

Romano, Octavio I. "The Chicano Movement in History." TQS Publications Online, 1997.

Roof, Judith, and Robyn Wiegman, eds. *Who Can Speak? Authority and Critical Identity*. Urbana, IL: U of Illinois P, 1995.

Roony, Ellen. "In a Word: Interview." Introduction. Gayatri Chakravorty Spivak. *Outside in the Teaching Machine*. New York: Routledge, 1993. 1–23.

Rose, Mike. *Lives on the Boundary: A Moving Account of the Struggles and Achievements of America's Educationally Underprepared*. New York: Penguin, 1990.

Rothgery, David. "'So What Do We Do Now?' Necessary Directionality as the Writing Teacher's Response to Racist, Sexist, Homophobic Papers." *College Composition and Communication* 44 (1993): 241–47.

Royster, Jacqueline Jones. "When the First Voice You Hear Is Not Your Own." *College Composition and Communication* 47 (1996): 29–40.

Royster, Jacqueline Jones, and Rebecca Greenberg Taylor. "Constructing Teacher Identity in the Basic Writing Classroom." *Journal of Basic Writing* 16 (Spring 1997): 27–50.

Royster, Jacqueline Jones, and Jean Williams. "History in the Spaces Left: African American Presence and Narratives of Composition Studies." *College Composition and Communication* 50 (1999): 563–84.

al-Saadawi, Nawal. *Woman at Point Zero*. Trans. Sherif Hetata. London: Zed Books, 1990.

Said, Edward. *Culture and Imperialism*. New York: Knopf, 1993.

——. "East Isn't East: The Impending End of the Age of Orientalism." *London Times Literary Supplement*. 3 Feb.1995, 3–6.

——. *Orientalism*. New York: Vintage, 1979.

——. "Thinking Ahead: After Survival, What Happens?" *Zmagazine* 7 April 2002 <http://www.zmag.or/content/Mideast/Saidfuture.cfm

San Miguel, Guadalupe, Jr. *"Let All of Them Take Heed": Mexican Americans and the Campaign for Educational Equality in Texas, 1910–1981*. Austin: U of Texas P, 1987.

Schell, Eileen. *Gypsy Academics and Mother-Teachers: Gender, Contingent Labor, and Writing Instruction*. Portsmouth, N.H.: Boynton/Cook, 1998..

Schell, Eileen, and Patricia Lambert Stock. *Moving a Mountain: Transforming the Role of Contingent Faculty in Composition Studies and Higher Education*. Urbana, IL: NCTE, 2001.

Schilb, John. *Between the Lines: Relating Composition Theory and Literary Theory.* Portsmouth, N.H.: Boynton/Cook, 1996.

———. "Composition and Poststructuralism: A Tale of Two Conferences." *College Composition and Communication* 40 (1989): 422–43.

Schroeder, Christopher, Helen Fox, and Patricia Bizzell, eds. *Alternative Discourses and the Academy.* Portsmouth, N.H.: Boynton/Cook, 2002.

Schwarz, Henry, and Sangeeta Ray. "Postcolonial Discourse: The Raw and the Cooked." *ARIEL: A Review of International English Literature* 26 (1995): 147–66.

Severino, Carol, Jan C. Guerra, and Johnnella E. Butler, eds. *Writing in Multicultural Settings.* New York: MLA, 1997.

Shaugnessy, Mina P. *Errors and Expectations: A Guide for the Teacher of Basic Writing.* New York: Oxford UP, 1977.

Shohat, Ella. "Notes on the Post-Colonial." *Social Text* 31/32 (1992): 99–113.

———. "The Struggle over Representation: Casting, Coalitions, and the Politics of Identification." *Late Imperial Culture.* Ed. Roman de la Campa, E. Ann Kaplan, and Michael Sprinker. London: Verso, 1995. 166–78.

Shor, Ira. *Freire for the Classroom: A Sourcebook for Liberatory Teaching.* Portsmouth, NH: Boynton-Cook, 1987.

———. *When Students Have Power.* Chicago: U of Chicago P, 1998.

Slemon, Stephen, and Helen Tiffin. Introduction. *Post-Colonial Criticism.* Spec. issue of *Kunapipi* 11 (1989): ix–xxiii.

Smitherman, Geneva. "Ebonics, King, and Oakland: Some Folk Don't Believe Fat Meat is Greasy." *Journal of English Linguistics* 26 (1998): 97–107.

Smitherman, Geneva, ed. *Black English and the Education of Black Children and Youth.* Detroit: Wayne State UP, 1981.

Soliday, Mary. "Translating Self and Difference through Literacy Narratives." *College English* 56 (1994): 511–26.

"Some Straight Talk on the Issue of Natural Hair." *Chicago Sun-Times* 13 Dec. 1998, N. pag.

Sommer, Doris. "No Secrets: Rigoberta's Guarded Truth." *Women's Studies* 20 (1991): 51–72.

Spivak, Gayatri Chakravorty. "Can the Subaltern Speak?" *Marxism and the Interpretation of Culture.* Ed. Cary Nelson and Lawrence Grossberg. Urbana, IL: U of Illinois P, 1988. 271–313.

———. *A Critique of Colonial Reason: Toward a History of the Vanishing Present.* Cambridge, MA: Harvard UP, 1999.

———. *In Other Worlds: Essays in Cultural Politics.* New York: Routledge, 1988.

———. *Outside in the Teaching Machine.* New York: Routledge, 1993.

———. "The Post-Colonial Critic." *The Post-Colonial Critic: Interviews, Strategies, Dialogues.* Ed. Sarah Harasym. New York: Routledge, 1990. 67–74.

———. "Postmarked Calcutta, India." Interview with Angela Ingram. Ed. Sarah Harasym. New York: Routledge, 1990. 75–94.

———. "Subaltern Talk." Interview. *The Spivak Reader.* Ed. Donna Landry and Gerald MacLean. New York: Routledge, 1996. 287–308.

———. "Transnationality and Multiculturalist Ideology." Ed. Bahri and Vasudeva. 64–89.

———. "Who Claims Alterity?" *Remaking History*. Ed. Barbara Kruger and Phil Mariani. Seattle: Bay, 1989. 269–92.

Stygall, Gail. "Resisting Privilege: Basic Writing and Foucault's Author Function." *College Composition and Communication* 45 (1994): 320–41.

Suleri, Sara. *The Rhetoric of English India*. Chicago: U of Chicago P, 1992.

"Summary of Data from Surveys by the Coalition on the Academic Workforce," 9 Jan. 2001. <http://www.theaha.org/caw/cawreport.htm>.

Supplement. 3 Feb. 1995, 3–6.

Swearingen, C. Jan. "Methinks Sor Juana Doth Protest Too Much! Tropes of Apology, Self-Deprecation, and Self-Abnegation in Seventeenth Century Women's Rhetoric." Address. Oregon State University Conference, "Feminisms and Rhetorics." August, 1997.

Swearingen, C. Jan, ed. *The Literacy/Orality Wars*. Spec. issue of *Pre/Text* 7 (1986).

Takaki, Ronald. "An Educated and Culturally Literate Person Must Study America's Multicultural Reality." *The Chronicle of Higher Education* 8 Mar. 1989, B1–B2.

Taylor, Jill McLean, Carol Gilligan, and Amy M. Sullivan. *Between Voice and Silence: Women and Girls*. Cambridge: Harvard UP, 1997.

Terrell, Tracy D. "The Natural Approach in English Education." *Schooling and Language Minority Students: A Theoretical Framework*. Los Angeles: Evaluation, Dissemination and Assessment Center, California State University, 1981: 117–46.

Tobin, Lad. *Writing Relationships: What Really Happens in the Composition Class*. Portsmouth, N.H.: Boynton/Cook, 1993.

Tompkins, Jane. "Fighting Words: Unlearning to Write the Critical Essay." *Georgia Review* 42 (1988): 585–90.

Urciuoli, Bonnie. *Exposing Prejudice: Puerto Rican Experiences of Language, Race, and Class*. Boulder: Westview Press, 1996.

Valdés, Guadalupe. "Bilingual Minorities and Language Issues in Writing: Toward Professionwide Responses to a New Challenge." *Written Communication* 9 (1992): 85–136.

Vatz, Richard. "The Myth of the Rhetorical Situation." *Philosophy and Rhetoric* 6 (1973): 154–61.

Velez, Diana L. *Reclaiming Medusa: Short Stories by Contemporary Puerto Rican Women*. Revised Edition. San Francisco: Aunt Lute, 1997.

Vélez-Ibáñez, Carlos G. *Border Visions: Mexican Cultures of the Southwest United States*. Tucson: U of Arizona P, 1996.

Villanueva, Jr., Victor. "Maybe a Colony? And Still Another Critique of the Composition Community." Address. College, Composition, and Communication Conference, 1997. Phoenix, Arizona.

———. *Bootstraps: From an American Academic of Color*. Urbana, IL: NCTE, 1993.

———. "On the Rhetoric and Precedents of Racism." *College Composition and Communication* 50 (1999): 645–61.

———. "Whose Voice Is It Anyway? Rodriguez's Speech in Retrospect." *English Journal* 76 (1987): 17–21.

Viswanathan, Gauri. *Masks of Conquest: Literary Study and British Rule in India.* New York: Columbia UP, 1989.

———. "Pedagogical Alternatives: Issues in Postcolonial Studies." Interview. *Between the Lines: South Asians and Postcoloniality.* Ed. Deepika Bahri and Mary Vasudeva. Philadelphia: Temple UP, 1996. 54–63.

Vitanza, Victor J. "An After/Word: Preparing to Meet the Faces That 'We' Will Have Met." Ed. Victor J. Vitanza. 217–257.

———. "Taking A-Count of a (Future-Anterior) History of Rhetoric as 'Libidinalized Marx-ism': (A PM Pastiche)." Ed. Victor J. Vitanza. 180–216.

———. ed. *Writing Histories of Rhetoric.* Carbondale, IL: Southern Illinois UP, 1994.

Walters, Keith, and Beverly J. Moss. 1993. "Rethinking Diversity: Axes of Difference in the Writing Classroom." *Theory and Practice in the Teaching of Writing: Rethinking the Discipline.* Ed. Lee Odell. Carbondale, IL: Southern Illinois UP, 1993.

Webster's Third New International Dictionary of the English Language. 1993.

Weiner, Tim. "A Guatemala Officer and the C.I.A." *The New York Times.* 26 Mar. 1997, 6.

Welch, Kathleen E. "Ideology and Freshman Textbook Production: The Place of Theory in Writing Pedagogy." *College Composition and Communication* 38 (1987): 269–82.

———. "Interpreting the Silent 'Aryan Model' of Histories of Classical Rhetoric: Martin Bernal, Terry Eagleton, and the Politics of Rhetoric and Composition Studies." Ed. Victor J. Vitanza, 38–48.

Wicomb, Zoe. "An Author's Agenda." *Critical Fictions: The Politics of Imaginative Writing.* Ed. Philomena Mariani. Seattle: Bay, 1991. 13–16.

Williams, Patrick, and Laura Christian. *Colonial Discourse and Post-Colonial Theory: A Reader.* New York: Columbia UP, 1994.

Wolff, Janice M. "Teaching in the Contact Zone: The Myth of Safe Houses." *Critical Theory and the Teaching of Literature: Politics, Curriculum, Pedagogy.* Ed. James F. Slevin and Art Young. Urbana, IL: NCTE, 1996. 316–27.

World Literature Written in English. 8 Sept.1999.<http://www.fas.nus.edu.sg/staff/jnl/wlwe/about.html>.

Wright, Richard. *Black Boy: A Record of Childhood and Youth.* New York: Harper, 1966.

Young, Robert J. C. *Colonial Desire: Hybridity in Theory, Culture, and Race.* London: Routledge, 1995.

Zentella, Ana Celia. "The Language Situation of Puerto Ricans." *Language Diversity: Problem or Resource?* Ed. Sandra Lee McKay and Sau-ling Cynthia Wong. New York: Newbury House, 1988. 140–65.

Contributors

Deepika Bahri teaches postcolonial literature and theory at Emory University. She has coedited *Between the Lines: South Asians and Postcoloniality* and has published articles in edited collections as well as in various journals, including *Ariel: A Review of International English Literature, Postmodern Culture,* and *College English.* Her book on aesthetics, politics, and postcolonial literature is forthcoming.

Martin Behr is an assistant professor of English at California State University, Northridge. His areas of research and teaching include rhetoric and composition, genre theory, postcolonial theory, and native North American literature.

Louise Rodríguez Connal earned her doctorate in rhetoric, composition, and the teaching of writing from the University of Arizona. Her education and her experiences as a Puerto Rican American led her to study the influence of hybridity and culture crossings. She has strong interest in postcolonial theories as they reveal the conditions of people of color living within USAmerica. Additionally, she is interested in education for minority students. Currently, she seeks to work with nonprofit agencies whose work is on literacy and preventing high-risk students from dropping out of school in the Phoenix area. Being born in New York and completing her early years in California, Dr. Rodríguez Connal uses her knowledge of Puerto Rican, Mexican, Chicano, and USAmerican cultures in her work.

David A. Dzaka is assistant professor of English at Messiah College, Grantham, where he teaches world literature, postcolonial literature, and a variety of courses in composition. A citizen of Ghana, he lived, studied, and taught English in various institutions in that country for many years before moving to the United States in 1996.

Pamela Gay teaches composition and creative writing at Binghamton University, SUNY, where she also directs the writing across the curriculum program. She has been teaching in an Internet-based classroom since 1997 and has directed two linked writing projects with her students and students from the University of Auckland, New Zealand, and the University of Ostrovo, Czech Republic. Gay is working on a forthcoming textbook, *Writers at Work: A Project Approach.*

R. Mark Hall teaches rhetoric, composition, and literacy studies at California State University, Chico. He directs the University Writing Center there and also writes about composition, literacy, and popular culture—including Oprah's Book Club.

Min-Zhan Lu is Professor of English at the University of Wisconsin-Milwaukee, where she teaches courses in life writing, critical theory, and composition. Her work focuses on the constructive uses of cultural dissonance in the teaching and learning of writing and on theories and practices of life writing as social acts. Her books include *Shanghai Quartet: The Crossings of Four Women of China* (2001), *Representing the "Other:" Basic Writers and the Teaching of Basic Writing* (1999) with Bruce Horner, and *Comp Tales: An Introduction to College Composition Through its Stories* (2000), coedited with Richard Haswell.

Andrea A. Lunsford is professor of English and director of the Program in Writing and Rhetoric at Stanford University. Formerly director of the Center for the Study and Teaching of Writing at Ohio State University, she has published widely on theories and practices of composition and rhetoric, on collaboration, and on issues of gender and diversity.

Jaime Armin Mejía, associate professor of English at Southwest Texas State University in San Marcos, Texas, teaches and studies rhetoric and composition as well as Chicana/o literature—fields in which he has long worked to develop literacy pedagogies. He is a native of the Lower Rio Grande Valley of South Texas, a borderlands area that continues to fuel his imagination for and wonder at intercultural contact between Mexican and North American cultures.

Gary A. Olson, professor of English, is the coordinator of the graduate program in rhetoric and composition at the University of South Florida. His most recent book is *Justifying Belief: Stanley Fish and the Work of Rhetoric,* an examination of the role of rhetoric in Fish's philosophical and legal writings.

Lahoucine Ouzgane is associate professor of English at the University of Alberta. His teaching and research interests include postcolonial literature and theory, composition and rhetoric, and masculinity studies. Some of his publications include articles on the postcolonial literature of North Africa and the Middle East, edited collections on postcolonial masculinities (in *Jouvert: A Journal of Postcolonial Studies,* 1998) and on African masculinities (in the *Journal of Men's Studies,* Spring 2002). He also coedited *JAC*'s 1998 special issue on postcolonial and composition studies. His *Studies in Islamic Masculinities* is forthcoming.

Aneil Rallin grew up in Bombay, lives in Los Angeles, and he does not drive. He is assistant professor of literature and writing studies and director of the General Education Writing Program at California State University, San Marcos. One of his interests is transgressive rhetorics.

Mary Rosner, associate professor of English, has long taught courses in various levels of composition as well as in Victorian literature and rhetoric. Her most recent research examines feminist readings of science and visual rhetoric.

C. Jan Swearingen is professor of English at Texas A&M University and past president (1998–2000) of the Rhetoric Society of America. Her history of western literacy and rhetoric, *Rhetoric and Irony: Western Literacy and Western Lies,* addresses attitudes toward privileged versus devalued literacies, oralities, and rhetorics in different periods. Her teaching and research interests include the history and theory of rhetoric, comparative and historical studies of literacy, rhetoric and religion, and the rhetorical history of women in western and nonwestern cultures. Her most recent book is an edited collection, *Rhetoric, the Polis, and the Global Village.*

Index

Abrahams, Roger, 249

activism, writing's relation to, 63–65

affirmative action, 79, 239, 252

African American Vernacular English. *See* Ebonics

African Americans: and Black literature, 253–54; in composition and rhetoric, 174–75

agency, 20, 51, 82, 93; compositionists fostering, 1–2, 4, 92

Alcoff, Linda, 128

"Aleph, The" (Borges), 58

al–Saadawi, Nawal, 124

Anzaldúa, Gloria, 12–14, 204–5, 211; acceptance of dominant writing, 17–18; activism of, 63–66; background of, 18–19, 33–34, 37–39; collaborations by, 36, 56–57; influences on, 58, 60–62; interviews with, 16, 22–26, 36–37; on mestizaje, 208–9; on prerequisites for innovation, 17, 19–21; relation with languages, 35, 52–53, 216; style of, 57–60, 62–63; on writing, 22–24, 35–36, 40–41; writing process of, 44–45, 54–56; writings of, 33–34, 54

Appiah, Kwame, 161

Aristotle, 203

"Arts of the Contact Zone" (Pratt), 30, 86, 96–97, 107; on autoethnographic texts, 184–85, 187; uses of, 105–6

Ashcroft, Bill, 72, 129, 211

assimilation, 183, 196

audience, 72, 184, 208; for Anzaldúa's writing, 36, 49–50; and ethos, 121–22; for testimonios, 125–26, 134, 139–42; writing for, 57–58

authors, 27, 88, 158; relation with audience, 121–22; student representations of, 29–30

authorship, of testimonios, 123–24, 132–34

autoethnographic texts, 184–87

Bakhtin, Mikhail, 132, 207–8, 218, 232

Baldwin, James, 243

Bauman, Zygmunt, 84

Belenky, Mary Field, 215

Berlin, James, 173

Between Voice and Silence: Women and Girls, Race and Relationship (Taylor, Gilligan, Sullivan), 214–15

Beverly, John, 123–25, 127, 133

Bhabha, Homi, 4, 42–43, 80, 90; on mimicry, 72, 82; on relations among cultures, 208–9

bilingual education: and Ebonics, 241–42, 244

bilingualism, 187; creation of, 176–77; and fluency in English, 21; identity construction in, 196–97; lack of attention to, 172, 174–76

Bitzer, Lloyd, 130

Bizzell, Patricia, 103–4, 215–17, 257n6

Black English and the Education of Black Children and Youth (Smitherman), 243

body, in writing, 23–24

Border Visions: Mexican Cultures of the Southwest United States (Vélez-Ibáñez), 188–93

Borderlands/La Frontera (Anzaldúa), 34, 54, 61

Britain, 157–58

Brodkey, Linda, 156

Brown, Stephen, 86–87

Burgos–Debray, Elizabeth, 123

Burke, Kenneth, 135, 139, 203

Campbell, Karlyn Kohrs, 132

"Can the Subaltern Speak?" (Spivak), 42, 89, 111–12, 115

Canada, 130–31

Carpenter, Edmond, 141–42

censorship, influence on writing, 46–47

Chicano/as, 63, 173–74. *See also* Latino/as; Texas Mexicans

Chiseri-Strater, Elizabeth, 228

class, in testimonios, 123, 126

Clément, Catherine, 118

Clifford, James, 210

Clinchy, Blythe McVicker, 215

Code, Lorraine, 107–8

code switching, 15, 18–19, 200; Anzaldúa's, 59–60; areas of use, 52–53

"Collaboration as 'Reflexive Dialogue'" (Qualley and Chiseri-Strater), 228

Colonial Desire (Young), 206–7

colonialism, 165, 172, 200; in contact zone concept, 96–98; and domination of the Other, 91–92; in education, 90, 201; effects of, 154, 160, 168, 206–7, 210; English in, 30, 43; pedagogy under, 160–63; resistance to, 30, 211–12

colonized, the, 17–18, 38, 115, 124

Colonizer and the Colonized, The (Memmi), 233–34

community, 131; myth of, 97, 103; representation of, 122, 124–25

composition, 15, 55, 94, 187; alternative models in, 19–21, 40, 62–63, 208; Anzaldúa's, 35–36, 44–45, 62–63; benefits of postcolonialism to, 16, 21, 26, 28, 30–31, 72–73; collaborations in, 36, 192–93; development of concepts in, 96; developmental frame in, 18–21; difficulty integrating postcolonialism and, 42–43, 67–68; effects of colonialism in, 17–18, 158, 168; effects of educational methods on, 163–64; hegemony through, 17–18, 36; inequity in relation to postcolonialism, 10, 32; innovation in, obstacles to, 47, 49–51; —, prerequisites for, 17, 19–20, 21; —, weighing degree of, 40–41, 46, 59; and literature, 10–11; materiality of, 22–25; as oppressive, 51–52, 156; postcolonialism's relation to, 31, 68, 70; relation to activism, 63–65; as remedial, 182–83; requirements for, 22–25; resistance to, 30, 158–60, 215; results of, 51–52, 205; standards in, 155–56, 159–60; strategies of, 29–30, 213–15; texts for, 13–14, 90–91; transculturalism through, 216–17; types of, 49–50; as undervalued, 10–11, 13–16. *See also* composition studies; style

composition process, 54–56, 160, 169; Anzaldúa's, 22–23, 44–45; body in, 23–24; for note form, 149–50

composition studies, 78, 153, 168, 172–73; academics speaking for student writers in, 26–27; in colonial education, 161–65; encounters with the Other in, 85–86; essay assignments in, 188–95; and postcolonialism, 25, 70–73, 76–77, 80, 82–83, 88–89; power relationships in, 93–94; students' culture in, 196–97, 202; students' speaking in, 215, 218; technology in, 219, 226–27; texts for, 175–76, 260n114; as university gatekeeper, 2, 63, 145–46, 152, 155–56; use of contact zones concept in, 87–88, 103

composition theory, 30, 40, 73, 86

compositionists: goals of, 1–3, 92; and postcolonialism, 2–4, 9. *See also* teachers

Consequences of Literacy, The (Goody), 249

contact language, 86–87

"Contact Zones and English Studies" (Bizzell), 103

contact zones concept, 185, 215, 257n6; definitions of, 102–4, 107, 258n3; evolution of, 96–99, 107; liberal version of, 88, 90; in pedagogy, 86–87, 92, 104–6, 257n9; types of contacts in, 107–8

context, in analyzing student writing, 30–31

Cortazar, Julio, 58

Cosby, Bill, 239, 244

critical literacy, 182–83, 197

Critical Theory, Cultural Politics, and Latin American Narrative, 96, 98

"Criticism in the Contact Zone" (Pratt), 96

culture, 65, 88, 203; clashes of, 97–99, 103–5, 214; in colonialism, 74, 206–7; and creation of bilingualism, 176–77; desire for unitary, 209–10; fear of changes in, 210–11; hierarchical comparison of, 136–38; of home vs. school, 246; of hybrids, 205–6; incorporating in composition classes, 196–97; internal diversity of, 68, 79–81; interplay among, 208–9; Inuit, 131–32; Mexican, 180; oral traditions in, 249–52; plurality of, 253–54; in postcolonialism, 78, 157; Puerto Rican, 215; of Texas Mexicans, 188–93; and transculturation, 200–1; transmission of knowledge in, 190, 192–93. *See also* contact zones concept

culture wars, 252

cultures of scholarship, 187–89, 194

Cushman, Dick, 134, 136

Daniell, Beth, 250

Davis, Deborah, 155

desire, 144, 150

developmental frame, in pedagogy, 18–21
Dialogic Imagination, The (Bakhtin), 207, 235
Dirlik, Arif, 73–74
discrimination. *See* oppression
drawing, relation to writing, 38–40
D'Souza, Dinesh, 127

Ebonics: as bilingual education, 241, 244;
    Oakland School Board's proposal for,
    239–43; orality of, 247, 249; and racism,
    241–42, 246; reactions against, 239,
    242–43, 245, 254; use in teaching stan-
    dard English, 241–43
economy: effects on Southwest and Texas
    Mexicans, 179–80; effects on writers,
    22–25; of Puerto Rico, 212
"Economy of Manichean Allegory, The"
    (JanMohamed), 91–92
Ede, Lisa, 69–70
education, 69, 165, 201; declining test scores,
    182–83; of Texas Mexicans, 177–79, 189
Elbow, Peter, 168
Emerson, Caryl, 234
emotions: choice of language for, 12, 18,
    52–53; in writing process, 44–45
Empire Writes Back, The (Ashcroft, Griffiths,
    Tiffin), 72
Engaged Pedagogy (hooks), 169
English, 52; association with colonialism,
    30, 43; in education, 18–19, 63, 177–79,
    241–42; fluency in, 21, 144, 147–48;
    hegemony of, 4, 52, 145, 231; imposed
    upon others, 10, 212, 239; as oppres-
    sive, 51–52, 167; scholarship in, 193,
    196; types of, 19, 60, 72–73, 240, 246;
    uses of, vs. Spanish, 12–13, 17–18; writ-
    ing in, vs. native language, 168–69. *See
    also* Ebonics; language
English departments, 182; composition un-
    dervalued in, 10–11, 13–16; as exclu-
    sionary, 172–73; response to declining
    test scores, 182–83
English studies, 10, 26, 103, 173, 194
Eskimo. *See* Inuit, *I, Nuligak*, testimonios
essays: assignments of, 159, 161–63, 188–95;
    in composition development, 166–67;
    vs. note forms, 143
ethics, 92; as encounter with Other, 85,
    115–16; and postmodernism, 84–85
ethnic minorities, 239; identity of, 29, 181–82,
    184; literacy studies for, 180–81, 183; as
    Other, 180–81; as teachers, 68

ethnographic realism, 134–37, 140
ethos: audience and, 121–22; of testimonios,
    125

Faigley, Lester, 173, 179–80
Fanon, Frantz, 42
feminism, 121–22. *See also* postcolonial femi-
    nists
feminist theory, 93
fiction, vs. nonfiction, 49–50
"Fourth Vision: Literate Language at
    Work, The" (Heath), 183–84
Fox, Helen, 158, 167
Fragments of Rationality (Faigley), 173
Freire, Paulo, 79, 161; influence of, 42, 169;
    use of theories of, 92–93, 257n8

Gates, Henry Louis, 7–8, 249, 251, 253–54
gender, in reticence to speak, 213–15
generational conflict, 214
genres, testimonios as, 129–32, 134, 136, 142
Ghana, 30, 157–65
Giroux, Henry, 79, 169, 257n8
"Globalization, Civilization Processes, and
    the Relocation of Languages and Cul-
    tures" (Mignolo), 187–88
globalization, effects on language, 187–88,
    193
Godzich, Wlad, 182–83
Goldberg, Whoopi, 239, 244
Goldberger, Nancy Rule, 215
Goody, Jack, 249
Gramsci, Antonio, 72
Greenbaum, Andrea, 4
Griffiths, Gareth, 72, 157, 211
"Growing up Chicana" (Anzaldúa), 61
Guaman Poma de Ayala, Felipe, 184–85,
    258n12
Guatemala, 260n16
Gupta, Sunil, 156
Guy–Sheftall, Beverly, 235

Hall, Stuart, 160
Hammersley, Martyn, 135
Haraway, Donna, 42
Harlow, Barbara, 123
Harris, Joseph, 87–88, 103
Havelock, Eric, 7, 247, 249
Heath, Shirley Brice, 29, 181–84, 250
Hinojosa, Rolando, 185–87, 198
Hoang, Haivan, 3, 5
Holmes, Hamilton, 252

Holquist, Michael, 235
homeless, discrimination against, 146–48
homosexuals, discrimination against, 148, 155
hooks, bell, 60, 79, 169, 214
"How to Tame a Wild Tongue" (Anzaldúa), 35
Hunter-Gault, Charlayne, 252–53
Hurston, Zora Neale, 243, 249
Hutcheon, Linda, 93
hybridity, 25, 66, 209; discourse of, 7, 215–16; and identity, 203–4, 206–7, 210–11; lack of location in, 80–81; postcolonialism on, 70–71; reactions to, 200, 205–6, 210–11, 216; and resistance, 200, 208; uses of, 201–2, 207–8, 211–12; uses of writing in, 216–17
Hymes, Dell, 138–39

I, Nuligak, 130–38, 140–42
identity, 35, 51, 119, 121, 191, 204, 230; class, 111–13; desire for fixed, 209–10; of hybrids, 206–8, 211; multiple, 33–34, 47–48, 116; on the Other, 91–93; stability of, 34, 216; USAmerican, 199–200
identity construction, 55–56, 179–83, 197; hybridity in, 201, 203–5
identity politics, 114
immigration/immigrants, 68, 80–81, 206, 213; control of, 147, 152, 154; discrimination against illegals, 148–49, 154–55; and USAmerican identity, 199–200
Imperial Eyes (Pratt), 96–98; reviews of, 99–103
In My Place (Hunter-Gault), 252–53
institutional locations, 25–26, 30, 75
Insurrections: Approaches to Resistance in Composition Studies (Greenbaum), 4
interviews, 15–17, 24
Inuit, 130–31. *See also I, Nuligak*
Ireland, Jeanette, 137

JAC: A Journal of Composition Theory, 3–4
Jamieson, Kathleen Hall, 130, 132
Jamieson, Sandra, 29, 174, 175–76
Jane Eyre, 58
JanMohamed, Abdul J., 42, 91–92
Jay, Gregory S., 126–27
Johnson, Mark, 135
Joiner, C. W., 240
Journal of Imperial and Commonwealth History, The, 99

King, C. Richard, 2
knowledge, 53–54, 60, 161
Kreisberg, Seth, 165
Krupat, Arnold, 136

Lakoff, George, 135
Lamb, Catherine, 107
language, 52, 244; contact, 86–87; desire for unitary, 213; discrimination for use of, 19, 62, 240; education in, 240–41; effects on identity, 35, 197, 205, 215; globalization's effects on, 193, 187–88; of home vs. school, 91, 246; hybrid, 207–8, 215–16; of hybrids, 205–6; oppression through, 38, 51–52; preferences of, 35, 59–60, 196; of Puerto Ricans, 30, 212, 215; standard vs. variants, 60, 72–73; transculturalism in, 200–2, 216; uses of, 72–73, 209; uses of English vs. Spanish, 12–13, 17–18, 52–53; writing in English vs. native, 168–69. *See also* English
"Language Situation of Puerto Ricans, The" (Zentella), 212–13
Latin America, testimonios from, 129
Latinas, writing by, 29–30, 213–15
Latour, Bruno, 95–96, 102, 107
Leith, Dick, 230
Lejeune, Philippe, 133
linguistics, 239–43
listservs, in composition studies, 218, 220–31
literacy: effects of, 250–51; orality and, 247–51; used in colonialism, 90
literacy studies, 180–81, 251–52
literary studies, 16, 173, 257n6
literature: Black, 243, 253–54; composition's relation to, 10–11; in contact zone concept, 97–98
Llorona, Theorizing Identity, Knowledge, Composition, La (Anzaldúa), 61, 64
Lucas, George, 247–48

Macedo, Donaldo, 169
Making Face, Making Soul/Haciendo Caras (ed. Anzaldúa), 34
Manguel, Alberto, 58
Mani, Lata, 72
Marcus, George, 134, 136
Marín, Lynda, 124
Martin Luther King, Jr., Elementary School Children v. Ann Arbor School District, 240, 243

Marx, Karl, 111–13
McCarthy, Cormac, 58
McGrath, Robin, 138
McLaughlin, Milbrey, 29, 181–84
McLuhan, Marshall, 249
McNeil, Robert, 244
McNeill, James, 138
McWilliam, H. O. A., 160
Meléndez, Nancy, 202
Memmi, Albert, 233–34
Menchú Tum, Rigoberta, 114, 122–25, 127, 260n15
mestiza: identity, 204–5; rhetoric, 23–24, 30, 34, 37, 204
mestizaje, 207–8
metaphor: and metonymy, 115, 119–20, 128; representation as, 113, 121
Metayer, Maurice, 132–37, 140–41
metonymy, 118; metaphor and, 115, 119–20, 128; representation as, 113–14, 121
Mexican Americans, bilingualism of, 174–77. See also Texas Mexicans
Mi querido Rafa (Hinojosa), 185–87
Mignolo, Walter D., 187–88, 193, 196
Milanés, Cecilia Rodríguez, 236
Miller, Carolyn, 130
Miller, Richard, 15, 88, 105–6
Miller, Susan, 173
Minh-ha, Trinh T., 26–27, 118–19, 260n114; on difference, 120–21; on rhetoric, 114, 122; on speaking for the Other, 114–15; on uses of writing, 216–17
modernism, assimilation in, 183
Mohanty, Chandra Talpade, 69–70, 154, 259n3
Mohanty, S. P., 93
Moi, Toril, 118
Mongia, Padmini, 157
Montejano, David, 177
Moraga, Cherrie, 33–34
Morrison, Toni, 58
Moss, Beverly, 250
multiculturalism, 87, 97, 231, 256n10; in composition studies, 68–69, 93–94; debate over, 219–25; fears about, 77–78, 251–52; and postcolonialism, 73, 76–77, 210; reactions against, 7, 77–78, 238–39, 252–54; texts for, 31, 68–69, 76, 173–74
multiple mediations, 72
Myerson, George, 230
myths/legends, 138–39, 247–48

Narayan, Uma, 228, 235
Neal, Elma A., 178
"Negotiating the Contact Zone" (Harris), 87–88
Nepantla concept, 12, 39, 54
"New Vocationalism," 183
nosotras concept, 17, 41–42, 62
note form, 23, 143, 145, 149–50, 156

Ong, Walter, 249
oppression, 88, 252; debate over, 222–23; divisions among victims of, 148, 152; and postcolonialism, 1, 75; responses to, 3, 63–65, 211; of Texas Mexicans, 177–78, 185–86; through language, 51–52
oral tradition, 167, 175, 247–51
oral-epic narrative, Star Wars as, 247–48
Other/other, 1; construction of, 92–93; in contact zones concept, 86–87; creation of, 26, 151–53, 155, 160; definition of, 75, 77, 223; dialogue with, 115, 234–35, 237; domination of, 91–92; encountering, 85, 89, 92, 94; ethnic minorities as, 180–81; in nosotras concept, 41–42; in postcolonialism, 75, 79; representation of, 114–15; speaking for, 26, 114–15, 121
Otherness/otherness, 87, 120
Outside in the Teaching Machine (Spivak), 117

Paredes, Américo, 175, 177
Parry, Benita, 90
pedagogy: Anzaldúa's, 37, 45–46; colonial, 158, 160–63; developmental frame in, 18–21; dialogue in, 233–37; for English, 241–42; ethical questions in, 86–87; goals of, 37, 47–49, 144, 154; postcolonial, 71–72, 158–60; power issues in, 89–92; representation in, 127–28; Sledd's, 14–15; students' reality in, 149, 196–97; use of contact zones concept in, 87–88, 104–6; using flare-ups in, 224, 226–29, 261n2. See also composition studies; postcolonial studies; teachers
Pedagogy of the Oppressed, The (Freire), 42
Pennycook, A., 164
Perry, Donna, 36–37
Philip, Marlene Nourbese, 150
plagiarism, 164
postcolonial, 65; definition of, 73–76, 157
Post-Colonial Critic, The (Spivak), 116
postcolonial feminists, 113, 124

postcolonial studies, 78; and composition
    studies, 25–26, 28, 30–31, 42–43; prob-
    lems of, 73–74, 79; subjects of, 26, 51,
    69; and testimonios, 129, 142
Post-Colonial Studies Reader, The (Ashcroft,
    Griffiths, Tiffin), 211
postcolonial theory, 1, 93
postcolonialism, 30, 59, 200; benefits to
    composition, 16, 21, 72–73, 82–83; col-
    laboration with composition studies,
    67–68, 73; and compositioners, 2–4, 9,
    12–13; and contact zone concept, 86,
    88–89; on difference, 71, 89, 120–21; as
    diversionary, 77–78; in English depart-
    ment hierarchy, 10–11; on ethos and
    audience, 121–22; in Ghana, 157–58; in
    Guatemala, 260n16; and hybridity,
    70–71, 211; literature of, 77–80, 89; loss
    of distinctions within, 79–80; and
    multiculturalism, 76–77, 87; relation
    to composition, 9–10, 12–13, 16, 68,
    70–72; and transnationalism, 70–71,
    76–77. *See also* postcolonial studies
Postmodern Ethics (Bauman), 84
postmodernism, 16, 93, 183; effects on sense
    of self, 179–80; and ethics, 84–85
poststructuralism, 16, 53, 126–27
power, 66, 82, 122, 146, 155, 157; in contact
    zone concept, 105, 107; definitions of,
    107; differentials in, 85–86, 97–98; in
    education, 60–61, 69–70, 89–92, 128,
    165–66; postcolonial studies examin-
    ing, 74–76; in relations among cultures,
    208–9; and representation, 112, 160;
    and voice, 227, 232–33
Power of Address, The (Leith and Myerson),
    230
Pratt, Mary Louise, 30, 258n12; on autoeth-
    nographic texts, 184–85, 187; on contact
    zones, 86–87, 96–99, 103, 105, 258n3;
    and reviews of *Imperial Eyes*, 99–103
precolonialism, search for connections to,
    53–54
*Predicament of Culture: Twentieth-Century
    Ethnography, Literature, and Art, The*
    (Clifford), 210
Preface to Plato (Havelock), 249
"Prieta, La" (Anzaldúa), 33, 61
Probyn, Elspeth, 153
Profession (MLA), 96–97
Puerto Ricans, 30, 201–2
Puerto Rico, 30, 212, 215

Qualley, Donna, 228, 237

race, 213–15, 252. *See also* Ebonics
Randall, Margaret, 124
Raspberry, William, 243–44
readers. *See* audience
reading postures, 16, 28–29, 31, 181
reality, 50, 52, 149; construction of, 51, 55–56;
    recreating, 56, 60, 65; teachers' per-
    spective as, 159–60
*Reclaiming Medusa: Short Stories by Contem-
    porary Puerto Rican Women* (Velez),
    216–17
Rendell, Ruth, 58
representation, 50, 72, 114, 117, 119, 126, 160,
    259n9; in autoethnographic texts,
    184–87; as function of rhetoric, 112–13;
    in pedagogy, 127–28; politics of, 30–31;
    processes within, 112–13, 121; strate-
    gies of, 110–11; and substitution, 118,
    127–28; in testimonios, 123–25, 129. *See
    also* self-representation
"Representing Audience" (Lunsford and
    Ede), 69–70
Research in African Literatures, 100–2
resistance, 90, 123, 155, 200, 209, 232; to
    composition, 158–60, 163–64, 166–67,
    215; and hybridity, 208, 211–12; and the
    subaltern, 81–82
Resistance Literature (Harlow), 123
rhetoric, 1, 156, 173, 216, 230, 249; forms of,
    129–30, 208; functions of, 111, 124, 204;
    as means of persuasion, 202–3; post-
    colonialism's relation to, 68, 70, 72;
    representation as function of, 112–13,
    121; of submission, 213–14; of testimo-
    nios, 125–26; transcultural, 200–2,
    204–5, 208, 212, 215–16; use of post-
    colonialism in, 82–83. *See also* mestiza,
    rhetoric
Rhetoric of Motives (Burke), 203
Rich, Adrienne, 149
Rimstead, Roxanne, 131
Rooney, Ellen, 116
Royster, Jacqueline Jones, 70–71, 80–81
Rushdie, Salman, 73, 80

Said, Edward, 4, 92, 179, 199–200
San Miguel, Guadalupe, Jr., 178
Sati (Mani), 72
Science in Action (Latour), 95–96
self, defining, 228–29

self-multiplication, 111, 116–17
self-representation, 27, 205, 208
sexuality, in Anzaldúa's writing, 47, 60
Shaughnessy, Mina, 167
Shohat, Ella, 76
"Signs Taken for Wonders" (Bhabha), 90
Sledd, James, 14–15, 19, 36, 61–62
Slemon, Stephen, 78
Smitherman, Geneva, 243
socioeconomics, effects on writing and
    writers, 23–25
Sommer, Doris, 124–26
Spanish, 12–13, 17–18, 52
"Speaking in Tongues: A Letter to Third
    World Women Writers" (Anzaldúa),
    36
Spivak, Gayatri, 26–27, 42, 76, 111–12, 118,
    148; influence of, 71–72, 122; self-multi-
    plication by, 116–17; on speaking for
    the Other, 114–16; on subaltern, 81, 89,
    259n9
Star Wars, as oral-epic, 247–48
Story of English, The (McNeil), 244
storytelling, 37–38. See also oral tradition
student writing: analysis of, 20–21; modes
    of soliciting, 30–31; responses to hate
    speech in, 106
students, 2–3, 29–30, 176; collaboration
    among, 192–93; and colonialism, 165,
    168–69; and composition norms, 17–20,
    20–21, 50–51; diversity among, 2, 25,
    32, 68; effects of developmental frame
    on composition by, 18, 20–21; empow-
    erment of, 1–2, 89; institutional loca-
    tions of, 25–26; language of, 14–15, 24,
    240–42; obstacles of, 22–23; others
    speaking for, 3, 26–27, 31; performance
    of, 20–21; relation with audience,
    121–22; relations with teachers, 161,
    233–37; representations of, 2, 89;
    teachers imagining, 28–29
style, 18, 35, 57–59, 167
subaltern, 89–90, 259n8, 259n9; use of con-
    cept, 72, 81–82. See also "Can the Sub-
    altern Speak?" (Spivak)
Subaltern Studies, 75, 81–82
subjectivity, 119, 121, 125, 158; in poststruc-
    turalism, 126–27; of women, 93, 124,
    213
Suleri, Sara, 93

Tartule, Jill Mattuck, 215

Taylor, Gilligan, Sullivan, 214–15
teachers, 154, 210; authority of, 86–87, 91–92,
    127; diversity among, 32, 68, 150–51;
    imagining student potentials, 28–29;
    part-time vs. tenured, 144–45, 150–51,
    153, 156; perspective as reality, 159–60;
    reading postures of, 28–29, 31; relations
    with students, 161, 165, 233–37; repre-
    sentations of, 27, 30; responsibility of,
    92, 144, 149; and student language, 147,
    212, 240
technology, 219, 226–27, 249
testimonios, 122–25; audience for, 139–40;
    by Canadian Eskimo, 130–34; collabo-
    ration in, 123–24, 132–34; as genre, 6,
    129–32, 134, 136, 142; rhetoric of,
    125–26
Texas, ending affirmative action, 239
Texas Mexicans, 196; cultures of scholar-
    ship of, 187–89; discrimination against,
    172–73, 177–79, 185–86; economic
    changes of, 179–80; re-valuing culture
    of, 188–93
Textual Carnivals (Miller), 173
This Bridge Called My Back: Writings by
    Radical Women of Color (Moraga and
    Anzaldúa), 33–34
Tiffin, Helen, 72, 78, 157, 211
"To Elsie" (Williams), 210–11
Tobin, Lad, 165
Tompkins, Jane, 107
"To(o) Queer the Writer" (Anzaldúa), 34
transculturalism, 200–2, 204–6, 212; prac-
    tices of, 207–8; rhetoric of, 215–16
Transforming Power: Domination, Empower-
    ment and Education (Kreisberg), 165
transnationalism, 71, 194; economics of,
    152–53; and hybridity, 80–81; and post-
    colonialism, 73, 76–78
truth, theory of objective, 135

Uncle Remus con chile (Paredes), 175
United States, 2, 4, 212; desire for single
    language and culture in, 200, 209–10,
    213; fear of change in, 210–11

Valdés, Guadalupe, 172, 176
values: and interplay among cultures,
    208
Vargas, Edwin, 202
Velez, Diana L., 216–17
Vélez-Ibáñez, Carlos G., 188–93, 196

Victorian Studies, 99–100

Viswanathan, Gauri, 74, 79

voice, 115, 237; Anzaldúa's, 33, 46, 64; and collaboration in testimonios, 132–33; connecting with person behind, 235–36; multiple, 47–48, 116–17, 119; power and, 232–33; recovery of, 64, 70; vs. silencing, 219, 225, 227

Walker, Alice, 243, 249

Wicomb, Zoe, 152

Williams, William Carlos, 210–11

"Witchfear among the Aivilik Eskimos" (Carpenter), 141–42

Wolff, Janice, 104–5

Woman, Native, Other: Writing Postcoloniality and Feminism (Minh-ha), 118–19

Woman at Point Zero (al-Saadawi), 124

women, 213; hesitation to write, 29–30; indirect writing strategies of, 29–30, 213–15; in Texas Mexican families, 188–93, 195–96

women's studies, 112–13

Women's Ways of Knowing: The Development of Self, Voice, and Mind, 215

"Working Together Across Difference" (Narayan), 228

World Literature Written in English, 100

Worsham, Lynn, 4

Wretched of the Earth, The (Fanon), 42

writers. *See* authors

writing. *See* composition

Young, Robert J. C., 206–7, 209

Zentella, Ana Celia, 212–13